MW01119818

SAGE was founded in 1965 by Sara Miller McCune to support the dissemination of usable knowledge by publishing innovative and high-quality research and teaching content. Today, we publish more than 750 journals, including those of more than 300 learned societies, more than 800 new books per year, and a growing range of library products including archives, data, case studies, reports, conference highlights, and video. SAGE remains majority-owned by our founder, and after Sara's lifetime will become owned by a charitable trust that secures our continued independence.

Los Angeles | London | Washington DC | New Delhi | Singapore | Boston

Disability, Gender, and the Trajectories of Power

Disability, Gender, and the Trajectories of Power

Edited by
Asha Hans

⑤SAGE   www.sagepublications.com
Los Angeles • London • New Delhi • Singapore • Washington DC • Boston

First published in 2015 by

SAGE Publications India Pvt Ltd
B1/I-1 Mohan Cooperative Industrial Area
Mathura Road, New Delhi 110 044, India
www.sagepub.in

SAGE Publications Inc
2455 Teller Road
Thousand Oaks, California 91320, USA

SAGE Publications Ltd
1 Oliver's Yard, 55 City Road
London EC1Y 1SP, United Kingdom

SAGE Publications Asia-Pacific Pte Ltd
3 Church Street
#10-04 Samsung Hub
Singapore 049483

Published by Vivek Mehra for SAGE Publications India Pvt Ltd, typeset at 10/12 pts Bembo by Diligent Typesetter, Delhi and printed at Chaman Enterprises, New Delhi.

Library of Congress Cataloging-in-Publication Data Available

ISBN: 978-93-515-0123-7 (HB)

The SAGE Team: Supriya Das, Sanghamitra Patowary, Mriga Maithel, Nand Kumar Jha, and Rajinder Kaur

Contents

List of Abbreviations

APL	Above Poverty Line
BPL	Below Poverty Line
CEDAW	Convention on the Elimination of All Forms of Discrimination Against Women
CRC	Convention on the Rights of the Child
CRPD	Convention on the Rights of Persons with Disabilities
CSW	Commission on the Status of Women
DPO	Disabled Persons' Organizations
DPPI	Disability, Pregnancy, and Parenthood International
DRM	Disability Rights Movement
DSM	Diagnostic and Statistical Manual of Mental Disorders
E.X.I.T.E.	Exploring Interests in Technology and Engineering
FGD	Focused Group Discussion
GIFT	Girls Institute for Technology
GR	General Recommendations (of CEDAW)
GSE	Gender in Science and Engineering
HI	Hearing Impaired
IAWS	Indian Association of Women's Studies
ICCPR	International Convention of Civil Political Rights
IGNOU	Indira Gandhi National Open University
ILO	International Labor Organization
MDAC	Mental Disability Advocacy Center
MHA	Mental Health Act
MNC	Multinational Corporation
MWDs	Married Women with Disabilities
NDF	Nawabshah Disability Forum
NGO	Nongovernment Organization
NHFDC	National Handicapped Finance and Development Corporation
NSSO	National Sample Survey Organization

OBC	Other Backward Classes
PD	Physically Disabled
PISA	Program for International Student Assessment
PNDT	Prenatal Diagnostic Techniques (Regulation and Prevention of Misuse) Act
RDE	Research in Disabilities Education
SC	Scheduled Castes
SCI-VIS	Science Camp for Interested Visually Impaired Students
SGSY	Swarnajayanti Gram Swarozgar Yojana
SHG	Self-Help Group
SMRC	Shanta Memorial Rehabilitation Centre
SMS	Short Messaging Service
ST	Scheduled Tribes
STEM	Science, Technology, Engineering, and Mathematics
UK	United Kingdom
UN	United Nations
UNCRPD	United Nations Convention on the Rights of Persons with Disabilities
UNDP	United Nations Development Program
UNESCO	United Nations Educational, Scientific and Cultural Organization
UNHCR	United Nations High Commissioner for Refugees
UNHRC	United Nations Human Rights Commission
UNICEF	United Nations International Children's Emergency Fund
UNSCR	United Nations Security Council Resolution
USAID	US Agency for International Development
VI	Visually Impaired
VRC	Vocational Rehabilitation Center
WB	World Bank
WHO	World Health Organization
WNUSP	World Network of Users and Survivors of Psychiatry

Preface and Acknowledgments

This book is being published at a time of change in disability politics—a time, as the title suggests, of transformation in gender relationships and emerging trajectories of power. The new order envisioned by the global disability human rights treaty, the Convention on the Rights of Persons with Disabilities (CRPD), is of a gender-equal and just humanity (Article 6). The new legal rights framework is being strengthened by other conventions, such as the Convention on the Elimination of All Forms of Discrimination Against Women (CEDAW) which focuses on women's rights, as does the ongoing Beijing+20 process. In countries across the globe, there are attempts to change national disability laws and amend them along the lines of the CRPD. The process is not easy, but women have been keeping watch over their exclusion in these latest laws. Another emerging trend has been the proliferation of writings by women with disabilities, such as Simi Linton (2006), Malini Chib (2011), and Shivani Gupta (2014), shaping the personal-is-political dimension. To conceptualize the gendered problematic, they have together tried to reclaim the political space that by rights is theirs.

There are women with great diversities emerging across the globe with creative viewpoints, new policy deliberations, and initiating processes of original writings and discourse. Their questioning of inequality and their arguments for an equal world are providing the strength to both the disability and the women's movement. This book is the product of a strong community of women and men who base their writings on critical thinking and their engagement with multiple women's voices. These arguments for a larger space in the politics of disability and feminism were hugely overdue, and it is significant that they are being accentuated.

The deliberations on issues that affect women, the violence everywhere, the marginalization and the invisibility, being replaced by an emergence of women politics, neglected across time, and laying new definitive equality guidelines at international and national levels provides hopefully a way to establish a new world order with equality and justice for all men and women.

This book brings together 12 chapters by feminist thinkers reflecting on issues that have been raised in recent years. To conceptualize the gendered problematic in Section One, together, Upali, Amrita/Satish, and Nilika/Mahima provide that subtle linkage between disability studies, data, and the paradigm shift in disability rights. They are involved as they want to transform the collectivity of our knowledge and revolutionize our ways of engaging with the world around us.

Throughout the history of disability studies, rarely has enough attention been given to bodies and sexuality as it is a woman's issue. The violence is not only physical, emotional, or legal (Chapter 5), but also of expression that transcends from private to public (Chapter 4). The women who wrote these chapters, especially in Section Two—Malini, Tina, Sandhya, Shubhangi, and Santoshi—came into the field of disability through a series of geographical, political, and intellectual disarticulations. Their journey is marked by struggles against State and society and charted at various levels. The contours of their identities formed through their experiences and consciousness in terms of feminism from a disability framework. The significance of these chapters in this section is the contribution to visioning grounded in feminist thought and experience.

Section Three provides the visions of democratic futures. The recent globalization of our issues, after the CRPD, necessitates an active deliberative focus on questions of future in comparative feminist thought and praxis. The writers Bhargavi, Stephanie, and Renu have mapped the trajectories in their own work, and the histories and self-determination to lay the ground for feminist praxis. Our hope is to see that their writings will draw attention to women's knowledge and the gaps they witness in policy spaces.

All the chapters in this volume emphasize on discriminations that are still left unattended despite many national ratifications of the CRPD and the growing loud voices of the disability community—from global to local. Another compelling reason for this book was the widespread discrimination, both old and new, which vitiates the environment, and if we are to remove these, we have to look at the strategies women are discussing. In its entirety, this book offers innovative and empirical research in the field of disability and feminist praxis. We have come to know through the process that critical analyses, tools, and our voices provide a more nuanced understanding of the world around us. We are involved, as we want to transform the collectivity of our knowledge and find new ways of engaging with the world around us. A possibility of revolutionary change is possible when we walk the path of political and intellectual thinking, and build on and anchor our ideologies and our struggles.

Acknowledgments

We continue to learn from our sisters, and thank them for treading a path that has opened up new avenues for us. Besides, the authors of the book are women who are symbols of leadership—Simi Linton, Judith Heuman, Mijoo Kim, Maria Soledad Cisternas Reyes, Maria Reina Venus Llagan, Charlotte McClain-Nhlapo, Myra Kovary, Carolyn Frohmader—and the large networks and women across the world—the International Network of Women with Disabilities, the Disabled Women's Network in Canada, Disabled Women in Africa, Women with Disabilities Australia, Women with Disabilities India Network—as well as many national and local networks from whom our ideologies and our knowledge have developed. These are besides the writers of this volume who have contributed so much to the movements and our understanding of disability.

I thank all the women who have molded the thoughts and writings in this book: Malini, the icon every woman looks up to and who laid the path to our understanding of sexuality; Bhargavi, with her wisdom and tremendous courage leading from the front to change the world; Tina, leading us through the policy sets across the globe; Stephanie, with her drive to get things right; Renu, who patiently but quietly works meticulously to get across her thoughts; Sandhya, who through grit and determination is trying to emerge out of a quiet world to challenges around her; Nilika and Mahima, dealing with high-profile gender issues that rarely get to reach our discussions; and Upali, Santoshi, and Shubhangi taking the issues forward from many angles that do not find space in our academic work. Satish Agnihotri, an administrator with intellectual insight, that is rare, has always been there to engage with any issue of gender as well as disability, and help us locate the spaces that link theory to policy and implementation, a rare gift that is available to only a few. Also, thanks goes to Amrita Patel, who has been a colleague and a student with a sharp intellect and the ability to focus on important gender issues.

I also recognize and honor the colleagues and friends whose support, ideas, and ideologies helped me through the rough paths of this world.

This work on gendered issues in disability started with the provocation of my brother Ashok, who is no longer with us, but who, over the decades, through his work at Shanta Memorial Rehabilitation Centre (SMRC), promoted and nurtured with humor and persistence the balance needed in life. None of this intellectual work would have been possible without the spiritual moorings of feminist thought he anchored us to, including the coeditor of my previous volume (Hans and Patri, 2003).

Finally, I want to acknowledge the people who have been engaged in making the book a reality: Reena at SMRC and Rajeshwari from San-sristi who helped in editing, Supriya Das of SAGE without whose support this book would not have been possible, and Anu, whose artwork on the cover so cleverly depicts the title of this book.

References

Chib, Malini. 2011. *One Little Finger*. New Delhi: SAGE Publications.

Gupta, Shivani. 2014. *No Looking Back: A True Story*. New Delhi: Rupa Publications India Pvt. Ltd.

Hans, Asha and Annie Patri. 2003. *Gender, Disability and Identity*. New Delhi: SAGE Publications.

Linton, Simi. 2006. *My Body Politic: A Memoir*. Ann Arbor: University of Michigan.

Introduction: Gendering the Disability Framework

The conceptual core of the framework presented is founded on the asser-tion that a nondiscriminatory approach is derived from the knowledge and expectation of women's well-being. A major assumption that influ-ences the analysis and the arguments presented in the chapters that follow is that equality is the germinal paradigm from which most major human institutions, such as the State, the economy, and the social relations of the family and community, have evolved. A second significant assumption of the framework and analyses is that the fundamental inequalities inherent in the multiple contemporary forms pose obstacles to the realization of the equality and justice of vast numbers of men and women. It is argued that these inequities must be challenged for realization of rights. Frustra-tion with the experience and the expectation of discrimination continues as these inequities constitute the widest and most serious threat to women with disabilities and, in some cases, to their survival. A third central assump-tion is that women's agencies have overcome many of the threats posed against them and have formulated multiple strategies to combat discrimina-tion, which need to be recognized. The key argument is that the present highly discriminatory system is not only incompatible to the protection and needs of women with disabilities, but also represents the foremost threat to their achievement of universal equal rights.

Emerging Feminist Disability Studies and Research[1]

Gendered disability research and the development of feminist disability studies are at a nascent stage in many parts of the world. Recent femi-nist research has spanned continents, covering a diversity of women and locales, and is increasing in magnitude and intensity. Despite the diversity of such research, challenges remain, as the gendered problématique linked to disability largely remains outside the feminist discourse. Much of this feminist research work linked to disability has been carried out by a variety of actors who are scholars, advocates, service providers, and policy makers.[2]

In general, many methodologies have been employed to understand the disability situation; however, few have been exhaustive or definitive from a gendered perspective. One of the outcomes is that feminist disability studies that intersect feminism with disability are not universally recognized as a full-fledged academic discourse. Although more research is needed, the ground has been set with works which introduce the social model and believe that it is imperative to link it to women's bodies. It is also important to recognize the change from a large research focus on victimhood of women with disabilities to the recognition of these women's agencies. This change is the first step toward comprehensive understanding of feminist disability; however, challenges remain regarding its inclusion not only in feminist disability research, but also in feminist research in general.

Gender inequality and injustice may become discrimination, which infiltrates into all stages of a woman's life and, in many ways, makes women invisible within the system. Within the larger framework of disability, the existing identity of men as dominant actors and their hegemonic control over women are absent and require a dialogue for transformative research. There are many facets of analyzing inclusion and invisibility, which have largely remained outside of disability research. Research must now increase its borders to include women's resilience and creativity in all aspects. To create a holistic analytical structure, gender must remain one of the many topical configurations with emerging sub-themes related to marginalized women with disabilities (deaf, blind, intellectual, psychosocial disability, and little women, widows, and single women), female children, elderly, and indigenous peoples.

Gender inequality and injustice may become discrimination, which permeates into all stages of a woman's life. Unfortunately, data are rarely disaggregated, and when available, are unreliable and limited for extensive analysis.[3] This data oversight means exclusion from structures and programs, creating an undemocratic system that keeps women on the margins. Therefore, it is important that while demanding universal disability, gender-disaggregated data, we link our general feminist research to women's voices.

Living within a Discriminatory System: Understanding Periphery Politics in Democratic Spaces

Living within different political systems, we witness discriminatory regimes that are characterized by inequities and deprivations. Within this order, democratic spaces are shrinking with the emergence of powerful actors, such as multinational corporations (MNCs) and international economic institutions. In this environment of greed and disparity between the rich and poor, women with disabilities find themselves limited to corner politics. In these spaces, they are confronted by insecurity in many forms, including insecurity related to food, livelihood, housing, increasing violence, and increasing health costs. As victims of a hegemonic system that sets its own unconstitutional rules of governing its polity, women are marginalized and women with disabilities are at the extreme periphery.

This core–periphery politics in the context of disability has rarely been challenged globally. Given that the democratic system was nonexistent until recently, except perhaps in very small island-like parts of the globe, there is no history of interrogating democratic fundamentals. Feudalism and colonialism in the developing world did not provide space for democratic structures; therefore, there is no history of protest by the women's movement of the disabled against undemocratic structures as women's roles were limited by a male-dominated political hierarchy.

In addition to women with disabilities being absent from national democratic structures, within the international system, there is an invisibility of their rights, even though nondiscrimination is a fundamental principle of international human rights law. This invisibility was observed in the international conferences until the United Nations (UN) Conference in Beijing (1995), when the issue and the women with disabilities and their allies made an appearance, although in a limited manner. This recognition did not convert to implementation of equal rights for women with disabilities. Differential treatment of women with disabilities continued to exist despite the standard-setting document of the Human Rights Declaration, which currently remains at the core of the global human rights regime. Most of the countries are signatories to many international conventions that protect human rights, such as the Convention on the Elimination of All Forms of Discrimination Against Women (CEDAW), UN Convention on the Rights of Persons with Disabilities (UNCRPD), and the Convention on the Elimination of All Forms of Racial Discrimination and are based on the promise of justice and equality to all, including women.

Today, in the search for women's equality, we must understand the normative foundation of democracy from a gendered perspective and question the threats to it. It is important to examine the role of those who have dominated the system at the cost of gendered equality from a disability perspective. To examine why women remain a part of a democratic system that is neither representative nor responsive to them, we must put a democratic framework in place that rests on gendered claims of justice, equality, and inclusion.

Within the existing trajectories of disability, justice, and equality, a new conceptualization should provide overarching principles that are inclusive of gender-related ideological elements and the understanding of current issues in a globalized world. We must question the inability of the system to remove many of the barriers created by the State, society, and family. This framework should enable us to analyze the challenges faced by researchers and practitioners in integrating gender under bounded situations as a result of a discriminatory system, in which a large group of women remain invisible and their needs remain unmet. A trajectory has to be ever moving upward, and not flat as in the case of women with disabilities. This reconstruction of gendered discrimination must develop clarity on these principles, especially as they are missing from disability research and praxis.

Justice and Equality

Ideologically, justice surfaces as the overarching normative principle under which disability policies should operate generally, and specifically within the broad structure of a disability-oriented feminist thought. Inequalities exist at various levels, but these can be removed by the adoption of a framework of justice. This framework should be able to create an environment where we do not have to raise the questions of survival, low quality of life, and insecurity of women.

Women's contribution to the justice and equality debate began in 1792. In her seminal work, "A Vindication of the Rights of Women," Mary Wollstonecraft wrote that justice, rather than charity, is wanted in the world. It is no historical irony that this statement fits into our present-day discussion related to women with disabilities. The general theories of justice have been grounded on the existence of various philosophical understandings and organizing principles (Rawls, 1971, 2001; Walzer, 1983). From a feminist perspective, the following two important notions of justice fit into our comprehension: giving women power over their own lives and the independence to live it the way they value it (Sen, 2009).This includes the important but ignored concept of *dignity*, on which little work has been done in relation to women and disability. Rawls' understanding of justice as fairness has also been debated (Nussbaum, 2001; Rawls, 2001: 5–8).[4] We can deduce from these writings that fairness and dignity are related and provide the foundation of fundamental rights. This notion resonates in Article I of the Universal Declaration of Human Rights, which states that all human beings are born free and equal in dignity and rights.

This book explores the foundation of justice within the normative framework of equality (Nussbaum, 2003, 2011; Sen, 2009). The justice–equality framework is not straightforward. For instance, in his writing of *Inequality Re-Examined*, Sen argues, "Equal consideration for all may demand very unequal treatment in favour of the disadvantaged" (1992). Providing for equality in a generic manner is insufficient; for instance, when a State is confronted by group inequity, special measures must be taken. States have discriminated legally in favor of women, race, caste, class, and even persons with disabilities when necessary. This is in line with Amartya Sen's theory of justice or what he calls normative social choice, which he states must be alive to both the fairness of the processes involved and the equity and efficiency of the substantive opportunities that people can enjoy (2009: 296). These arguments raise the following questions: Why does discrimination exist? Who is accountable? Why does the State not implement the process of rights it provides for? Why is there a weak implementation process? Who gains and who loses if laws are not implemented properly? It is critical that we question the State's implementation of the concepts of equality and justice, and their dispensation to persons living within its boundaries, specifically from a feminist perspective.

In the context of disability, Article 13 of UNCRPD on access to justice requires the abolishing of rules that limit or establish as void the capacity of persons with disabilities to testify, thus, connecting this Article with the issue of legal capacity. Although it addresses justice dispensation, it does not do so for the ideological basis, making the section rather narrow (UN

Enable). Justice in its philosophical understanding is broader than justice dispensation. Although the ideological foundation of UNCRPD is based on the concept of justice, it must be developed further so that it can be implemented in its entirety. Overall, eliminating inequalities in the space of *being* is what matters at the end of the day.

It can be argued that the subject of equality is central to the perception of disability within the broad parameters of justice. There can be inequality in the space of rights, gender being the prime example that affects the choice of many women, especially the marginalized. The aforementioned international conventions, the many disability-related laws formulated to provide equality, stipulate that States must end discrimination both in law and in practice. Under the UNCRPD (Article 5.1), for instance, State parties recognize that all persons are equal before and under the law, and are entitled without any discrimination to the equal protection and equal benefit of the law.

It is necessary to extend discourses beyond Article 5 and to develop a multidimensional principle of equality that has space for women. In this, we can relate our legislative reform to CEDAW. As Indira Jaisingh, a feminist lawyer, writes, CEDAW's contribution to the "improvement in the status of women worldwide is that it has given us a definition of equality which addresses both direct and indirect discrimination, and evaluates the goal of equality by looking at impact and outcome rather than looking at the form of law" (2011: 4). Jaisingh's argument reflects that CEDAW is one of the only global instruments to provide substantive equality to women. The aim of substantive equality is to take into account the role of gender in the existing power structures and to extend beyond the concept of discrimination on the grounds of sex or gender. Rather than outlawing discrimination on the basis of sex, it aims to eliminate discrimination against women. It is not sufficient to provide equal rights as they apply to men, as such rights may not provide space for the full equality of women.

To secure equal rights for women with disabilities, response measures must address the discrimination that women with disabilities encounter and how they can access their fundamental rights for justice. In this context, we must examine the laws drafted for the inclusion of women's rights and women's equal access to these laws, policies, government programs, and decision-making processes. It is also imperative that women with disabilities access substantive equality. To achieve this goal, we must investigate the many hurdles confronting women in their public and private roles.

The Body Politic: Violence and Torture

The fundamental relationship between patriarchy and violence suggests the use of a gender process to interpret and analyze the linkage. Patriarchal control is visible in many forms and is typically violent in nature. Such control is perpetrated on women with disabilities by various actors— family, personal assistants, teachers, doctors, and a range of other service providers. Ranging from traditional to today's extended patriarchy, the core characteristic of systemic violence exists and maintains the hierarchical order.

The normalcy and ethical acceptability of any and all categories of violence must be challenged as we seek to comprehend the interrelationships among forms of violence.[5] Among these, domestic violence, rape, and torture are all fundamental elements of sex- and gender-based violence. The multiple forms of gender violence serve different functions in perpetuating patriarchy. We must critically understand the bases of patriarchal strength and inconsistencies to create change toward achieving gender equality, and moving away from controlled and unequal situations.

Violence is used in many modes, ranging from structural to sociocultural violence, which reinforces gender disparity. Its aim is to not only cause physical and psychological harm, but also to abuse human dignity. For the difficult task of creating a violence-free society, we must understand that women with disabilities are more vulnerable to violence because they lack a civil society network backup. They are also less literate, unskilled, and more isolated than other women. Some groups among these women face more violence than others, for instance, women with intellectual or psychosocial disability and the deaf and blind. To change this unequal situation, power must be restructured between the perpetrators and the women who experience violence. The first step in this restructuring of power is to recognize that violence can be prevented.

The system that sanctions violence against women, diminishing the rule of human rights, raises issues of how to replace the present system with a gender-equal, disability-centered system of nonviolent institutions. Although some remedial steps are being taken in the present system to reform a few of its most egregious effects, the formidable violent structure stands strong in a democratic space.

One of the issues that must be raised are the forms of violence related to torture (see Article 15 of UNCRPD in UN Enable). According to the UN Special Rapporteur on the right to health:

> The right to be free from torture and other cruel, inhuman, or degrading treatment cannot be violated under any circumstance, and governments must take immediate action to address it. Women are often provided inadequate time and information to consent to sterilization procedures, or are never told or discover later that they have been sterilized. Policies and legislation sanctioning nonconsensual treatments... including sterilizations... violate the right to physical and mental integrity and may constitute torture and ill-treatment. (UN Human Rights Council, 2009)

The UN Committee Against Torture, which monitors and interprets the Convention Against Torture and Other Cruel, Inhuman or Degrading Treatment or Punishment, and the UN Special Rapporteur on Torture have stated that violence, including domestic violence, can be torture.[6] These two documents provide a basis on which to develop advocacy. The Torture Convention provides an absolute prohibition against torture in both the public and private spheres, thus, linking it to domestic violence. The convention is grounded in the principle of the inviolability of universal human dignity integral to human philosophy developed over time and the whole body of international human rights standards.

Torture is not an aberration; rather, it is a manifestation of a system that is insensitive to violence. This is an order that exists in and is maintained by patriarchy. Significantly, gendered violence is sexually inflicted. How does this relate to disability? The most obvious relation is the invisibility of persons with disabilities, on whom violence (especially sexual violence) is perpetuated and not circumvented due to these individuals' limited power and low position in the gender power order. Patriarchy sustains and integrates the holistic system of violence through coercion and repression. Most of this violence is manifested as a power structure of not only male power over female power, but is also extended in the case of disability to female power over women with disabilities. This order posits a hierarchy of moral inclusion and exclusion divided by those with more value than others. Examples include a parent battering a young child for not being able to meet the *normal* standards of studying, locking up or beating a girl with intellectual disability because she does not understand the societal gendered norms, and using forced hysterectomy on a young girl because she does not comprehend the standards of hygiene or may be *raped*, leading to pregnancy. These examples establish the similarity between torture and violence in disability situations, as the perpetrators enjoy impunity despite the cruelty and an escalation of harm that results in avoidable and severe physical and mental torture.

In this book, we argue that there is a need for critical consciousness of basic ethics of human relationships, moral reflection, and citizens' social and civic responsibilities. We must advocate for the eradication of torture, so as to overcome the socialization of the culture of violence embedded in our societies. In addition to individuals' responsibilities, the Convention stipulates that "the States obligation to prevent torture also applies to all persons who act ... at the behest of the State Party" (para 7, General Comments). Hospitals, which are care institutions supported by the State, come directly under the obligations, as "no exceptional circumstances whatsoever may be invoked by a State Party to justify acts of torture ..." (para 5). We must clearly understand the system of violence that produces torture and the network of responsibility for its continuation. Through our research, we need to develop an understanding of the interrelationships among all forms of violence and the essential gendered nature of the patriarchal structures and relationships that comprise the culture of violence that characterizes this society and State.

The Issue of Motherhood and Right to Be Born

This issue is addressed in this book because the ethical context that is linked to disability creates an environment of extreme discrimination against women with disabilities with regard to childbearing.[7] The discourse on motherhood is a continuation of a long-standing feminist theory of its glorification; however, there has been a tendency to place women with disability on the periphery and sometimes outside of this discourse. Motherhood is a conscious choice. In the case of disability, it is burdened by various compulsions laid down by society and the health system. Encircled by patriarchy, poverty, and little social support, most women with disabilities feel threatened by the state of pregnancy. Women with disability are threatened because of the society, which views them as asexual beings sited within an inaccessible health system that has little knowledge of their concerns, and face with social stigmatization that marginalizes them more than men. Therefore, they are both excluded and placed on the sidelines.

Mothers are blamed for giving birth to a child with a disability as punishment for their personal doing. In the eyes of the community, this justifies the departure of their spouse and the withdrawal of family support. Not only do they have little access to health care, as previously mentioned, they are categorized as asexual. This barring from sexuality means that they have no choice for motherhood. The implication that they are not true *women* reminds us of the Aristotelian suggestion of women as men with disabilities (Aristotle, 1944; Garland, 1995). Because marriage and childbirth are fundamental rights, the exclusion of women with disability places them as noncitizens within the nation.

Meenu Sikand, from Canada, paints a poignant picture of motherhood:

> My strong network of family, friends and other resources was ready to support me during and after the pregnancy. So, here I was Pregnant. My body experienced changes and I started to have many questions on my mind that my doctors were unable or unwilling to answer. While answering, they used phrases such as, "or a normal woman the experience will be ..." or, "Under normal circumstances, the delivery plan will be ..." I started to feel very agitated and hated the word "Normal." I simply wanted to know about the care I would need or delivery plan my doctor would follow. I wanted answers specific to my situation, not some hypothetical scenario. (2002)

She received few answers and stated, "I was so thrilled to be pregnant, but at the same time I was reaching the lowest point of my life" (ibid.).

Although many global programs have not engaged in eugenic programs of sterilization, they do show similarities with such programs in the context of disability. According to eugenics, it is possible and desirable, through selective breeding and the elimination of undesirable individuals, to alter the hereditary qualities of a race or population. Newborns with disabilities are killed before they are born, usually as disability simply is considered to be a burden. In India, the Prenatal Diagnostic Techniques (Regulation and Prevention of Misuse) Act, 1994, was enacted and brought into operation on January 1, 1996, to check sex selection. It was enlarged in scope to include pre-conceptual diagnostics through an amendment in 2002. A major issue that remains unresolved is the legitimate abortion of the disabled fetus provided for in the Act. The outcome of the Act is the strengthening of social construction of disability as an affliction that can be removed by technology when the aim should be to create gender equality.

This linkage of disability of giving women the right to remove an *unfit* child is a product of eugenistic thought. The growing sanctity given to technology in the name of the perfect is an abuse of human rights. This is more obvious in the context of women's reproductive rights when a woman is asked to terminate her pregnancy if the fetus is *disabled*.[8] Even genetic counseling is provided under a Pre-conception and Prenatal Diagnostic Techniques Act in India so that the disabled may be selected for destruction.[9] Thus, there is an existing unethical divide in the law, which considers testing for gender selection as illegal while testing for disabilities as legal.

The development of Nano-Bio-Info-Cogno-Synbio technology has swept the globe, breaking barriers wherever these have been constructed. There is little or no information or transparency of these new technologies, and they are used without people receiving information or providing consent (Hans, 2006). Researchers are redefining human geography, and modern explorers are elaborating a new human map (based on genes) that could alter human views and perceptions of normality and abnormality, particularly in the field of procreation. This is where technology comes in, or, as Wolbring argues, the nondisabled, non-transhumanism view of the human body as *defective* and all individuals as *impaired* or *defective* with the potential to be improved to enhance physical and cognitive performance (Swanson, 2006). This can be observed in the impacts of prenatal testing and screening on women (Peters and Lawson, 2002). Wolbring views society's increasing drive for human enhancement or perfection as damaging to any individual who does not meet the expected standards. For example, the ultimate societal direction could be to give a cochlear implant to an individual who is deaf, presuming that he or she is deficient—to the horror of some parents and others in the deaf community who value deaf culture (quoted in Swanson, 2006).

Concerns about genetic determination in the context of women have been voiced by some writers. New developments make possible a whole new branch of technology that intervenes in the processes of life itself, and, to some extent, shapes and reshapes human nature to our own designs. It also widens the gap between those with and those without disability, as we search to perfect the human body. New technologies pose further risks to women with disabilities and their control over their bodies. This search for perfection also creates exclusiveness as such that a disability might be viewed as a medical problem with little relation to its social context. Historically, the perfection of the body has played an important role, and the Adonis and Cleopatra syndromes have dominated the world society. It is, therefore, not surprising that the new technologies will assist in furthering this dimension of human desires.

Technology is becoming a barrier in the achievement of rights. Hi-tech companies patent our lives with their new reproductive technologies using human tissues or DNA (deoxyribonucleic acid). Among the new technologies, the *Red Biotechnology* being introduced as the answer to perfection means that our bodies are no longer our own. Rather, they are marketed by companies that make a profit while people become testing grounds. The aim is always to improve, enhance, and move forward. The cloning of animals or food is one strategy to achieve perfection, but this is only the beginning. La Fontaine saw it as the aim to attain a *perfect* body, which places the body in the same context as inanimate subjects such as architecture and household goods (2003: 43). The *perfect* human body is always visualized as without *defects*, and disabled bodies are considered as aberrations. The technological search for perfection gives rise to the conception that perfection can be purchased, which results in the discarding of the imperfect. When some disabled women marry, they are viewed as having defective wombs that will produce disabled children. Disabled women are considered incapable of bearing and rearing healthy children; thus, more than 80 percent of disabled women remain unmarried.

The marketing of next-generation assisted fertility technologies provides an example of the divide between the medical and social/human approach. This attainment of *perfection* promoted by family members or physicians comes at the cost of removing those with disabilities. In many countries where this practice exists on a large scale, new technologies are being tested. One of these tests has been the use of a synthetic malarial chemical called quinacrine. Quinacrine was tested in India, Bangladesh, Vietnam, and other poor countries even though the drug caused chemical sterilization (Dasgupta, 2005). Like many other earlier contraceptives, it has been used on women without their consent. This practice is not new; MNCs and medical institutions have often tested drugs (especially birth control drugs) on women, including those with disabilities, without their knowledge and consent.

Although contraceptives provide some women with reproductive choices, for other women, they assist in the violation of human rights. Women's rights are violated when women's wombs become testing grounds for New Reproductive Technologies (NRTs). They can become disabled through such testing. For women who are already disabled, the situation is far worse. To understand this emerging phenomenon, further research must be carried out. There are no national guidelines for existing unethical practices that open women's wombs to the free marketplace for use, while denying them basic rights and justice. Within the disability movement, especially women must question and contest these technologies. Each new day, a new technology emerges. We must be prepared to meet the challenges that these technologies pose to our freedom and identities.

The recent feminist queries reflect the dilemma in the debate.

> How do we understand and respond to a woman's right over her body, vis-à-vis the rights of her "unborn child," in a way that is both consistent and progressive? And how do we understand and define disability, including its point of origin, in a way that resonates with feminist principles we want to espouse? (Sama Health, 2012)

These queries require further projection within feminist debates on the use of reproductive technologies. Women organize across the world to seek justice, but the presence of women with disabilities within these movements is limited. The issues confronting women with disabilities may be different and must, therefore, be addressed by the women's movement and the disability movement. There must be solidarity in our approach, as the powers of technology and its promoters are too strong to be confronted alone or by a small group of researchers.

Diversities and Struggles for Recognition

The heterogeneity of disability issues is linked to the diversity of disability groups. In the persisting hierarchy, some groups find themselves at the bottom. Among these, near-excluded groups are women with multiple disabilities—those with psychosocial disability—and women from indigenous populations. There has been also little research on women in conflict and disaster situations.[10]

There is little or no work on gendered issues of autism. Generally, it has been perceived that groups with autism, such as those with psychosocial disability "continue to be denied the 'four key pillars of minority rights'," as identified by the UN's Special Rapporteur on Minority Issues, Rita Izsák: "[P]rotection of existence and prevention of violence against minorities; promotion and protection of minority identity; equality and non-discrimination; and the right to effective participation in all areas of public, economic and social life." The violence against those with autism is extensive and includes behavior modification, institutionalization, and abusive medical and therapeutic practices, such as electric shocks or *packing.* They, therefore, hide their condition for fear of discrimination. Erich Kofmel, the President of Autistic Minority International, argues for awareness which would lead to acceptance, recognition, and respect for autistics as autism acceptance will ensure full and equal participation in all areas of public, economic, and social life (2014).

Previous studies have shown that extensive discrimination prevails against women with intellectual and psychosocial disabilities in the form of forced segregation, socially sanctioned abuse, and State dehumanization structures, stigma, forced hysterectomies and sterilization, and harm by service providers, personal assistants, and family members.[11] Devalued and objectified, they have no rights and are treated as medical objects that are manipulated with drugs and confined like wild and dangerous animals. According to Tina Minkowitz, psychiatry lockup is:

> I believe a form of deprivation of legal capacity since your decision-making rights in a wide range of areas are stripped, particularly your rights to decide about your daily life and your future, and your right to protect your own body against invasion with unwanted medical procedures/substances.[12]

Most women who enter mental asylums rarely find their way back home, as they are discarded for life.

One of the key provisions of UNCRPD is Article 12 and legal capacity. In many countries, women with both intellectual and psychosocial disabilities are denied the right to legal capacity. The authority to act rests with their guardians/any other third person, which includes their right to manage property, money, and place of residence. This is due to laws linked to mental health that create a specific regime of detention and forced treatment based on the grounds that the person has mental illness.

More women have been incarcerated in mental asylums/psychiatric wards or even within the home because any anger that they express earns them the title of *mad*. Women are expected to be patient, quiet, and to not get angry or raise their voice. Such behavior is considered inappropriate and warranting lockup. They are then subjected to drugs and invasive medical procedures. They are deprived of legal capacity, with no authority to manage property or to get married. At the least, they are placed under guardianship with few rights.

As Tina Minkowitz, of the Center for the Human Rights of Users and Survivors of Psychiatry, writes,

> I also think the issues of disproportionate rights and responsibilities, which relates to legal capacity, has both a gender and a disability dimension.

Women have more responsibilities than rights, it is harder for women to enforce rights and this leads to a situation where even formal legal capacity can be a cipher.[13]

***

The struggle for feminist disability rights must change and be comprehensive if it is to pay wide-ranging dividends. We must adopt an approach that is universal and joins mainstream struggles in the long run. Otherwise, it will end with women fighting for their narrowly focused *disability* rights, which may not be our final goal. Countries with high poverty, little access to resources, and high inequality require our attention because if the countries change, we benefit. We must supplement our efforts by drawing power from other struggles. An indigenous woman with a disability should find an equally good platform within the indigenous rights platform. Human diversity can only be accommodated if people move together and recognize their multiplicity of needs. Women need more avenues to raise concerns to achieve equality in a rather unequal world. This may not be easy; therefore, the struggle from a separate platform for disability rights cannot be relinquished altogether for a larger cause, but must continue while drawing strength from other movements.

Notes

1. Disability studies from a gendered perspective have found little grounding, though earlier Avery (1994) had attempted to link feminism with disability studies. Important work has been carried out by R.G. Thomson (2005). However, there is no work related to women from the developing countries.
2. Among these, senior bureaucrats, academics, researchers, and activists have contributed to disability research from a feminist perspective. See Addlakha (2013), Fine and Asch (2009), Hans and Patri (2003), Hans et al. (2013), Mason (2004), Mintz (2007), Morris (1991), and Wendell (1996).
3. The *World Report on Disability* suggests that the prevalence of disability is 15 percent and the variation of disability ranges from 1 percent to 30 percent, but across all countries, all vulnerable groups, such as women had a higher prevalence of 19.2 percent females versus 12.0 percent male (World Health Organization [WHO] and World Bank [WB], 2011: 27–29, 261). The WB, projecting data on women, concludes that women with disabilities make up a sizeable proportion of the global population, and a majority of the population of persons with disabilities in developing countries. Although firm statistics

have been difficult to acquire, current researches estimate that women with disabilities make up at least 10 percent of all women globally (WHO). They comprise three quarters of all disabled people in low and middle-income countries (US Agency for International Development [USAID]). 65–70 percent of women with disabilities in low and middle-income countries live in rural areas (USAID). Women in general are more likely than men to become disabled because of poorer working conditions, poor access to quality healthcare, and gender-based violence (International Labor Organization [ILO]). Literacy rates for women with disabilities globally may be as low as 1 percent (United Nations Development Program [UNDP]).

4. Nussbaum (2001) criticizes Rawls for stereotyping citizens in the role of rough equals who relate because they can benefit each other, saying "Instead of picturing one another as rough equals making a bargain, we may be better off thinking of one another as people with varying degrees of capacity and disability, in a variety of different relationships of interdependency with one another."

5. The Declaration on the Elimination of Violence Against Women, adopted in 1993, defines violence against women as "any act of gender-based violence that results in, or is likely to result in, physical, sexual or psychological harm or suffering to women, including threats of such acts, coercion or arbitrary deprivation of liberty, whether occurring in public or in private life" (UN General Assembly, 1993).

6. Violence/torture can be physical, such as beating, burning, asphyxiation, pulling out nails, mutilating, rape and other sexual molestation. It can also be psychological, such as threat to create fear and sexual humiliation.

7. One of the works related to maternity and maternity leave is in a book about *Julianna's* standpoint a tension-filled, contradictory, and ironic statement of what life entails for a pregnant woman with disabilities. The book revolves around her story, displaying the ways in which she pieced together data and insights (Buzzanell, 2003).

8. For a discourse on bioethics and disability, see Amundson and Tresky (2007), and Asch (1990, 1999, 2002). Lombardo (2008) has linked disability to eugenics.

9. Some work has been done providing the systematic bias against the disabled in the structure and practice of genetic counseling (Patterson and Satz, 2002).

10. The most comprehensive work that has come recently is by Mitchell and Karr (2014); however, gender is not a focus.

11. The term intellectual disability was adopted during the process of negotiations of the text of the UNCRPD in place of mental retardation because the word mental has been used in derogatory ways. The term psychosocial, used by the World Network of Users and Survivors of Psychiatry, could not be adopted but is increasingly utilized. As UNCRPD moves away from the medical model, the removal of medical terminology such as psychiatric disability, mentally ill and health is being debated.

12. Personal communication. 2013.

13. Personal communication. 2013.

Bibliography

Addlakha, Renu (ed.). 2013. *Disability Studies in India*. Delhi: Routledge.

Amundson, R. and S. Tresky. 2007. "On a Bioethical Challenge to Disability Rights," *Journal of Medicine and Philosophy*, 32 (6): 541–561.

Aristotle. 1944. *Generation of Animals*, translated by A. L. Peck. Cambridge: Harvard University Press.

Asch, A. 1990. "The Meeting of Disability and Bioethics: A Beginning Rapprochement," in B. S. Duncan and D. Woods (eds), *Ethical Issues in Disability and Rehabilitation: An International Perspective*, pp. 85–89. New York: World Rehabilitation Fund, World Institute on Disability and Rehabilitation International.

————. 1999. "Prenatal Diagnosis and Selective Abortion: A Challenge to Practice and Policy," *American Journal of Public Health*, 89 (11): 1649–1657.

————. 2002. "Disability and Reproductive Rights," in J. A. Baer (ed.), *Historical and Multicultural Encyclopedia of Female Reproductive Rights in the United States*, pp. 64–66. Westport, CT: Greenwood Press.

Avery, H. 1994. "Feminist Issues in Built Environment Education," *Journal of Art and Design Education*, 13 (1): 65–71.

Buzzanell, P. M. 2003. "A Feminist Standpoint Analysis of Maternity and Maternity Leave for Women with Disabilities," *Women and Language*, 26 (2): 53–65.

Das, Rajashri Dasgupta. 2005. "Quinacrine Sterilization in India: Women's Health and Medical Ethics Still at Risk." A publication of the Population and Development Program at Hampshire College, (34): 1–4.

Fine, Michelle and Adrienne Asch. 2009. *Women with Disabilities: Essays in Psychology, Culture and Politics*. Philadelphia: Temple University Press.

Garland, Robert. 1995. *The Eye of the Beholder: Deformity and Disability in the Graeco-Roman World* (second edition). London: Bristol Classical Press.

Hans, Asha. 2006. "Gender, Technology and Disability in the South," *Development*, 49: 123–127.

Hans, Asha and Annie Patri (eds). 2003. *Women, Disability and Identity*, pp. 43–55. New Delhi: SAGE Publications.

Hans, A., A. Patel, and S. B. Agnihotri. 2013. "Need for a Framework for Combined Disability and Gender Budgeting," in Renu Addlakha (ed.), *Disability Studies in India*. Delhi: Routledge.

Health, Sama. 2012. *Advancing Feminist Debates on Reproductive Technologies—A Seminar*, March 30. Available online at http://samawomenshealth.wordpress.com/2012/03/30/advancing-feminist-debates-on-reproductive-technologies-a-seminar-3-2/ (downloaded on 19.05.2012).

Jaisingh, I. (ed.). 2011. "Introduction," in *Illusive Equality Constitutional Guarantees and Legal Regimes in South Asia, Malaysia and China*, p. 4. New Delhi: Women Unlimited.

Kofmel, Erich. 01.06.2014. "Comments on Draft General Comment No. 35 of the Human Rights Committee on Article 9 of the International Covenant on Civil and Political Rights." Geneva: Autistic Minority International.

La Fontaine, Michelle. 2003. "Perfect? An Analysis of the Global Genetic Fix," in Asha Hans and Annie Patri (eds), *Women, Disability and Identity*, pp. 43–55. New Delhi: SAGE Publications.

Lombardo, P. 2008. *Three Generations, No Imbeciles: Eugenics, the Supreme Court, and Buck v. Bell*. Baltimore: Johns Hopkins Press.

Mason, Grimley. 2004. *Working Without Odds: Stories of Disabled Women's Work Lives*. Boston: NE University Press of New England.

Mintz, Susannah B. 2007. *Unruly Bodies: Life Writings by Women with Disabilities*. Chapel Hill, USA: University of New Carolina Press.

Mitchell, David and Valerie Karr. 2014. *Crisis Conflict and Disability Ensuring Equality*. Oxford: Routledge.

Morris, Jenny. 1991. *Pride Against Prejudice*. Philadelphia: New Society Publishers.

Nussbaum, M. 2001. "The Enduring Significance of John Rawls," *The Chronicle of Higher Education*, July 20.

———. 2003. "Capabilities as Fundamental Entitlements: Sen and Social Justice," *Feminist Economist*, 9 (2–3): 33–59.

———. 2011. "Capabilities, Entitlements, Rights: Supplementation and Critique," *Journal of Human Development and Capabilities*, 12 (1): 23–37.

Patterson, A. and M. Satz. 2002. "Genetic Counseling and the Disabled: Feminism Examines the Stance of Those Who Stand at the Gate," *Hypatia*, 17 (3): 118–142.

Peters, Yvonne and Karen Lawson. 2002. "The Ethical and Human Rights Implications of Prenatal Technologies: The Need for Federal Leadership and Regulation" for Prairie Women's Health Centre of Excellence. Available online at http://www.pwhce.ca/pdf/petersLawson.pdf (downloaded on 29.12.2014).

Rawls, J. 1971. *A Theory of Justice*. Cambridge: Harvard University Press.

———. 2001. *Justice as Fairness: A Restatement*. Cambridge: Harvard University Press.

Sen, A. 1992. *Inequality Re-Examined*. New York: Russell Sage Foundation/Cambridge: Harvard University Press.

———. 2009. *The Idea of Justice*. London: Allen Lane/Penguin Books.

Sikand, M. December 2002. International Persons with Disabilities Day Featured Article. Available online at http://sci.rutgers.edu/forum/showthread.php?31489-Sikand-Meenu (downloaded on 28.01.2015).

Thomson, R. G. 2005. "Feminist Disability Studies," *Signs: Journal of Women in Culture and Society*, 30 (2): 1557–1587.

United Nations Conference in Beijing. 1995. Fourth World Conference on Women. China - September 1995 Action for Equality, Development and Peace, Beijing. For details, see Report UN Document A/CONF.177/20/Rev.1. Available online at http://www.un.org/womenwatch/daw/beijing/pdf/Beijing%20full%20report%20E.pdf (downloaded on 26.12.2014).

United Nations Enable: Development and Human Rights for all Web Page. Available online at http://www.un.org/disabilities/ (downloaded on 26.12.2014).

UN General Assembly. 1993. "Declaration on the Elimination of Violence Against Women," Res. 48/104, 48 U.N. GAOR Supp. (No. 49) at 217, U.N. Doc. A/48/49 (1993), Article 1.

———. August 10, 2009. "Right of Everyone to the Enjoyment of the Highest Attainable Standard of Physical and Mental Health," Note/by the Secretary-General, A/64/272. Available online at http://www.refworld.org/docid/4aa762e30.html (downloaded on 18.12.2014).

UN Human Rights Council. August 10, 2009. "Right of Everyone to the Enjoyment of the Highest Attainable Standard of Physical and Mental Health," report submitted by Anand Grover, Special Rapporteur, A/64/272, 2009, para 55. Available online at //www.refworld.org/docid/4aa762e30.html (downloaded on 03.02.2015).

Walzer, Michael. 1983. *Spheres of Justice*. New York: Basic Books.

Wendell, Susan. 1996. *The Rejected Body: Feminist Philosophical Reflections on Disability*. New York: Routledge.

WB. 2009. "Women with Disability (Articles 3 and 6)." Available online at http://web.worldbank.org/WBSITE/EXTERNAL/TOPICS/EXTSOCIALPROTECTION/EXTDISABILITY/0,,contentMDK:20193528~menuPK:418895~pagePK:148956~piPK:216618~theSitePK:282699,00.html (downloaded on 20.07.2013).

WHO and WB. 2011. *World Report on Disability*. Geneva: WHO.

Wolbring, Gregor. "An Ardent Advocate," *abilities*. Available online at https://abilities.ca/gregor-wolbring/ (downloaded on 30.12.2014).

DISABILITY: A GENDERED PROBLEMATIC AND CONCEPTUALIZATION

SECTION ONE

1

A Gendered Perspective of Disability Studies
Upali Chakravarti

Introduction

The emergence of disability studies is often attributed to the increased politicization of persons with disabilities in different countries, including the growth of social movements by persons with disabilities, such as the Independent Living Movement in the United States, the Self-Advocacy Movement in Sweden, and struggles by persons with disabilities in British residential institutions for greater control over their own lives. A range of issues have been identified as triggers for the emergence of disability studies: the social disadvantages experienced by persons with disabilities, their politicization through civil rights and equal opportunities campaigns, and social policy responses.

There has not been much work on disability in India vis-à-vis services or provisions; academic discussions about disability have just begun. Some played a catalytic role to provide impetus to disability campaigns. Despite the aforementioned developments in recent decades, the struggle of persons with disabilities in India for recognition and policy interventions has been long and arduous. Thus, while the academic field in the last decade or so has opened up to disability-related issues, economic, social, and political contexts of disability still await attention. Furthermore, there is a need to explore the gender dimensions of the issues as mentioned earlier. Rigorous studies on disability are also required in order to sensitize both the State and civil society to make changes that are imperative for a humane and just society for everyone in India. Across the world today, the disability movement is about citizenship and human rights, and disability studies must, therefore, find a balance between activism and academic work in order to impact policies for persons with disabilities in India.

This chapter will provide an overview of studies that have dwelt on disability in the contexts of political economy, gender, and care. The political economy is an important arena within which many questions and issues relating to disability can be analyzed and understood. It shapes the way a society defines disability, the services it makes available, facilitates access to employment and to self, and the identity development of disabled persons. Gender and sexuality are two critical issues in disability studies as they form an integral part of the experiences of persons with disabilities. Many of the struggles of the disabled are that they should not be stereotyped on the basis of appearance, since what most people first do is to categorize others based on their physical appearance—the body image. This body image shapes the sense of being and the self-identity that a person chooses. Further, while it is important to focus on the struggles of disabled people to make a place in the *normal* world— a struggle that is not to be undermined—it is important also to dwell on the stories and struggles of those who too make the same journey, the families of the disabled persons. Therefore, focus is required on the importance of the care of the disabled, from the perspective of both giving and receiving care.

A review of literature on the subject of disability shows that the issue of disability and the experiences of persons with disabilities have received scant consideration in the academic arena. The two disciplines that have worked in the area of disability, to some extent, are medicine and psychology. However, in both disciplines, the predominant context of reference is medical. Further, the discipline of psychology not only views disability as a *problem*, but also emphasizes the need for *adjustment* by the disabled persons to the *normal* environment. None of the other academic disciplines, such as sociology, history, political science, anthropology, or social policy, have developed theories or understandings other than basing studies in a medical context. The focal points of discussion within the disciplines, particularly medical sociology and anthropology, often get restricted to distinguishing illness, health, and disability, again indicating a strong leaning toward the medical model of disability.

Another crucial aspect that dominates the understanding of disability is the highly individualized nature attributed to the issue of disability. Apart from the medical condition that informs the approach to disability, it is viewed as an individual problem that must be handled or dealt with at the individual level. This view, thus, relegates the issue of disability outside the purview of studies that try to understand the nature of social relations in the relevant field of inquiry.

The two aforementioned approaches to disability have led many disability rights activists as well as academicians with disability, such as I. K. Zola, Meekosha, and Jenny Morris (Shakespeare et al., 1996: 182–205) to delve deeper into history and identify the real causes for the exclusion of disabled persons from the larger studies of society, politics, and economics.

Thereafter, the dominant views of disability as individual and medical problems were challenged, mostly by disabled persons themselves, beginning in the Western countries. The restrictions placed on disabled persons' abilities and lives due to these narrow views were the first seeds of the development of disability studies as a separate field of inquiry.

Barnes et al. drew attention to some of the limitations prior to the 1980s in disability studies; they argued that some exceptions aside, academic interest in disability was confined almost exclusively to conventional, individualistic, medical explanations, and even where others had become involved, they tended to reproduce disability uncritically within these frameworks (2002: 3).

A notable example is Erving Goffman's (1968) account of the interactions between the *normal* and *abnormal*, entitled *Stigma* (Barnes et al., 2002: 3).

According to Barnes et al., during the late 1960s and 1970s, though sociological studies drew attention to various economic and social consequences of the ascription of a conventional *disabled* identity, none made any serious attempt to question its ideological underpinnings—what has been variously called the *individual, medical,* or *personal tragedy* model of disability (ibid.: 4). Further, Barnes et al. note that the challenge to orthodox views came not from within the academy, but from the disabled people themselves. Inspired by the political and social upheavals during the 1960s and 1970s, disabled people began to organize collectively in increasingly large numbers to protest against their incarceration in residential institutions, their poverty, and the discrimination they encountered (ibid.).

According to them, the British experience is considered important, since it generated a radical and controversial new approach to theory and practice, now referred to as the *social model of disability* (ibid.: 4–5). The activities of grassroot organizations controlled and run by disabled people are important and provided a fertile ground in which disabled activists could explore and reconfigure the whole notion of disability. An impressive body of work emerged which implicitly, rather than explicitly, drew on personal experience, and these sociological insights constituted a direct challenge to conventional thinking and practice on disability. Thus, *disability* is not a product of individual failings, but is socially created (Barnes et al., 2002: 5). Rather than identifying disability as an individual limitation, the social model identifies society as the problem and looks to fundamental political and cultural changes to generate solutions (ibid.). These shifts in activist understandings of disability were mirrored by disability studies with a new emphasis on the structural and cultural forces that shape the lives of disabled people, and led to the generation of an increasingly complex body of knowledge. These include the debates on an appropriate definition of disability; the cultural context of the responses to disability; the ideological construction of disability mainly through the medicalization and individualization of disability; approaches to constructing disabled identities from the perspective of psychology, social psychology, sociology, race, and gender; and social construction of disability mainly from the political, economic, and social policy perspectives. In the recent years, we have also witnessed an increasing focus on the important issue of gender and disability. The last theme encompasses within it not only gender issues related to disabled persons, but also the broader feminist perspective on disability, ethics, and care.

Disability and Its Experience/ Experiencing Disability

According to Barbara Fawcett, for nearly all writers in the disability arena, fearful of the continued imposition of able-bodied agendas and perspectives, personal experience continues to occupy a position of central importance (Fawcett, 2000: 43). Oliver further adds that the personal response of individuals to their disabilities cannot be understood merely as a reaction to trauma or tragedy, but have to be located within a framework that takes into account both history and ideology (Oliver cited in Barnes et al., 1999: 60). For example, anthropologist Robert Murphy was struck by paralysis due to a tumor in his spinal cord at the age of 48. This became the occasion for writing a book entitled *The Body Silent* (1990) based on his own experience of disability and coping with it. However, he also uses his personal experience to make a generalized analysis of disability. As he puts it, the book is not "my autobiography, but the history of the impact of a quite remarkable illness upon my status as a member of society, for it has visited upon me a disease of social relations no less real than the paralysis of the body" (Murphy, 1990: 4). Another example is that of an eminent disabled sociologist, Zola:

> I realized how meager are our attempts to write and to do research about adjustment and adaptation. It would be nice if, at some point, growing up ends and maturity begins, or if one could say that successful adjustment and adaptation to a particular difficulty has been achieved. For most problems, or perhaps for most basic life issues, there is no single time for such a resolution to occur. For the problems must be faced, evaluated, redefined, and readapted to, again and again and again. And I knew now that this applied to myself. No matter how much I was admired by others or by myself, there was still much more I had to face. "My Polio" and "My Accident" were not just my past; they were part of my present and my future. (1982: 84)

One of the first books to challenge the *able-bodied* orthodoxy was Paul Hunt's edited collection *Stigma: The Experience of Disability* (1966). It comprises 12 personal accounts of disability from six disabled men and six disabled women. The aim was to avoid *sentimental autobiography*. Hunt argues, "the problem of disability lies not only in the impairment of function and its effects on us individually, but also, more importantly in the area of our relationship with 'normal' people" (Hunt, 1999, in Barnes et al., 1999: 77).

The challenge to analyze disability as a form of social oppression has scarcely been acknowledged within academic social science writings. However, the work of Paul Abberley represents some of the most sophisticated discussions of understanding disability as social oppression (Barnes et al., 1999: 79). Abberley emphasizes that a theoretically informed account must recognize the historical specificity of the experience of disability (ibid.). He developed his approach to disability as social oppression through the comparable work on sexism and racism. Abberley argues that the biological element in disabled people's oppression—impairment—is far more real than its counterparts for women and black people—sex and skin. Indeed, for many disabled people, "the biological difference... is itself a part of the oppression." Further, according to Abberley, a social oppression theory of disability must address this materially, rather than socially constructed difference, for at least two reasons. First, it comprises the bedrock on which conventional views of disability are based. Second, the extent of internalized oppression forms a major barrier to the development of a "political consciousness among disabled people" (Abberley, 1987, cited in Barnes et al., 1999: 79).

According to American social theorist Iris Young's study, entitled *Justice and the Politics of Difference* (1990), the demand for social justice has shifted from distributive aims to a wider canvas of decision making, division of labor, and culture, as well as "the importance of social group differences in structuring social relations and oppression." Young accounts that oppression comprises five different dimensions: exploitation, marginalization, powerlessness, cultural imperialism, and violence (Young, 1990, cited in Barnes et al., 1999: 81). According to Young, isolation and exclusion associated with marginalization form central elements in the experience of disabled people.

The Gendered Experience of Disability

Disabled people have often been represented as *without gender*, as *asexual* creatures, as freaks of nature, monstrous, the *other* to the social norm. In this way, it may be assumed that for disabled people, gender has little bearing. Yet, the image of disability may be intensified by gender—for women, a sense of intensified passivity and helplessness, for men a *corrupted* masculinity generated by enforced dependence. Moreover, these images have real consequences in terms of education, employment, living arrangements, personal relationships, victimization, and abuse that in turn reinforce the images in the public sphere. The gendered experience of disability reveals sustained patterns of difference between men and women (Meekosha, 2004: 3).

Disabled men and women narrate their experiences in significantly gendered terms, with both the content and styles reflecting the way in which gender expectations are modulated by disability status (ibid.: 10). According to Meekosha, both gender and disability have traditionally been seen as a product of biology. Gender, as a result of biology, has been thought to determine all manners of social behavior on the part of men and women. In a similar way, disability, as biology, has been seen as determining disabled people's choices and behavior. In the 1970s, feminists attempted to differentiate between gender and sex (the social from the biological) to counter the argument of women being naturally inferior and weak. Even disability theorists attempted to separate disability from impairment (the social from the biological) (ibid.: 11).

Meekosha further states that it is no longer adequate to separate the social from the biological in this dichotomous way. The social relations of gender and the social relations of disability are now viewed as much more complex and nuanced. Because the model drew on political economy, it emphasized political and economic processes that generate disabling environments (Meekosha, 2004: 12).

There has been a slowness to accept the relationship between gender and disability. According to Morris, the Disabled People's Movement, as with other political movements, has been dominated by men—both as theorists and as holders of important leadership and organizational posts. Also, non-disabled feminists are criticized for the failure to address disability issues or for simply repeating disablist ideas (Morris and Begum, 1991, in Barnes et al., 1999: 87).

According to Barnes et al. (1999), one of the earliest attempts to relate women's experience was Jo Campling's *Better Lives for Disabled Women* (1979) followed shortly by her innovative collection of essays *Images of Ourselves: Women with Disabilities Talking* (Barnes et al., 1999: 87). Although grounded in an individual perspective, these stressed common concerns about personal relationships, sexuality, motherhood, education, employment, and culture.

One of the first attempts to set these experiences within a wider theoretical framework was made by two American writers, Michelle Fine and Adrienne Asch (ibid.). They found that disabled women experienced a similar but more acute pattern of discrimination to women generally. Similarly, Susan Lonsdale's *Women and Disability* (1990) documents a range of social and economic disadvantages which largely replicate gender divisions in the general population (ibid.).

The writings on and by disabled women have gone beyond bringing disabled women into the disability theory, to consider more radical revisions in a social barriers approach. Rosemarie Garland Thomson (2004: 75) has pointed out that the goal of feminist disability studies is to augment the terms and confront the limits of the ways we understand human diversity, the materiality of body, multiculturalism, and the social formations that interpret bodily differences (ibid.). Simi Linton (1998) has suggested that studying disability is "a prism through which we can gain a broader understanding of society and human experience" (ibid.: 76).

Like women, disabled people's politicization has its roots in the assertion that *the personal is political*, that their personal experiences of being denied opportunities are not to be explained by their bodily limitations, but by the disabling social, environmental, and attitudinal barriers which are a daily part of their lives. However, over the past few decades, there has been a debate between the feminist and disability philosophy. Some feminists who view feminist theorizing from a disability perspective, such as Morris (1991) and Wendell (1989, 1996), are disturbed by evidence that feminism has not overcome a *residual allegiance to normalcy*. Indeed, some discussions of disability by feminists seem to proceed by laying aside feminism's own affiliations with liberation, self-affirmation, and inclusiveness. It is considered that because feminist philosophy is woman centered, and most women do not identify as being disabled themselves; the interests and emphases of feminist thinkers are not always congruent with those of activists aspiring to liberate the disabled from oppressive social arrangements or of scholars formulating liberatory theories that guide and justify doing so. Two conversations where the alliance between feminist philosophy and the philosophy of disability is strained relate to women's liberty to shape their own relationships and their liberty to reproduce. Thus, the interplay of biological and social identities—whether these are innate, imposed, or embraced—has become a subject of first-order importance in disability studies as well as in feminist theory.

In their article, "Smashing Icons," Marian Blackwell-Stratten, Mary Lou Breslin, Arlene Brynne Mayerson, and Susan Bailey (1988) discuss the political priorities of disabled and non-disabled feminists, showing how there are both links and differences. They make three key points: first, that being disabled and female is a unique dual status, different from other women; second, that while nondisabled and disabled women may agree on issues, the solutions may be different; and third, that disabled women experience *double* discrimination (Shakespeare et al., 1996: 182–205).

On the other hand, according to Jenny Morris, a focus on *gender and disability* should not be about examining the so-called *double disadvantage* experienced by disabled women. Such a focus feels disempowering to disabled women. It is also an inevitable consequence of treating disabled women's concerns as a *minority interest*, as an optional add-on to the concerns of both feminist analysis and to that of the DRM (Morris, 1998: 4). According to Morris, disabled women have to find a way of making experiences visible, sharing them with each other and with nondisabled people in a way which, while drawing attention to the difficulties, does not undermine the wish to assert self-worth. Morris argues that feminist writing does not usually victimize the (nondisabled) women whose lives are the subject of research and analysis. Feminist analyses of women's oppression are themselves a way of asserting resistance, of struggling against oppression. The studies of women's experiences—although they are studies of the difficulties that women face in their lives—rarely present them as passive victims (Morris, 1998: 5).

Thus, the interrelationship between gender and disability is a multi-faceted issue and is not in fact solely about women and girls, for both are social constructs which affect men as well as women. Gender, as a social construct, can be experienced in an oppressive way by men and boys as well as by women and girls, and there is a danger that if we do not acknowledge the influence and interaction of both in men and women's lives, any analysis or account of disabled people's lives can only be incomplete (ibid.: 11). At the same time, while it is true that the disability movement needs to adapt and change if it is to be fully representative, it is also the case that other movements and communities need to adapt and recognize their disabled members.

Disability and Sexuality

Historically, the DRM has focused its energy on issues more amenable to social change, such as access to the built environment, education, and employment (Shuttleworth, 2007: 2). By virtually ignoring the sexual issues relevant to disabled people, the DRM, thus, reinforced the individualized and medicalized view of disability and sexuality that held sway (ibid.).

The issue of disability and sexuality was and is still perceived by many disabled people as an individual problem, and it has remained virtually unacknowledged in mainstream culture. From the early 1980s through the mid-1990s, a few activists and scholars attempted to put sexuality on the political and research agendas of the DRM and of academic disability studies (ibid.).

The need to think about relationship between disability and sexuality is being stressed in recent writings. It is often recognized that women with disabilities are generally considered to be asexual or de-sexual not just in terms of not having sexual desires, but also in terms of not being *attractive*; hence, not attracting attention to themselves. Many disabled women have discussed this by drawing examples from their own personal experiences. Another important issue related to disability and sexuality is that of marriage and sexual reproduction. Anne Finger notes sadly that it is not just medical experts who are guilty of ignoring the reproductive and sexual rights and needs of people with disabilities (1992). Also, the movements for sexual and reproductive freedom have paid little attention to disability issues. Further, according to Finger, because the initial focus of the women's movement was set by women who were overwhelmingly non-disabled (as well as young and middle-class), the agenda of reproductive rights has tended to focus on the right to abortion as the central issue. Yet, for disabled women, the right to bear and rear children is as much if not more at risk (Finger, 1992).

Disabled feminist scholars have argued that because reproduction is seen as a *women's issue*, it is often relegated to the back burner. They feel that it is crucial that the DRM starts to deal with it head on. Even in the absence of outright bans on reproduction, the attitude that disabled people should not have children is widely held. Disabled women and men are still sometimes subject to forced and coerced sterilizations, including hysterectomies performed without medical justification, to prevent the *bother* of menstruation in the case of girls (ibid.).

Commenting on the DRM, many disabled men and women feel that it has certainly not put sexual rights at the forefront of its agenda. Finger states, "Sexuality is often the source of our deepest oppression; it is also often the source of our deepest pain" (ibid.). According to Finger, it is easier to talk about and formulate strategies for changing discrimination in employment, education, and housing than to talk about exclusion from sexuality and reproduction. Also, although it is changing, the DRM has tended to focus its energies on lobbying legislators and creating an image of *the able disabled*, which has obscured the range of ways disability is experienced as a disadvantage (ibid.).

In India, the disability discourse has primarily focused on issues related to the medical management, the education, and the employment of persons with disabilities. This is a crucial step in the disability movement, because it has resulted in the legislation for affirmative action and other policy moves (Addlakha, 2007: 3). However, since the focus of discussion and activities both by the State and the non-government organization (NGO) sector is still confined to enhancing the educational and employment opportunities of differently abled persons, other critical areas of concern, such as their fertility, sexual behavior, and reproductive health, have not yet found articulation in the public discourse (ibid.).

Not only in India but worldwide, persons with disabilities emerge as a sexually disenfranchised segment of the population. There is, in fact, a general social rejection of their sexuality. Consequently, disabled sexuality is an important area in the discipline of disability studies, more particularly feminist disability studies. Even in the Indian context, preliminary work in this domain has been undertaken by feminist researchers in the social sciences (Addlakha, 1999, 2001, 2005; Addlakha and Das, 2001; Ghai, 2003; Hans and Patri, 2003; Mehrotra, 2004, 2006).

Among these writers, Renu Addlakha highlights the dilemmas faced by young persons with disabilities, as they struggle to construct their sexual identities within dominant heteronormative discourses of conjugality in the Indian context. She argues that the absence of role models with disabilities and negative social perceptions of persons with disabilities are the major stumbling blocks for young people with disabilities as they struggle to cope with both the pain and excitement of growing up in general, and the personal challenges posed by disability in particular (Addlakha, 1999, 2001, 2005; Addlakha and Das, 2001; Ghai, 2003; Hans and Patri, 2003; Mehrotra, 2004, 2006).

Disability and Caring

Care for children, the elderly, and those with a disability is a major part of the work that needs to be done in any society and in most societies, it is a source of unfairness. Any theory of justice needs to think about the problem from the beginning, in the design of the basic institutions. In her book, dealing with the ideologies of caring, Dalley (1988) has focused on dependent people and women who usually care for them. Dalley highlights the ideology, the pattern of beliefs and attitudes, which underlie action. In particular, she draws attention to the competing ideologies upon which alternative social policies for the provision of care for dependent people are based, namely, familism and collectivism.

Analyzing the meaning of caring, and taking the example at the affective level, Dalley states that a distinction can be made between *caring for* and *caring about*. The first is to do with the tasks of tending another person; the second is to do with the feelings for another person (Parker and Graham, cited in Dalley, 1988: 8). Caring for and caring about are deemed to form a unitary, integral part of a woman's nature (which cannot be offloaded in the *normal* state of affairs). In the *extra-normal* situation of a child being chronically dependent beyond the constraints of dependence dictated by its age—through sickness and disability—the mother automatically extends and is expected to extend her *caring for* function. Just as the affective links which form at birth are tied to the mechanical links of servicing and maintenance in the case of healthy children, similarly, the same affective links in the case of disabled and chronically dependent family members get tied to the servicing and maintenance functions.

For most women, especially working-class women, the model results in triple burden—child rearing, housework, and wage labor. The nuclear family and the roles associated with it may not always exist in concrete form, but as an ideological construct; it is of crucial significance. Dalley points out that to be critical of community care policies is not to be critical of the importance of caring for and caring about, or of the necessity of enabling disabled and chronically dependent people to live *normalized* and *ordinary* lives; nor is it to deny that people want to be cared for in familiar surroundings, and to be cared about by people about whom they themselves also care.

In a review article, based on a number of works, published in the *New York Times*, Martha Nussbaum (2001: 34–37) develops further the arguments on disability and society on the basis of three books on the issue of caring for dependent persons (Kittay, 1999). She notes that much of the work of caring for a dependent is unpaid; nor is it recognized by the market as work. Yet, it has a large effect on the rest of such a worker's life. For persons who can afford hired help, most of it is drawn from women who are paid low wages; generally, they are also not as respected by society as they should be for performing a vital social service. According to Nussbaum, studies show that the work of caring for dependents at home is a crucial issue affecting the social equality of women. Holding that women are often subtly coerced by social norms into shouldering the burden of caring for a dependent, one scholar argues that any solution to the problem has different parts. One is the reallocation of domestic responsibilities between men and women in the home. The second is the role of the State: the State may lighten the burden of people who care for the dependents through a wide range of policies (Nussbaum, 2001). The supports could be financial, human resources, and/or institutional in nature. Access to these supports by the family should be automatic, rather than bureaucratic.

Another area in the issue of disability and caring is that of disabled women as caregivers as well as receivers of care. Jenny Morris was involved in a collective project with other spinal cord-injured women who need personal assistance in their daily lives, and experienced the different ways of receiving such assistance; she found that neither the feminist perspective nor that of the disabled people's movement adequately represented disabled women's experiences of receiving support in their daily lives (Morris, 1998: 6).

Karin Barron (1997), who has conducted extensive research on the lives of young women with disabilities, observes that great value is placed on the womanly art of caring for dependents, but the traditional dependent position of young women with disabilities prevents them from occupying, and, therefore, from demonstrating any aptitude for, this role (Alcoff and Kittay, 2007: 133). According to Rosemarie Garland Thomson, the controversial feminist ethic of care also has been criticized by feminist disability scholars for undermining symmetrical, reciprocal relations among disabled and non-disabled women, as well as for suggesting that care is the sole responsibility of women (1997: 26). In many situations, because of the lack of a support system, caregivers themselves undergo a lot of stress and health problems that are not adequately recognized as either a disability or a health issue.

Disability and Ethics

Bioethics is another area where feminist thinking, while making its mark, at least initially occluded disability perspectives. Feminist bioethicists, most often, have aligned with the principle that women are owed control of their own bodies. While this idea may appear compatible with the value of self-determination promoted by much disability philosophy, some bioethicists, including some who are feminists, have adopted medicalized views of disability, and, in doing so, have argued that the prospect of bearing a disabled child justifies, or even obligates termination of the pregnancy (Purdy, 1995; see also *Stanford Encyclopedia of Philosophy*, 2009). A related, but not identical, position challenges *Baby Doe* laws in the United States that prohibit hospitals from denying neonates with disabilities effective life-saving treatment, arguing that parents should be free to decide whether their child's life will be worth living.[1]

Feminist bioethicist Adrienne Asch has carefully distinguished between a woman's right to terminate her pregnancy and the moral constraints on her terminating the life of her newborn child. Disability does not diminish the claims of neonates, nor of other individuals with disabilities, to the necessities of life (Asch, 1990, 2002; Asch and Geller, 1996; Asch et al., 2003; Kittay, 2005).

Disability scholars generally have objected to the unfounded presumption that being disabled makes life not worth living, or at least makes the lives of people with disabilities less gratifying and valuable than those of non-disabled people. However, the social isolation to which disabled individuals often are condemned results in non-disabled people being misinformed about their potential for satisfying lives. Terminating a pregnancy because the resulting child may have impairment reduces the individual to the disability, but people with disabilities are as much a sum of many different strengths and flaws as non-disabled people are (Parens and Asch, 2000).

The objectionable presumptive devaluing of life with a disability is not compatible with a full and equitable commitment to reproductive liberty. Philosophers as well as policy makers have invoked the supposed inescapable suffering of disabled people as a reason for barring women with disabilities from using reproductive technology (for example, pre-implantation genetic diagnosis) to bear children like themselves, narrowing these women's reproductive choices. At the same time, according to Eva Kittay, social policies that pertain to disabled people also affect their family members, friends, and professional caregivers (Kittay, 2001, cited in Alcoff and Kittay, 2007: 133). So, feminist disability theory should recognize that disability affects the identities of many people beyond the 600 million worldwide who are themselves disabled (Herr et al., 2003, cited in Alcoff and Kittay, 2007).

According to Asch and Fine, women have won the right to abortion as a part of the right to control their bodies. If a woman decides that she wants to abort rather than carry to term a fetus with Down syndrome, she has the right to make this decision; but the more information she has, the better her decision can be (Asch and Fine, 1998: 237). Grief-stricken, shocked, and anxious parents who may seek to end the lives of their *imperfect* infants should be counseled, educated, and told about the treatment the child will receive whether or not the parents agree. We should work toward a policy in which the State picks up the medical expenses associated with such treatment. Parents may be removed if they so desire from responsibility at which point the State has to act to protect infants (ibid.: 238–239).

In India, the issue of bioethics, especially with regard to reproductive rights, is complex and is not just limited to the right to abortion, but the Prenatal Diagnostic Techniques (Regulation and Prevention of Misuse) Act or PNDT Act, 1994, also has a bearing on sex selection and disability. The PNDT Act states that abortion on the basis of sex is prohibited; however; it is permitted on the basis of disability. This consequently results in legitimization of one kind of selection versus another. In a study by Ghai and Johri, they argue that first, the concept of individual choice which is reified through the PNDT Act is socially constructed and contextually located; second, that while a pro-choice perspective is important to feminists, the thoughtless use of prenatal testing could reduce, rather than expand, women's choices (2008: 291). The disability community in India is so involved with issues of basic survival that there is as yet no space for discussion of the implications of new reproductive technologies. There is a need to make efforts to incorporate the perspectives of disabled individuals in genetic counselors' education and practice, thereby reforming the society's view about the disabled (Ghai and Johri, 2008: 312).

The State has the major responsibility of assisting disabled children and their families throughout life. Not only does the government have the obligation to absorb the medical and social service expenses that disabled children entail, it also has the obligation to provide parents with extensive information about life with a disability. In addition, they must assist the parents in finding alternative homes for children if the parents do not feel prepared to raise them (ibid.).

Like feminism, the DRM entails a commitment to self-determination and a shared sense of community. Disabled adults are among the most important advocates for disabled children, and they must participate in the decisions about the lives and policies affecting the lives of such children.

Viewing the literature on disability, it can be seen that disability, like any other human issue, has multifarious perspectives. However, it has to be remembered that these studies are mainly from the Western countries which have had a history of welfare state, social and economic policies, and provisions for the disabled, strong civil and political movements on the issue of human rights, and, above all, scholars who have recognized the lacunae or injustice of State policy locally as well as globally to be able to critique it objectively. For instance, they have recognized the negative side of capitalism, privatization, and globalization and its severe/harsh impact on persons with disabilities next only to women and children.

Disability studies in India should not merely end up recording the number of services provided, number of institutions opened, and number of rehabilitation professionals certified, or having a predominantly segregated and medical approach to the issue of disability even in the centers or departments of disability studies. The emerging field of disability studies in India must be integrated with the curricula at the levels of school, college, and university, with the content being much more analytical and positively critical, and must have an active component that can bring about social, political, and economic change for the better prospects of the disabled people of rural and urban India.

Today, the disability movement all the world over is about citizenship and human rights, and disability studies must find a balance of activism and academic work to impact the policies being made for disabled persons in India. By drawing attention to the economic, social, and political contexts of disability as well as incorporating a gender perspective in all rigorous studies, a critical role can be played in generating further scholarship and in sensitizing both the State and civil society to make changes that are imperative for a humane and just society for all. From this overview, we can see that a beginning has been made; there is a need to build on that.

Note

1. The primary case was a 1982 incident involving *Baby Doe*, a Bloomington, Indiana baby with Down syndrome, whose parents declined surgery to fix esophageal atresia with tracheoesophageal fistula, leading to the baby's death. The surgeon general of the United States at the time of this incident, C. Everett Koop, argued that the child was denied treatment (and food and water) not because the treatment was risky, but rather because the child was mentally retarded. Koop commented publicly that he disagreed with such withholding of treatment. In his decades as a pediatric surgeon, Dr Koop had repaired hundreds of such defects, with a continually improving rate of success. By 1982, success was nearly certain if the surgery was performed. A similar situation in 1983, involving a *Baby Jane Doe*, again brought the issue of withholding treatment for newborns with disabilities to public attention. In this case, *Baby Jane Doe* was born with spina bifida, an abnormally small head, and hydrocephaly. Dr Koop advocated medical treatment despite the severity of the condition and the limited outcomes that would result. Koop's efforts to educate the Congress about this issue ultimately led to the Baby Doe Amendment (United States Code Annotated Title 42, Chapter 67, Section 5106a). On October 9, 1984, the amendment extended the laws defining child abuse to include the withholding of fluids, food, and medically indicated treatment from disabled children. The law came into effect on June 1, 1985.

Bibliography

Addlakha, R. 1999. "Living with Chronic Schizophrenia: An Ethnographic Account of Family Burden and Coping Strategies," *Indian Journal of Psychiatry*, 41 (2): 91–95.

Addlakha. 2001. "Lay and Medical Diagnoses of Psychiatric Disorder and the Normative Construction of Femininity," in B. V. Davar (ed.), *Mental Health from a Gender Perspective*, pp. 313–333. New Delhi: SAGE Publications.

———. 2005. "Affliction and Testimony: A Reading of the Diary of Parvati Devi," *Indian Journal of Gender Studies*, 12 (1): 63–82.

———. 2007. "Gender, Subjectivity and Sexual Identity: How Young People with Disabilities Conceptualise the Body, Sex and Marriage in Urban India," Occasional Paper no. 46, Centre for Women's Development Studies, New Delhi.

Addlakha, Renu and Veena Das. 2001. "Disability and Domestic Citizenship: Voice, Gender, and the Making of the Subject," *Public Culture*, 13 (3): 511–531.

Alcoff, L. and E. F. Kittay (eds). 2007. *The Blackwell Guide to Feminist Philosophy*. UK: Blackwell Publishing Ltd.

Asch, A. 1990. "The Meeting of Disability and Bioethics: A Beginning Rapprochement," in B. S. Duncan and D. Woods (eds), *Ethical Issues in Disability and Rehabilitation: An International Perspective*, pp. 85–89. New York: World Rehabilitation Fund, World Institute on Disability and Rehabilitation International.

———. 2002. "Disability and Reproductive Rights," in J. A. Baer (ed.), *Historical and Multicultural Encyclopedia of Female Reproductive Rights in the United States*, pp. 64–67. Westport, CT: Greenwood Press.

Asch, A. and M. Fine (eds). 1998. "Shared Dreams: A Left Perspective on Disability Rights and Reproductive Rights," in *Women with Disabilities: Essays in Psychology, Culture, and Politics*, pp. 297–305. Philadelphia: Temple University Press.

Asch, A. and G. Geller. 1996. "Feminism, Bioethics and Genetics," in S. M. Wolf (ed.), *Feminism and Bioethics: Beyond Reproduction*, pp. 318–350. New York: Oxford University Press.

Asch, A., L. O. Gostin, and D. M. Johnson. 2003. "Respecting Persons with Disabilities and Preventing Disability: Is There a Conflict?" in S. S. Herr, L. O. Gostin, and H. H. Koh (eds), *The Human Rights of People with Intellectual Disabilities*, pp. 319–346. New York: Oxford University Press.

Barnes, C., M. Oliver, and L. Barton (eds). 2002. *Disability Studies Today*. Cambridge: Polity Press.

Barnes, C. et al. 1999. *Exploring Disability*. Cambridge: Polity Press.

Barron, Karin. 1997. Disability and Gender : Autonomy as an Indication of Adulthood (English), Doctoral thesis, Uppsala: Acta Universitatis Upsaliensis.

Dalley, G. 1988. *Ideologies of Caring: Rethinking Community and Collectivism*. London: Macmillan Education.

Fawcett, B. 2000. *Feminist Perspectives on Disability*. London: Pearson Education Limited.

Finger, A. 1992. "Forbidden Fruit," *New Internationalist*, (233): 8–10.

Ghai, Anita. 2003. *(Dis)embodied Form: Issues of Disabled Women*. Delhi: Shakti Books.

Ghai, A. and R. Johri. 2008. "Prenatal Diagnosis: Where Do We Draw the Line?" *Indian Journal of Gender Studies Special Issue: Disability, Gender and Society*, 15(2): 290–313.

Hans, Asha and Annie Patri. 2003. *Women, Identity and Disability*. Delhi: SAGE Publications.

Kittay, E.F. 1999. *Love's Labour: Essays on Women, Equality and Dependency*. New York: Routledge.

————. 2001. "When Care Is Just and Justice Is Caring: The Case of the Care for the Mentally Retarded," *Public Culture*, 13(3): 557–579.

————. 2005. "At the Margins of Moral Personhood," *Ethics*, 116(1): 100–131.

Lonsdale, Susan. 1990. *Women and Disability*. London: Macmillan.

Marian, Blackwell-Stratton, Mary Lou Breslin, and Arlene Byrnne Mayerson. 1988. "Smashing Icons: Disabled Women and the Disability and Women's Movements" in Michelle Fine and Adrienne Asch (eds), *Women with Disabilities: Essays in Psychology, Culture and Politics*, pp. 306–332. Philadelphia, PA: Temple University.

Meekosha, H. 2004. "Gender and Disability," draft entry for *SAGE Encyclopaedia of Disability*. Available online at http://disability-studies.leeds.ac.uk/files/library/meekosha-meekosha.pdf (downloaded on 29.12.2014).

Mehrotra, N. 2004. "Women, Disability and Social Support in Rural Haryana," *Economic and Political Weekly*, 39 (52): 5640–5644.

————. 2006. "Negotiating Gender and Disability in Rural Haryana," *Sociological Bulletin*, 55 (3): 406–427.

Morris, J. 1991. *Pride Against Prejudice: Transforming Attitudes to Disability*. London: Women's Press.

————. 1998. "Feminism, Gender and Disability," paper presented at a seminar in Sydney, Australia. Available online at http://disability-studies.leeds.ac.uk/files/library/morris-gender-and-disability.pdf (downloaded on 28.12.2014).

Murphy, R. F. 1990. *The Body Silent*. New York: W. W. Norton.

Nussbaum, M. 2001. "Disabled Lives: Who Cares?" *New York Review of Books*, xlviii (1): 34–37.

Parens, E. and A. Asch (eds). 2000. *Prenatal Testing and Disability Rights*. Washington, D.C.: Georgetown University Press.

Purdy, L. M. 1995. "Loving Future People," in J. C. Callahan (ed.), *Reproductions, Ethics and the Law: Feminist Perspectives*, pp. 300–327. Indianapolis: Indian University Press.

Shakespeare, T., K. Gillespie-Sells, and D. Davies (eds). 1996. "Making a Change," in *The Sexual Politics of Disability: Untold Desires*, chapter 7. Cassell. Available online at http://www.leeds.ac.uk/disabilitystudies/archiveuk/gillespie%20sells/chapter7.pdf (downloaded on 28.12.2014).

Shuttleworth, R. 2007. "Introduction to Special Issue, Critical Research and Policy Debates in Disability and Sexuality Studies," *Sexuality Research & Social Policy Journal of NSRC*, 4 (1). Available online at http://www.newint.org/features/1992/07/05/fruit/ (downloaded on 28.12.2014).

Stanford Encyclopedia of Philosophy. 2009. "Feminist Perspectives on Disability." Available online at http://plato.stanford.edu/entries/feminism-disability/ (downloaded on 28.12.2014).

Thomson, Rosemarie Garland. 1997. *Extraordinary Bodies: Figuring Physical Disability in American Culture and Literature*. New York: Columbia University Press.

———. 2004. "Integrating Disability, Transforming Feminist Theory," in B. G. Smith and B. Hutchison (eds), *Gendering Disability*, pp. 73–106. New Jersey: Rutgers University Press.

Wendell, S. 1989. "Toward a Feminist Theory of Disability," *Hypatia*, 4 (2): 104–124.

———. 1996. *The Rejected Body: Feminist Philosophical Reflections on Disability*. London: Routledge.

Young, Iris Marion. 1990. *Justice and the Politics of Difference*. Princeton: Princeton University Press.

Zola, Irving K. 1982. "Social and Cultural Disincentives to Independent Living," *Archives of Physical Medicine and Rehabilitation*, 63: 394–397.

2

Women with Disabilities: How Do They Fare in Our Society?

S. B. Agnihotri and Amrita Patel

This chapter looks at the status of women with disability in four states of India: Andhra Pradesh, Chhattisgarh, Odisha, and West Bengal. Women with disability represent a confluence of two divides in the society—gender and disability. While each of the divides has been studied independently, if not in isolation, the two have rarely been studied together.[1]

The writings first trace the contours of the available demographic data on the population of persons with disability in the four states and its gender dimension. Incidences of different disabilities are analyzed separately and presented in order to identify clusters of high and low incidence. Implication of such clustering is examined. An analytical framework linking impairment and disability is then analyzed through the structure of barriers. It uses the capabilities framework of Amartya Sen to examine the disadvantages faced by a person with a disability in the space of outcomes, that is, how does the person function in the society in the context of her disability. Functional characteristics of a person with disability create difficulties in utilizing commodities to achieve certain outcomes. This can be mitigated to some extent using certain technologies: aids and appliances come under such a category. However, the bigger problem that one faces is of the entitlement failures of the persons with disabilities in general and women with disabilities in particular.

Women with Disability—The Macro Picture

This section looks at the demographic data from Census 2001 and Census 2011 on women with disabilities.[2] Deficiencies in the census data and debate over definitions notwithstanding, data from population Census

2001 are internally consistent, and allow a robust comparison of certain indicators relating to disabilities. The definitions of the types of disabilities have been further streamlined in the 2011 Census.[3] The four states covered in the study do form a contiguous region. This facilitates analysis of certain parameters at the district level, and highlights certain clusters of high and low incidence of disability.

The total population with disabilities of India as per Census 2011 is 2.68 billions, representing 2.11 percent of the total population of the country. In the four states under consideration, this incidence ranges from 2.21 percent in West Bengal to 2.97 percent in Odisha. Obviously, contribution of Odisha and West Bengal to the population with disabilities in the country is higher than their contribution to the overall population, while Andhra Pradesh and Chhattisgarh make a lower contribution.

It is instructive to see the incidence of disability in the male and the female population of the four states. It is observed that unlike many countries, the incidence of disability among men is invariably higher than that among women in all the states and in all population segments.[4]

This is also corroborated by the sex ratio of the population with disability of the four states. The disability sex ratio is the highest in Chhattisgarh (871), while West Bengal has the lowest overall (790). Odisha and Andhra Pradesh fall under the intermediate range with the sex ratio of the disability population being 844 and 851 respectively.

Sex ratios of different disabilities indicate a similar pattern (see Table 2.1). Chhattisgarh, by and large, has higher sex ratios in all disabilities with the

Table 2.1
Sex Ratio of Different Disabilities

Type of Disability	Odisha	Chattisgarh	West Bengal	Andhra Pradesh
Total	844	871	790	851
In Seeing	928	983	901	1006
In Hearing	930	926	902	999
In Speech	779	822	814	805
In Movement	699	756	576	643
Mental Retardation	796	889	790	884
Mental Illness	870	913	755	937
Any Other	840	838	765	912
Multiple Disability	913	1007	843	832

Source: 2011 Census.

exception of those with *hearing* and *any other* category. Similarly, West Bengal has the lowest sex ratio in all impairments except *in speech*, the lowest being the case of *in-movement* impairment. Low sex ratio (less women per 1000 men) amongst those with physical disability in all the states is consistent with the pattern observed in the received literature, as a large number of men suffer from these disabilities in course of their participation in the workforce.

Data on sex ratios in rural and urban areas indicate that urban areas usually show lower sex ratios in all the disabilities and all the states.[5] Why it may be so needs closer investigation. It must be borne in mind, however, that the urban population is considerably smaller compared to the rural population.

One can see that the persons with visual and movement disability account for about 40–45 percent of the total women with disabilities in all the states.

A noteworthy aspect is the high number of women with disabilities with intellectual/mental disability in urban West Bengal. The rural to urban ratio is nearly 2:1, which is the highest in all the states under study and among all types of disabilities (as per the 2001 Census). Whether the lower number of women with disabilities compared to their male counterparts is on account of underreporting, biological reasons, or occupational reasons, it is an issue that needs resolution through a more detailed study.

At the same time, the lower number of women with disabilities in urban areas has a positive program implication. Since training, transportation, marketing, and monitoring infrastructure in the urban areas is stronger, it should be possible to implement the programs for women with disabilities in urban areas on a saturation basis. This will include pension programs as well as vocational training programs and the consequential marketing support needed by the women with disabilities.

Clusters of Low and High Incidence and Their Implications

We now turn to the incidence of different disabilities at the district level so as to identify clear clusters of high and low incidence. The cluster of high incidence in terms of the percentage of the population with disabilities is surprisingly similar across different impairments and spans a belt consisting of the districts of Raipur and Bilaspur in Chhattisgarh, Bolangir, Sambalpur, and Bargarh, along with the scattered location of Ganjam in Odisha and South 24 Parganas in West Bengal. This pattern remains so even if we look for high incidence by gender. As such, there is a clear case for going into the likely causes of this pattern and, more importantly, the likely measures which will improve the lot of the women with disabilities in these districts.

Regarding the clusters of low incidence of disability that we find in the different states, an issue may remain regarding the quality of enumeration in these districts. While recording the high incidence of disability provides a clear evidence of the problem, recording low incidence may not give similarly a clear evidence of absence of disability. Still it may be possible to take up such clusters for *saturation coverage* in terms of welfare schemes, such as pension. This will either ensure a complete coverage which is a desirable program goal or bring out un-enumerated cases, which is a desirable monitoring goal.

The macro data on disability, thus, shows certain consistent trends. It reveals regions that make a higher contribution to the population with disabilities compared to their share of national population. It shows that the sex ratios among those with disabilities are highly masculine, and most so among persons with physical disabilities. Urban sex ratios among those with disabilities too are more masculine than the rural ones.

District-level maps show a clear cluster of few districts in Chhattisgarh and Odisha with high incidence of disability. The pattern of high incidence remains as such whether we map it by gender or by impairment. This is intriguing and needs a closer analysis.

The low incidence clusters are spread across all states. But this may partly be attributed to quality of enumeration as well. An interesting approach for these districts will be to take up a scheme, such as pension, to a saturation level.

We have looked at the macro population data as it is. We next look at the data related to other parameters, for example, literacy and workforce population. Before exploring these, we first explore the question of what converts impairment into a disability, for what we have analyzed so far is essentially impairment. By itself, impairment may not translate into disability. It is the social organization that mediates such translation and dictates whether, and to what extent, persons with impairment get their entitlements.

When Do Impairments become Disability? And How Do the Gender and Disability Disadvantages Combine?

This brief discussion elaborates an analytical framework to examine when impairment becomes disability. In doing so, it uses the entitlement framework of Amartya Sen along with the capabilities approach to human well-being (Sen, 1999). Elaborating as to how *barriers* convert impairment into a *disability*, we explore how the gender barrier aggravates disability further. While entitlements relate to the command a person can have over a commodity basket, capabilities relate to the use to which the person can put the commodity basket into actual outcomes through personal characteristics. Impairment is one such characteristic that may affect his/her ability to convert the concerned commodity basket into an outcome. This can worsen further if there are barriers, both social and physical, that impede the outcome. The situation can be mitigated, at least partly, through removal of such barriers and provision of suitable technology and social infrastructure.

Among different barriers, gender acts as one important barrier affecting a person's ability to extend a command over commodities as well as her ability to use the commodity set to get a desired outcome. This is looked at in some detail. Different combinations of these two disadvantages are possible; one of these could be a nonlinear and multiplicative combination. If you are a woman and have a disability, you may face the worst of both the worlds.

Does the assertion that the gender disadvantage aggravate the disability disadvantage further stand scrutiny through available secondary data? Analysis of the secondary data does indeed show this to be the case, even though much of the available data, including disability data, is *gender-insensitive*. This is seen right from the stage of giving disability certificates, access to literacy or education, acquisition of skills, chance to convert the skill into income—whether through wage employment or self-employment, and so on. Even in noneconomic issues, such as marriage, stability of marriage, or violence in domestic as well as public sphere, gender and disability combine adversely. An interesting case is of participation in the Self-Help Group (SHG) Movement. Within the sample of women's SHGs, gender discrimination should be nonexistent, at least in principle. Yet the representation of women with disabilities in SHGs is abysmally low, indicating a lack of sensitization on part of SHGs. It is not out of place to indicate here that women with intellectual disabilities emerge as the most disadvantaged among women with disabilities themselves. This aspect is elaborated in more detail while analyzing primary data.

Regarding the gender gap in entitlements among the persons with disability, it is noticed that the gap is lower in schemes where coverage of the target group is very high, for example, grant of certificates or schemes that involve direct transfer of resources, such as pensions. Where mobilization or capacity building of persons with disability is involved, the gender gap is large. This raises an important issue regarding implementation of different welfare schemes. It also raises an issue of strategy. Is universal coverage of certain small groups, through direct transfer, an effective way of reaching vulnerable women with disabilities? Widows, among the women with disabilities, are one such prime small group that may benefit from such an approach through grant of pensions.

Entitlements and *functioning*

In *Inequality Re-Examined*, Sen (1995) identifies the space of outcomes or functioning as the most appropriate space for examining inequalities that a person may face. Inequalities exist at various levels. There is inequality in the *endowments* that a person has, and people differ in various physical characteristics, skill levels, state of health, and so on. But these inequalities can be modified as far as the entitlements of the person are concerned. An unemployed person can be given allowance, wage increase can be imposed, skills can be enhanced, and access to commodities can be facilitated through the public distribution system, and so on. There could be inequality in the space of entitlements themselves, income inequality being the prime example affecting the choice of commodities a person can have.

But commodities by themselves may mean very little. How these are put to their intended use decides the actual outcomes or *functioning* of a person. Is the person able to live a long life? Is the quality of life tolerable? Is he/she able to acquire skills and put these to use for earning a sustainable livelihood? These are questions and issues related to the *being* of the person. Inequalities in the space of *being* is what matters at the end of the day.

Impairment figures at different stages of this sequence spanning endowments to functioning. These could affect entitlements of a person in a straightforward manner, for example, a person with a visual disability may not find much use for a bicycle. But cases of entitlement failure may also occur through the organizational aspects in the society, for example, a person with hearing impairment may not get a data entry operator's job or same wages for a given job merely on account of disability. Even after he/she gets her entitlements, impairment may affect him/her ability to put these to a specific use; for example, a student with a physical disability may get admission to a school, but may not be able to attend classes on the first or second floor. Or he/she may get a job, but may not be able to commute to his/her place of work in the absence of a tricycle. Barriers can, thus, be physical, social, or attitudinal, and can result in entitlement failure or impairment of the *freedom to function*, that is, capabilities of a person.

While this may be the case for all persons with disability, an additional fault line or feature gets added to the process—the gender dimension. Given that gender does introduce entitlement failures through social and attitudinal barriers and the conversion of these into outcomes, it is not surprising to imagine that the combination of disability and gender may be aggravating the entitlement failure, as well as the well-being, in an accentuated way, and not as a mere combination of the two. In practical terms, it would mean that the gender gap in, say, literacy in the general population, may in fact be sharper among persons with disability. The same argument can be extended to a host of other entitlements and functioning: admissions to schools, access to scholarships, skill acquisition, support for wage or self-employment, ability to get married, or *appear in public without a feeling of shame*, and so on.

We analyze relevant secondary data available from the four states to examine the above assertion. However, much of the public domain data are gender-insensitive, even the one for the persons with disability. This itself calls for a conscious effort to make gender- and disability-disaggregated data available for policy purposes. Nevertheless, data that are available do show accentuation of entitlement failure and well-being failure when the twin disadvantages combine. This *accentuated failure* is also seen when we add another disadvantage to the situation: widowhood or mental disability. Widowhood represents a sharp fault line within gender, while mental disability represents an equally sharp fault line within disability.

Disability Certificates

One can start with the very basic data on disability certificates. Interestingly, no gender-disaggregated data is available in three of the states. In Odisha, disability certificates were made available to 61 percent men and only 39 percent women (Government of Odisha, 2006a). One could, thus, notice that the gender gap in giving disability certificates is sharp, particularly where the coverage levels need to be universal as an effective antidote to gender gap. Nevertheless, this is a good indicator of the first barrier to access that women with disabilities may face vis-à-vis the system.

Literacy

Next coverage that needs focus is literacy, a more basic indicator than formal education. It is noteworthy that the gender gap in literacy among those with disabilities is greater than that in the overall population. The gap tends to reduce at higher levels of literacy, as seen from the literacy rates in urban areas for the women with disabilities. Till the time of completing this chapter, the literacy data of the population with disability as per the 2011 Census was still not available.

It is instructive to look at the distribution of illiteracy in the region under consideration from the 2001 Census. It is seen that there is a cluster of low literacy rate (<34 percent) among persons with disability in rural areas, covering the Bastar–Koraput–Kalahandi–Visakhapatnam–Vizianagaram belt. The same cluster stands out for low level of rural female literacy among women with disability, but at a far lower cutoff level (<18 percent). At the higher end of the literacy rate, the cluster of coastal Odisha and West Bengal stands out with a cutoff level of 34 percent and above for rural female literacy which remains the same for the rural literacy rate of 49 percent among persons with disability. One could notice that the gender gap narrows down as literacy levels go up, that is, the female literacy of population with disability is the highest in West Bengal (41.9 percent), which also has the lowest gender gap in literacy (18.8 percent) (see Table 2.2).

Table 2.2
Female Literacy of Persons with Disability

Country/State	Persons	Male	Female	Gap
India	49.3	58.1	37.3	20.8
West Bengal	52.7	60.8	41.9	18.8
Odisha	48.8	60.1	34.6	25.5
Andhra Pradesh	44.2	53.2	32.4	20.8
Chattisgarh	48.1	60	33.3	26.7

Source: Census 2001.

Access to Education

Enrollment into primary or secondary education comes up next in the ladder. A gender-wise breakup of enrollment of students with disability, or children with special needs as they are termed, is not available across the states. This is the first sign of a gender-insensitive database, and it is necessary to step up advocacy efforts to ensure that the Sarva Shiksha Abhiyan data are made available by gender for children with disability.

For the present, we can look at the data from special schools and scholarships for students with disability and compare the gender gap with that in the gross enrollment ratios for the total student population. In Andhra Pradesh, the 2003–2004 data from 111 special schools revealed a 2:1 ratio between the male (6,401) and female students (3,502). The ratio has improved during 2004–2005 to 7,504: 4,119 (Government of Andhra Pradesh, 2006c). The gender gap is quite large, indicating yet again the access problem. As we go up the ladder of facilities and educational levels, the gap widens further. The homes and hostels for students with disability, crowded as these are, accommodate 1,009 male students and only 290 female students (ibid.).[6] Similarly, in Odisha, the special schools supported by the state government have 2028 male and 917 female students, while the special schools supported by the central government have 884 male and 448 female students (Government of Odisha, 2006b). While Andhra Pradesh and Odisha have the data segregated by gender, no such breakup could be obtained in Chhattisgarh and West Bengal.

Vocational Training

Vocational Rehabilitation Centers (VRCs) are national centers of vocational training and rehabilitation of persons with disability. The gender-wise segregated data available with these centers indicates that less than one-fourth women either join or are rehabilitated.

Disability Pension

For persons having access to disability pension, the gender gap can be expected to be minimal and, in fact, in favor of the female beneficiaries in the older age group. However, data from two districts of West Bengal and one district of Andhra Pradesh show that women with disabilities constitute only 30–40 percent of the recipients of disability pension (Government of West Bengal, 2006). In Odisha, where state-level data was available, the variance is between 60 percent for males and 40 percent for females (Government of Odisha, 2006b). This is one imbalance that can and needs to be immediately corrected.

Access to Health Services and Aids and Appliances

Like pensions, aids and appliances represent direct transfer of assets. Distribution of aids and appliances is another robust indicator of the extent of access and the gender gap thereof. Once again, the data from Artificial Limbs Manufacturing Corporation of India, Bhubaneswar, reveals a 2:1 ratio among the male and the female beneficiaries. Likewise, the data from Visakhapatnam shows a breakup of 1,253 males and 458 women with disabilities having received appliances. In Mayurbhanj district in Odisha, the figure was 4,998 and 1,453 in 2004–2005, and 3,941 and 2,021 respectively during 2005–2006. While the gender gap declined, the access inequality is quite clear. This is against a backdrop of a proactive district-level campaign for such distribution.[7] West Bengal and Chhattisgarh do not have gender-wise breakup of beneficiaries.

Interestingly enough, the National Policy for Persons with Disability (2006) guideline itself stipulates a recommended level of 25 percent coverage for women. While the breakup by value of the assets is not available, it is highly likely that the gender gap goes up as the asset value increases.

The issue of distribution of free or subsidized assets is essentially an issue of access. This point is corroborated by the data on evaluation of persons with disability by the VRC in Bhubaneswar. Of the total number of persons with disability that have been evaluated by the center from 1983 to August 2006, 30,795 have been males and only 10,133 females (Government of India, 2006). A similar picture is seen in the multipurpose identification camps in Visakhapatnam—4,207 men and 2,595 women (Government of Andhra Pradesh, 2006b).

Access to Employment

The picture regarding access to employment can be judged by the following parameters:

- Workforce participation as per Census 2001 data
- Registration in the employment exchange and actual placement thereof
- Membership of SHGs
- Access to loans for self-employment.

Workforce Participation as Per Census 2001 Data: A striking pattern that one notices is the low work participation among the women with disabilities in the urban areas. While in rural areas, the number of women with disabilities workers is half–one-third of the number of male

workers with disability; the ratio comes down to one-fifth–one-sixth in urban areas (occasionally one-fourth). This pattern is seen in all the states without any exception. This is really surprising given the larger scope for work, awareness, and more proximate presence of government and non-government organizations (NGOs) in the urban areas. Another surprising result is the low sex ratio among the workers in West Bengal compared to the other states.

Registration in the Employment Exchange and Jobs Thereof: This represents the opportunities available in the formal sector to women with disabilities. Data from West Bengal reveals that there were 10,034 persons with disability applicants on the live register, of which female applicants were only 2,369 in the month of July 2006. The ratio for the overall population figure in the state is higher with 74 million total applicants, out of which there were 20 million female applicants in the state. Six hundred and twenty women with disabilities were able to get employment against a total of 2,234 persons with disability (about 28 percent) (Government of West Bengal, 2006).

In Odisha, placement for five years has been only nine percent though there has been a steady rise in registration but decline in live registration (Government of Odisha, 2006c). The track record of Andhra Pradesh in terms of providing jobs in government has steadily improved. In the first 100 roster cycles, six women with visual disabilities have been given jobs as compared to 31 hearing-impaired (HI) men and 56 men with physical disabilities. In the second 100 roster cycles, while 131 HI women were given jobs, 106 visually impaired (VI) men and 156 men with physical disabilities benefited. In the third 100 roster cycles, 256 women with physical disabilities were given jobs, and 206 men with visual disability and 231 with hearing impairment were provided jobs (Government of Andhra Pradesh, 1997). No gender-disaggregated data was available from Chhattisgarh.

Self-Employment Programs: Women with disabilities involved in self-employment programs are likely to face less inconvenience in terms of mobility, caregiver's support, and so on. Moreover, their repayment track record is known to be better compared to the male beneficiaries. Yet their representation in the self-employment programs does not appear to cross the *25 percent barrier*. This is substantiated by the gender-wise breakup of National Handicapped Finance and Development Corporation (NHFDC) beneficiaries since inception (that is, during 1997–2006).

The Economic Rehabilitation Scheme in Andhra Pradesh indicates coverage of 137 women with disabilities as recipients of subsidy against 342 men (Government of Andhra Pradesh, 2006a).

Participation in the SHG Activities: The picture under the *Swarna-jayanti Gram Swarozgar Yojana (*SGSY) is no better—82 *women with disabilities* against 204 men (ibid). A similarly dismal pattern was noticed in the SGSY in Odisha at Raygada and Khordha districts. The report on the SHGs in Chhattisgarh shows very low participation of *women with disabilities*. Out of a total of 7,797 SHGs in Raipur with 89,477 female members, only 225 members are *women with disabilities*. Same is the case in Bilaspur district. Out of its 6,523 SHGs, with a total number of 78,752 female members, only 83 members are *women with disabilities* [SHGs (Women), 2006].[8] There is reportedly no exclusive SHG for women with disabilities in both the districts. The situation is better in Visakhapatnam district in Andhra Pradesh. Out of total 5,994 members in SHGs, while males with disabilities have a higher presence with 3,778 members, there are 2,216 disabled female members (Government of Andhra Pradesh, 2006b).

One can, thus, see a clear gender gap within the disability domain that is often worse than what obtains in the overall population. Such gap is less in simpler entitlements that are easy to administer, for example, certificates or pensions. However, the gap starts increasing as we move on to processes requiring more organizations of inputs. The access inequality of the women with disabilities goes up as one moves up the *value chain* of the entitlements. Such inequality can be mitigated if we try to universalize the coverage. Interestingly, government-led entitlements seem to offer a better deal to women with disabilities than those left in the private domain. This is brought out sharply in the case of participation in the SHGs.

Among the persons with disability, as there is a competition over the limited assistance available, men tend to access the benefits disproportionately at least in the initial stages. Where the coverage is very large or a quota is fixed, women with disabilities do appear to get the benefit. Among the SHGs, since its members are themselves struggling to improve their economic lot, they have little time for the women with disabilities. This is particularly so since there is no mandated inclusion of women with disabilities in a given SHG, nor is there a stipulation about forming SHGs exclusively for women with disabilities.

The double disadvantage faced by the women with disabilities is clearly borne out through the secondary data. We will look at what the primary data reveal about the nature and the processes of deprivation.

Where Does the Shoe Pinch?
Analyzing the Primary Data

This section analyzes the primary data from a sample of 320 women with disabilities in eight districts of the four states. Two districts were selected from each of the states and 40 respondents were interviewed in each district. Focused group discussions (FGDs) were also held with different stakeholders. The purpose of the primary survey and the FGDs was to see the situation of women with disabilities in different contexts firsthand and to draw some conclusions about the programs for their well-being and empowerment.

The primary data is analyzed in terms of the demographic parameters, entitlements as they are obtained from the field, as against what the secondary data reveal, the perception of the women with disabilities and other stakeholders about the processes and reasons for entitlement failures and the barriers to well-being. A number of insights emerge on policy as well as program implementation.

The Survey

The study involved a survey in eight districts of the four states of Andhra Pradesh, Chhattisgarh, Odisha, and West Bengal. Two districts were selected from each state, keeping in mind the rural–urban representation. In each state, the district covering the state capital was selected, as this would be the seat of most privileges, more awareness, more government and NGO presence, and so on. Though all districts were supposed to have urban and rural populations, Hyderabad and Kolkata were exceptions as they did not have a rural population. As a result, the selection of rural respondents had to be suitably increased in Visakhapatnam and South 24 Parganas. The rural–urban representation was kept close to 80:20 to provide more representation to rural women.

The sampling has been purposive and not in proportion of the population of the district or the incidence of disability in the given state. It was a conscious decision to take 80 women with disabilities respondents from each state, that is, 40 respondents per district. It was further decided to give comparable representation to each major type of disability as per census classification, for example, physical (locomotor), visual, hearing, including speech and intellectual (mental), even though their incidence differs significantly from each other.[9]

Age Distribution of the Women with Disabilities

The age distribution of the respondents was categorized in five age groups by type of disability. The age group of 14–17 years fell outside the marriage and political range, but was important in the context of education and skill acquisition. It is also an age where livelihood options can be decided. The next three age groups, clubbed together from ages of 18–45 years, account for approximately 72 percent of the respondents. This large group needs study and intervention in the context of skills, employment, higher education, decision making, and political participation, etc. The smallest group of about 8 percent belonging to the oldest age group (46–60 years) would require interventions, such as health, pension, etc. Issues such as violence and social exclusion, however, cut across all age groups.

The age distribution among the sample women with disabilities shows lower longevity, particularly for the intellectually disabled and the HI. Their presence in the 37–45 age group is itself low and certainly so in the 45–60 age group. This pattern is similar across all states. (This has important policy implications in terms of safety net for women with intellectual disabilities beyond the age of 35 years.) Cross-tabulation of the Census 2001 data for age distribution among women with disabilities of different disabilities will be helpful in this context.

Marital Status and Family Support

About one in six women with disabilities in the sample tended to be married. But the state-wise variation is significant, from 1:9 in Odisha to 1:4 in Andhra Pradesh. The marriage prospects for women with disabilities do not differ much by urban or rural location (except in urban Chhattisgarh where all respondents are unmarried, which is a non-representative situation). Age-wise, married women appear clustered around the 26–36 age group with very few getting married in the 18–25 age group.

Interestingly, women with disabilities among the respondents were found to have married persons without disabilities against the general impression that they marry only those with disabilities. While this may be a strengthening factor, it is only partially so, as most illiterate women with disabilities married illiterate men and mostly were wage earners who do not necessarily provide support, especially economic. The poverty levels of the women, therefore, remain high, as 79 percent married women remained below the poverty level in contrast to 67 percent unmarried.

Marital Status by Disability Types: Analysis of the marital status by disability types shows a higher proportion of persons with physical disabilities

among those married, followed by the VI and those with hearing impairment. Women with intellectual disabilities do tend to remain unmarried. However, in terms of percentage of married among the women with disabilities category, VI enjoy a higher rank, followed by physical disability and HI. This has implications on the care of women with intellectual disabilities. It also suggests that the 2001 Census data need to be cross-tabulated by marital status and disability types for better targeting of policy and programs.

Marital Status by Caste, Economic Status, and Level of Education: Analysis of the marital status by caste, economic status, and level of education indicates that the chances of marriage of women with disabilities among the below poverty line (BPL) category (13 percent) are higher compared to the above poverty line (APL) category (4 percent). Similarly, the chances of marriage for women with disabilities among the scheduled castes (SC) (one in four) are higher than those among the general category (one in five). This pattern is more or less same across all the four states. In Odisha, however, where chances of marriage are low in the overall sample, the incidence of marriage among women with disabilities in the BPL category is also low. Both these trends conform to the hold that hypergamy has over the APL and the caste Hindu households.

The hold of hypergamy is further corroborated when we look at the breakup among the unmarried and the married in terms of education level. Among those women educated to the level of intermediate schooling and higher, hardly any women with disabilities are married. This is in line with the pattern of more qualified women finding it more difficult to get a hypergamous match. For the women with disabilities, the gap is rather sharp. The pattern is similar across states. Curiously, in West Bengal, there are no married women with disabilities even in the high school category.

An important aspect of the marital status is the employment status vis-à-vis the unmarried women with disabilities. We find considerable unemployment among the married as well as the unmarried respondents, but the more disturbing aspect is the status of widows, with eight out of 10 respondents being unemployed. Widow women with disabilities are the worse off in terms of economic status. This once again supports the hypothesis that disabilities multiply, and widowhood combining with gender and disability increases vulnerability nonlinearly. Even if the sample is small, this may have important policy implications, and this *most vulnerable group* may need some pension support.

Role of the Family as *Caregivers:* Given the preponderance of unmarried among the women with disabilities, it is important to look at the support structure that they have. This is particularly important since a significant number of unmarried women were severely disabled. Their high numbers have policy implications in the context of livelihood and dignified survival, which must be taken into account, as well as social inclusion.

In the absence of a credible, state-supported social security system, families play an important role. The study probed the role of families from the twin perspective, of being facilitators or a hindrance. Besides dependence on parents, respondents' reliance on siblings and others was high. With majority living even in rural areas in nuclear families, what emerge are the limited support structures available to the women. With caregiving being limited to parents and siblings, the family emerges as a unit in the lives of the women, and the role of siblings thus becomes recognized as central to their well-being.

Women-headed Households: An important subset of households that need the attention of the policy makers as well as program managers are the women-headed households. Disability-wise analysis of these women-headed households did not include women with mental conditions as expected. Contrary to common perceptions, a relatively large number of women-headed households include the women with disabilities themselves and mothers. This sizeable number of households, being headed by women, poses critical questions in terms of the safety net of provision and empowerment. It strengthens the view above that mothers and women with disabilities form a dyad, and this assumes significance when assessing the needs of the women as inclusion of mothers is essential.

Women-headed households have defining characteristics of illiteracy or low literacy, highly unemployment, little training and assets (mostly in the form of livestock and not houses or land), and often severe and profound disability. These create a picture where women are found living on the margins without any structures and in need of comprehensive support, both economic and extended.

The Entitlement Failure

While the aforementioned analysis highlights some of the demographic features of the respondents, it is important to examine their entitlements and their view about factors that facilitate access to entitlements and failures that occur, if any.

Disability Certificates: Possession of a disability certificate indicates access to the system and resources. The study, therefore, paid importance to this aspect in the selection process of the women participating in the survey. This was done to overcome the problem of wrong assessment of disability by the investigators in the field, and enabled the selection of the severely disabled who were central to this study. Yet only 67 percent of the respondents were found to be in possession of the disability certificates, intellectual disability being the most deprived (51 percent), while 80 percent of the respondents with physical disabilities had certificates. Curiously, the least number of women in Andhra Pradesh possessed the certificates.

The inability of the team to find all the women who possess disability certificates across all states confirms the issue being highlighted by the disability groups that disability certificates are difficult to obtain. The average of the disability-wise range of possession, for instance, is low for women with mental conditions, but higher for those with mobility conditions. The limited possession of certificates by women with intellectual disability is a matter of concern as their access to resources is constrained from the beginning.

The issues highlighted from the field were the corruption involved in obtaining certificates as well as mention of the right percentage of disability which might be very high for some with disability while less for those who are severely disabled. The women complained of harassment in the obtaining of certificates, far distances to travel to get them, and the few number of days on which they are given out by the concerned authorities.

Educational Levels: The snapshot of educational level among the married and the unmarried women with disabilities given above does reveal a high incidence of illiteracy with above 50 percent women with disabilities respondents being illiterates. Among the unmarried respondents, however, we find more participation at school level and above. This clearly shows that the schooling percentage is higher among the general women with disabilities, followed by the Other Backward Classes (OBC), Backward Classes/Socioeconomically Backward Classes (BC/SEBC), and then the SCs and Scheduled Tribes (STs).

Does educational level confer any benefit on the women with disabilities? High school education and above does show higher employability, and illiteracy the least. Given the reality that a significant proportion of the women with disabilities will remain unmarried, this data suggests that a strong emphasis has to be placed on the schooling of girls with disability so that they can be self supporting.

There are as expected variations in literacy among disabilities. The largest share of the illiterate at the bottom of the pyramid as expected were those with mental conditions, with the HI placed a little higher. A woman with a mental condition, with no certificate and no education, remains excluded from every facility the state may provide (except pension perhaps). It reflects the inadequacy of education provided to this group.

When stipends are being provided and still more than half the women are illiterate, it reflects on the inadequacy of the education system. The exceptions are those who reach primary level, which is sufficient for many to enter the self-employment schemes. Those educated beyond this level, especially highly qualified, have not been able to fulfill their aspirations of acquiring employment.

The process was not smooth for the literates even when they entered the institutes, with over one-third (35 percent) reportedly facing some difficulty or other. Accessibility remained a major issue for women with mobility problems, but was not limited to physical accessibility alone, thus, highlighting the complexities within the concerns of accessibility. Besides architectural barriers and especially absence of ramps and toilets, there were the problems of traveling long distances to reach the institutes and harassment by bus drivers. Among them was the lack of disability-friendly toilet facility which after a certain age becomes a cause for drop-outs. These are not insurmountable problems as suggestions from the field indicated. NGOs, such as Sulabh Shauchalaya and UNICEF, which provide toilets should be required to set up accessible toilets, and specific government orders as per the Persons With Disabilities (Equal Opportunities, Protection of Rights and Full Participation) Act, 1995, if given whenever money is released, would make it easier to carry out the policy.

Besides physical and structural barriers, the most difficult barriers are human, related to the people who come in touch with the disabled—family, caregivers, teachers, vehicle drivers, etc. The first is the attitude of families toward girl child education and especially a girl child with a disability.

In the school itself, lack of trained staff and ill treatment of those with disabilities by both students and teachers creates barriers. All these are not impossible tasks and can be overcome by situating support structures wherever required. The lack of sensitization among teachers and students is a significant cause of dropouts. Teachers' sensitization remains a big challenge that needs to be addressed. In Kolkata, a parent alleged that her daughter admitted to a so-called *normal* school was excluded from the activities by other children and authorities did not play a role to integrate the children. Integration is not difficult; as another parent admitted, where initially no one used to mix with her daughter, nor visit their house, as they thought that disability was infectious and their children would be affected, but later when provided explanation they came to know about the disability and its cause and they now include them in their activities. Sometimes, superstitions come in the way of all protective laws and conventions.

The multiple challenges women face in accessing education could be overcome if provisions of the Act and other government orders were followed. Two important suggestions that emerged were the enforced monitoring of reservations of seats in schools which are being disregarded and which right from the start excluded disabled from the system. The other smaller step was of scholarship application forms being made available in schools and colleges. This step, those with disabilities felt, would reduce the dropout rate, especially after class 10. This could be further strengthened by provision of free residential schools and, above all, education at the doorstep for girls with severe disabilities who could not travel. It may be worthwhile to look at the possibility of a *friend* or a *mentor* of the women with disabilities student program through National Social Service (NSS) or a similar program. This can help create required capacity in the long term in different schools. It may also be possible to experiment with a *mobile teacher*—a trained special educator who can provide teaching at the doorstep for students with severe disabilities.

Vocational Training: A clear relationship has been found among education, livelihood, and vocational training, especially when illiteracy is high. In this study, clear vacuum was observed in the linking of the three, more so where the marginalized groups are concerned, with only 17.5 percent respondents having availed vocational training. The coverage also varies by disabilities as well as by states, with women with visual disability and Andhra Pradesh topping the list and West Bengal at the bottom. Training is not accessed because it is not designed to be accessible. When most of those with disabilities are isolated from formal structures, it is highly probable that their information levels would be low as the study indicated. No steps have been taken to make the information available to them, whether it is of the facility itself or the availability of scholarship. What with familial barriers to cross and little guidance by teachers, it is not unexpected that level of training would be so low.

The nonformal training structures to which the women apply are not usually equipped to provide services except to any women with physical disability. Even those women with physical disability find the physical barriers at the workplace difficult to handle. Though most women spoke of desires to enter government training institutes as they are low cost and recognition of certification when applying for jobs is high, they could rarely access them.

The linkage between training and jobs is missing. To begin with, the trainees get the wrong training and are faced with missing backward–forward linkages. While the respondents joined the trained as it is available, only 32 percent of them could find it useful for any economic activity, that is, either wage or self-employment. As such, most training is a waste of time and resources. The women have little skills and what they have may not be marketable.

The women themselves are aware that their poverty stands in the way of acquisition of skill. This adverse situation is compounded by multiple barriers which are physical, attitudinal, and professional, such as identification of unsuitable trades. Many could also take up trades with some physical adaptations, but while a computer is considered as an aid in acquiring employment for the general population and facilities for which are available, the same is not the case of occupational therapy and specialized aids and appliances needed for making the women employable. The problem of social exclusion and mobility gets further compounded by nonavailability of sheltered or residential training linked to production centers.

Aids and Appliances: Nonavailability of aids and appliances to more than three-fourth of the respondents represents one more barrier to accessing education training and jobs. The clear disability-wise variations, with women with visual conditions accessing less, need further investigation. There is also a need to assess the appropriateness of aids being manufactured in a gender-indifferent manner.

Transportation: Most FGDs and narratives took up the issue of transportation from various angles. While lack of it in rural areas was highlighted and was predictable, significantly, the majority said that they are dependent on caregivers to accompany them, and this needs understanding and support from a national perspective and implementation at the state level, especially for rural women's access to bus services. The respondents were highly critical of the treatment meted out to them by the bus staff, rude behavior, refusal to carry them, and extra money demanded for carrying wheelchairs.

Workforce Participation: Livelihood is dependent to some extent on literacy and training, and as mentioned, the missing linkages in the process keep many women with disabilities out of the workforce. There is a considerable regional variation, with Andhra emerging as more sensitive to women's work participation on the whole and with emphasis of self-help activities.

Employment: It is well known that employment is generally much lower for those with disabilities than for others, but there is a further divide when it comes to involvement of women with disabilities in livelihood and other activities by disability. In general, women with mobility condition fare better, while no employer wants to employ women with disabilities in the intellectual disability category as they do not reach an acceptable level of education or skill to be employable. The inaccessibility of employment in the private sector for women with disabilities is an indicator of the low public–private partnerships available and the low awareness of women's capabilities found to be unemployed. The substantially high range of unemployment among the unmarried and marginalized women is again a loss to the state economy.

Awareness again emerges as an important factor. The problem does not stop here because those who do get into the mainstream, except in government jobs, can rarely sustain them. State variation in unemployment rates with a very low rate in Andhra Pradesh was surprising, while limited variation in the other three states put West Bengal's progressive governance in the same league as Odisha and Chhattisgarh. The high rate of unemployment in general remains a cause of concern.

It is not that those with disabilities are unemployable, as seen in the case of a woman with multiple disabilities from West Bengal employed in a multinational corporation (MNC). Field examples showed that women can achieve high levels of employment if barriers both physical and attitudinal are removed.[10] To improve the situation, state-specific initiative and awareness creation is required with a focus on the type of disability.

Self-Employment: The livelihood options available in the formal sector are poor for the women with disabilities. Nominal representation in the service and production/trade sector leaves the women who engage with it only as wage earners (the highest representation being in Andhra in the service sector). They are not able to join the agricultural workforce due to their disabilities. Not being able to participate in agriculture leaves women with very few avenues in the rural areas and this aspect needs special attention. This unskilled workforce has no social security in the form of pensions or insurance. While skill remains a matter of concern, the unavailability of a social net creates issues linked to food insecurity and survival.

With low wage employment, self-employment is the only other option; but even here the work participation is not encouraging. Again, women with mobility problems were found to take up self-employment more readily, while those unfortunately with mental conditions were left outside the sector with no space for inclusion. However, emergence of women as small entrepreneurs provides a niche which should be explored. Among the states, Andhra Pradesh and then Odisha are the ones in which more women with disabilities are seen to be self-employed. The low-earning potential in urban West Bengal exposes the myth that urbanization could create better job opportunities for women with disabilities.

Micro Credit: Micro credit, often depicted as the panacea for women's economic independence in India, has opened its door only partially to women with disabilities. Though SGSY, in particular, provides 3 percent reservation for disability, the participation of women as seen from secondary and primary sources was disappointing. The states of Andhra and Odisha are well known for the micro credit revolution, but even in these states, especially in Odisha, the revolution has sidestepped the women with disabilities. The discrepancy between awareness and access is very high. It is also surprising that the women do not join exclusive SHGs. Even the limited number of women who could get in and adapt to the system well faced noncooperation. The low awareness level of the respondents implies that the SHG Movement has not pervaded each section of the society and barriers for the groups remain. But these can be lifted with some effort at inclusion through awareness creation among local political bodies and bankers.

Access to Schemes: Schemes available to women with disabilities come from the poverty alleviation programs, in general, and some from special schemes meant for those with disabilities. Among the schemes linked to micro credit are loans which are exclusive and meant for those with disabilities as well as general loans, especially as part of micro credit.[11]

As is becoming obvious throughout the study, the awareness level on entitlements is extremely low. It is not, therefore, unexpected that women with disability are not provided loans and all women with disabilities except for some in physical disability are excluded. State-wise, Andhra again emerges as the highest loan disburser, and not surprisingly, Odisha with its impressive track record in the SHG Movement does not show up as doing enough.

Many women do not access schemes as they are not aware of their entitlements. What is surprising is their low awareness on generally well-known schemes, such as Sampoorna Grameen Rozgar Yojana, Prime Minister Rozgar Yojana, Indira Awas Yojana, etc. in general, and specific schemes meant for those with disabilities such as NHFDC in particular. Their low awareness on related institutes such as VRCs, polytechnics, and special schools adds to the inaccessibility of women to their entitlements. Even for those aware of them, the complexity of the selection process, bankers' low faith in their abilities, corruption at all levels, mobility problem, and lack of family support emerge as major barriers.

The only awareness on pensions is also predictable as the disbursement process is easier. As most of the money goes for this scheme, it would be thought that women would access these, but contrary to the common perception: this is incorrect.

There is, thus, a clear need to step up the micro credit avenue for *women with disabilities* and their greater inclusion in SHGs, either inclusive or exclusive. This is particularly crucial for women with more severe disability.

Assets and Family Support: The link between poverty and disability is evident from the large population of women who fall BPL. A more accurate picture emerges when we see these women in the context of the assets they or their families possess. If expenses on disability in the form of hospitals and health-related transportation cost, caregiver's expenditure, aids and appliances, and their maintenance are taken into account, many women who are APL would also fall below the line. Another complexity is the large number of unmarried women who are part of this poor group who are also illiterate and unemployed, with few having received training. The majority of the women in the study fall in the category of the most deprived of population with access to training in the country.

Among those who fall BPL expectedly are those with mental conditions. Most of these women are asset-less; the very few who have assets in the form of house and land would still not convert their disability into ability. State variation shows some women in Odisha and Andhra Pradesh possess self-assets while most in West Bengal do not. Disability-wise, the asset holders at the lowest level are women with mental conditions. Though among those with disabilities the largest number who possess assets are those with visual conditions, the difference is marginal.

The variation between BPL and APL possessors of land is low, so most women are on the margins. More families in contrast own assets, but within these, women have little rights. This large number are the poorest of the poor and the state-specific variation is only in Andhra Pradesh where assets are owned by both APL and BPL women, whereas in other states, only APL women own assets.

Social Exclusion: The dilemma, of the women acknowledging in public any violence perpetuated against them, was revealed when there was a clear discrepancy in the survey and narratives. Whilst lesser women acknowledged it in the surveys which were conducted publicly, in the narratives, most women spoke of multiple locations of violence. Feminist research has been suggesting that women are reluctant to report violence due to the social stigma attached. It is, therefore, not surprising that this group is reluctant to acknowledge it publicly.

A variation as per disability shows up as women with mobility and psychosocial conditions, the two most visible disabilities, are excluded from social–cultural locations. In their narratives, they spoke of different levels of exclusion and discrimination. In the FGDs and narratives, the frustration of the women at the social stigma attached to disability which manifested itself in many ways emerged as a major concern. Use of objectionable names, hiding them from public, and a show of pity and sympathy reinforces their already low esteem. Found across all the regions, it must be nationally the same.

While they encounter problems within the community and state institutions, the families also act as barriers. Families usually blame the condition of disability on karma and become important agents in *women with disabilities* sociocultural nonparticipation, especially in states such as Odisha and Andhra where a small group not only face stigma but are abandoned from birth or childhood, some with old grandparents where they can neither be looked after properly nor access their needs.

Violence is the most extreme form of discrimination, and when it is within the family, it is difficult to assess.[12] In the case of women with disabilities, there is a difference in the definition of domestic violence because they face it all through their life cycle. The survey reported violence in both the parental home and in marriage. The Domestic Violence Bill needs to take into account the high level of cruelty faced by women whose physical and mental conditions make them more vulnerable than others. Women's reporting of verbal and physical abuse created emotional and physical trauma.

Women with disabilities such as those with mental and hearing conditions do not speak for themselves. When their mothers (as in the survey) become spokespersons, it is possible that the truth is hidden. In the narratives, women openly spoke of domestic, mental, and physical violence at home, in the workplace, and in public spaces. As literacy and employment are low, the violence reported is more at home than in the educational institutions and workplaces; but these institutions cannot be excluded when designing protection strategies which need to be comprehensive.

There is an equally clear relationship between violence perpetuations and underreporting, but a larger picture emerges when settlement issues are taken up. Family reconciliation still remains the best means of settlement and not legal or institutional means. This is not only because women's knowledge on laws and the institutions is low, but also due to lack of family support in taking the issue forward for structural settlement and making the violence public.

State-wise differentiations were indicated with higher violence in most areas, except physical, which was concentrated in Chhattisgarh, followed by West Bengal, Odisha, and Andhra Pradesh.

Decision Making and Political Participation: Low decision-making power, as provided by data in the study, is in keeping with the emerging picture in this study of the low status of the women with disabilities. It is also in keeping with the other findings that women with mental conditions are completely excluded from decision making. Most of those who do decide do so within the family.

With regard to political participation, the inclusion in the voters' list does not convert to voting. Among those women who did not exercise their voting rights were mostly those with mental or physical conditions. This is in keeping with the knowledge that most booths are not accessible to women with physical disabilities, and those with intellectual disabilities are not allowed to vote.

This was confirmed in the FGDs and narratives where women mentioned this as a denial of their rights. The study also breaks the myth that women with disability are more dependent on decision making, including political decisions, on parents or husbands. What was encouraging was that women had made an entry into politics even if they lost. These efforts will provide markers for many other women.

Access to Health Services: The data provides valuable insights into the health of women with disabilities. A high range of women born with disability or disease suggests the absence of health services for person with disabilities. This is reinforced by the data that most women were disabled by these two causes, in birth for those with the hearing and mental conditions, and by disease for those with mobility and visual conditions.

The data suggests that most disabilities could have been prevented. Prevention of disability remains a major gap in the system. Appropriate prevention strategies need to be devised. Low awareness of Human Immunodeficiency Virus (HIV) makes the group more open to the disease which is dangerous considering its rising prevalence in India. The disabled are more prone as there is no available disability-friendly awareness materials, and interest in the group is lacking.

Access to health was near universal in Chhattisgarh with Odisha coming up with friendly treatment, but specialized needs, such as physiotherapy and occupational therapy as well as specialized institutions, were available only to a few. Women having access to medical treatment in general, for reasons other than disability, was lower signifying that the other *hidden* health problems, such as reproductive care, are not availed. If disability is to be treated, professional services have to be made available at the village level; otherwise, the majority of those with disabilities will be deprived of essential health services. The deprivation continues when there is non-completion of treatment of the majority of women when the reason of treatment *not having any impact* substantiates the conclusion that not enough specialized services are available. State-wise, though Chhattisgarh showed high access to treatment, completion of treatment fell by half.

In disability, especially when people have to live with it all their lives, chronic diseases among at least a fifth of the population suggest high poverty. This was confirmed by the BPL data that the chronically ill are also more deprived which is perhaps a reason for being BPL. The highest cases being from Andhra Pradesh indicates that state-specific measures to be taken.

***

This chapter presents an analytical framework linking impairment and disability through the structure of barriers.

It is submitted next that the disadvantages of gender and disability aggravate the existing gender gap among persons with disability in various aspects of entitlements and functioning. This *not so obvious* assertion is then examined with reference to the secondary data available from the four states. In doing so, the first problem one faces concerns the nature of the data. Much of the public domain data is gender-insensitive, and even more disability-insensitive. Nevertheless, the available data does show an accentuated gender divide in the disabled population whether we look at literacy, schooling, and access to work or employment. Gender gap in literacy among persons with disability is stronger than in the overall population, and so is the gap in schooling, access to skills, and avenues of self-employment through loans. This aggravation cuts across state boundaries.

Within gender, widowhood represents another disadvantage. Similarly within disability, mental disability represents additional disadvantage. Analysis of primary data indicates that widows and women with intellectual disabilities are perhaps the most vulnerable among the women with disabilities. This has important implications on the design of welfare programs for women with disabilities. The Disability Pension Scheme should perhaps aim to cover this group on a 100 percent basis on priority. Analysis of the primary data also reveals areas where it is imperative that the 2001 Census data is cross-tabulated to further corroborate or contradict some of the trends seen for the women with disabilities. Markedly lower longevity among the intellectual disability group is one case in point in this regard.

The patterns and the process by which disadvantages multiply rather than merely add are analyzed further through the primary level data and the FGDs.

It is important to analyze the pattern of allocation of government funds in the field of disability. Budget analysis is a nascent area of analysis. But it has been undertaken in this study to make a beginning. As the allocation figures for disability are not available by gender, the analysis is done for the sector as a whole. Even if the analysis is preliminary, it provides important insights in terms of the gap between the budget estimates and the actual expenditure as well as the per capita allocation figures. If consistently done over a longer cross-sectional and temporal database, budget analysis can emerge as an important advocacy as well as a monitoring tool.

The insights obtained through the aforementioned analysis themselves indicate some of the solutions. While program interventions in the field of disability have made considerable headway in the past few years, they do lack the structure to monitor the lot of women with disabilities in a systematic manner. Besides the gender-neutral aspects of program implementation, there is a serious need to address the problem of sexual vulnerability of women with disabilities in the younger age group. This is one aspect of the problem that the women with disabilities face and which needs urgent resolution.

Analysis of the primary data provides useful insights about the sociodemographic parameters of women with disabilities. The age profile of the respondents brings in the issue of longevity, particularly among those with intellectual disabilities. This has important implications on the policy for a social safety net, particularly since the intellectually disabled also happens to be the most deprived group among the women with disabilities in terms of various entitlements.

Analysis of the marital status brings out various nuances. First is the harsh reality of the low likelihood of marriage. This is particularly strong among those with intellectual disability. Second is the hold of the norms of hypergamy. Third is the emergence of widows as the more vulnerable among the married women with disabilities.

Literacy and educational level do present the rather disturbing picture of entitlement failure. Yet schooling does provide employment hope to the girl child with disability and it must be an important component of any strategy to improve their lot.

The story of entitlement continues as we move up the *value chain*: the disability certificates, access to skills, the wage/self-employment opportunities thereof, aids and appliances, health checkup, the security aspects, and the decision making. Lack of awareness owing to lack of information appears to be the first and the major bottleneck. Beyond this too, it is an uphill task for the women with disabilities to get their entitlements.

The community environment is not conducive to better self-esteem and productive engagement with the workplace. The family too leaves a lot to be desired. Starting with the stigma and the hidden and not-so-hidden prejudices, the women with disabilities have to face the specter of violence and abuse. This is the most unacceptable part of the entitlement failure and will need an urgent resolution. The recent protective legislation against domestic violence toward women could provide a right beginning in this regard.

Notes

1. This chapter is based on a study on multistate socioeconomic study of women with disabilities in India.
2. Census 2001: The First Report on Disability in India (referred to in this chapter as Census 2001).
3. There are eight categories of disability in the 2011 Census: in seeing, in hearing, in speech, in movement, mental retardation, mental illness, any other, and multiple disability.
4. In Hong Kong, for instance, it was observed that men always outnumbered women until recently, especially in the 20–39 age group. Hong Kong Equal Opportunities Commission. We as one.
5. As per the Census 2001.
6. Government of Andhra Pradesh Disabled Welfare Department. District Review Committee Meeting held on May 6, 2006.
7. District Magistrate. 2006. Personal Communication. Mayurbhanj.
8. Government of Chhattisgarh. 2006. Unpublished SHGs, (Women) and State.

9. It may be noted that the incidences of disability of different types as reported by Census 2001 and National Sample Survey Organization (NSSO), differ significantly. Census data on visual disability is subject to certain controversy owing perhaps to the way visual disability is defined. But this aspect is beyond the scope of this study and not crucial either. However, the 2011 Census gives a revised definition: in seeing, one-eyed persons were treated as disabled in the 2001 Census, but not so in the 2011 Census. A simple test was done to ascertain blurred vision.

10. I am a young woman with Cerebral Palsy using a wheelchair for mobility. I have complex communication needs and I communicate by pointing to an alphabet board or through a personal computer, with a head pointer. I also use a Tracker Ball, which is a special mouse, since I cannot operate the normal mouse. My head pointer is my lifeline as it enables me to communicate as well as fulfill my passion for painting. I have a full time friend, my Didi, who has been with me ever since I was eight months old. I completed my B.Com from Indira Gandhi National Open University. I have been employed as an executive in reputed corporate house, working as a computer programmer and am perhaps the only adult with severe multiple disabilities in Kolkata who has worked in such offices! (interview conducted in West Bengal)

11. During the period subsequent to the study done in 2007 (on which this chapter is based), there have been an increase in the number of schemes for persons with disability both at the central level as well as in many of the states. However, none of the schemes are particularly for women with disability, barring a few exceptions like the hostels for women with disability in Odisha.

12. Examples of violence narrated:

    • A girl suffering from cerebral palsy has been found to be frequently raped by the villagers and blamed for the rape.
    • A woman with a mobility condition married to a person with disability is battered. Assetless and completely dependent on her family, she is abused by her brothers.
    • Another woman with mental condition is battered by her sisters-in-law.
    • A woman with a mobility condition was tortured and electric shocks were used on her; ultimately, she was driven away from her workplace. After returning to her parents' house, she is now abused by her sisters-in-law, even though she does work at home and her pension is taken by her family.
    • A woman with a mobility condition and unmarried is psychologically abused by the village women who call her names and do not like them taking help from their husbands.
    • A neighbor tried to molest a woman with a hearing condition.
    • Married to a person without disability, a woman with mobility impairment faced violence by her husband which started after the initial year of

marriage. Finally, she was deserted. She later sought a divorce and now depends on old parents.

- Hysterectomy is very common on women with mental conditions.
- There are cases of false promises to marry and desertions.

Bibliography

Government of Andhra Pradesh. 1997. Unpublished. "Abstract." WD&CW Department.

———. 2006a. Assistant Director, Disabled Welfare, Visakhapatnam.

———. 2006b. Director, Disabled Welfare, Visakhapatnam.

———. 2006c. Director of Education.

Government of India. 2006. Vocational Rehabilitation Center for Handicapped, Bhubaneswar.

Government of Odisha. 2006a. *Annual Report on Women and Child Welfare.* Bhubaneswar: Department of Women and Child Development.

———. 2006b. *Annual Report on Handicapped Welfare.* Bhubaneswar: Department of Women and Child Development.

———. 2006c. Special Employment Exchange for Physically Handicapped Persons.

Government of West Bengal. 2006. Office of the Controller of Vagrancy, Visakhapatnam.

———. March 2006. Special Employment Exchange for the Physically Handicapped Persons. *Progress Report on the Working of the Directorate of Employment.* West Bengal.

Sen, Amartya. 1995. *Inequality Re-Examined.* Oxford: Oxford University Press.

———. 1999. *Commodities and Capabilities.* Oxford: Oxford University Press.

3

Women with Psychosocial Disabilities: Shifting the Lens from Medical to Social

Nilika Mehrotra and Mahima Nayar

For a long time, women were absent from most health research. Gradually, *women's health* was recognized as a specialized area. But this recognition came with a price, especially in the area of mental health where any behavior of women which did not fit with the normative feminine constructs of the time was understood as illness, and efforts were made to *treat* it largely from a medical model. This kind of *treatment* made women more vulnerable to exploitation, which resulted in silencing their voices. With the social model of disability as its background, this chapter attempts to explore how women's psychosocial disability is often a result of their socioeconomic circumstances. It looks at the *medical interpretation* of distress and examines the different pathways through which women have exercised their agency in order to deal with psychosocial disabilities. It focuses on the women's movement and cultural ways of healing. Through these explorations, we also want to establish how these ways of healing are legitimate paths through which women move toward health.

Health involves multiple facets of life—emotional, physical, social, as well as spiritual. Health is a precondition for most of the activities we define as human: our culture, economy, child raising, laughter, sex, work, freedom of choice, the affirmation of our rights—all are in some way dependent on the health of the individual and the community. In situations where freedoms are denied, education not provided, and work not done, or environments in which violence, inequity, and exclusion are common, there are often negative effects on health (Sharpe, 2010). This means that health includes the influence of society and environment. Health is determined by the interaction of economic, political, and social forces. Understanding the significance of this interaction means an appreciation of the interconnectedness between models of development pursued around the world and systems of domination which reduce the capacities of people, especially poor people, to sustainably lead their lives (Dan, 1994). In the fifth International Conference on Women's Health Issues, 1992, it was recognized that structural adjustment, now operative in about 80 countries, has increased the caring burden on women by withdrawal of the state from service provision in many areas. There is an erosion of women's access to food, shelter, occupation, and education, resulting in the deterioration of women's health. The realm of women's health is vast and includes issues ranging from malnutrition, anemia, and other micronutrient deficiencies to reproductive health issues, as well as sexual harassment, domestic abuse, violence against women, depression, and other problems related to aging, gender inequities, and the obstruction of their basic human rights. Women's health also relates to the appropriate status that a woman should enjoy, her right to assert, and decide for herself the number of children she wants to have and the time she should have them.

Historically, women have been absent from most health research as maleness has been regarded as the norm and women's female characteristics constitute deviations. The critique of women's health experience reflects the negative consequences of their being defined only in relation to and by men. When they are defined only in relation to men, women's suffering becomes invisible, or if it is visible, then it is only defined as deviance. A feminist critique of medicine is concerned with issues of power, both as it shapes health, illness, and recovery, and as it determines forms of and access to health care and research. In India, during the 1970s, the preoccupation with family planning led to the neglect of many other women's health issues. A progressive shift in policy occurred in 1996, spurred by the women's heath movement and the 1994 International Conference on Population Development, which moved from a target-based approach to reducing fertility to an emphasis on women's individual reproductive life choices and her rights over her body (Mukhopadhyay, 1998). In addition, a life cycle approach, including both reproductive and non-reproductive dimensions of health, was then promoted as the new women's health paradigm (World Bank, 1998). With the broadening of the concept of women's health, many issues which had been previously neglected came into prominence. The feminist critique of medicine begins with the recognition of dominant and subordinate social roles in society: male and female social roles are unequal, and men's gender role is more highly valued than women's (Hamilton, 1994: 60). Unequal gender roles have profound effect on women's physical and mental health.

The women's movement, which was responsible for the broadening of the concept of women's health, also helped in the development of the Disability Rights Movement (DRM). According to Mehrotra (2011), the strong presence of women's movements, and the interest and push of international agencies created a more conducive space for the political mobilization of marginalized groups, such as the disabled. With the DRM gaining prominence, there was a greater recognition of social factors which are responsible for disability. The social model of disability gave visibility to the problems that women with psychosocial disability faced. This is because when viewed from a purely medical model, the difficulties and the disability arising from distress remained largely unrecognized or were reinterpreted to fit into the *medical paradigm*. Women's behavior, which was in some ways a reaction to their circumstances wherein they were silenced and made invisible, was very quickly categorized as mental illness. The ways to *correct* this was through largely medical procedures through which the behavior was controlled. Through this chapter, we want to understand women's psychosocial distress through the lens of disability, and not through the mental illness paradigm. This is because the notion of *mental illness* will always remain a medicalized one, linked to psychiatric labeling, over being determined by law (Dhanda, 2000), and linked with negative social descriptors alienating women from themselves, their mind-bodies, and their lifeworlds. The gender discourse could look at *disability* as an alternative way of constructing identities of persons and women who experience psychological distress and disability (Davar, 2000). Use of disability language over a *mental illness* language helps in remaining close to the personal experience of the women.

In this chapter, we focus on psychosocial disabilities that women experience largely as a result of facing inequalities and the socioeconomic environs that they live in. It attempts to link women's mental health, distress, and suffering with the macro-level factors. The first section explores the location of women and how their geographical or social situation influences their mental health. The second section presents briefly the understanding of madness, medicalization thesis, and how this was refuted by feminists. Here, we explore alternative ways of healing focusing on the women's movement and cultural ways of healing. We seek to explore the experience of women with psychosocial disabilities from the two axes primarily used to formulate the social model of disability—socioeconomic discrimination and the medicalization of disability and its relationship to health care.

I

Location of Women and Psychosocial Disability

Women's diverse locations in terms of class, caste, region, ethnicity, and religion determine to a certain extent the kind of issues, problems, and discrimination that they face. In urban spaces, where the struggle for survival is continuous, women often find themselves in spaces which by their very nature are oppressive. One of the determinants of health is poverty. The attention to the poverty–health nexus can be attributed to a broadening conceptualization of poverty, accompanying a renewed commitment to poverty alleviation (WB, 1990). Poverty is now viewed as multidimensional, embodying more than material deprivation. Levels of and risks for health are key dimensions of poverty. The implications are not negligible: raising living standards may not be sufficient to combat poverty if the health of the poor does not also improve (Wagstaff, 2002). Previously, it had been thought that absolute poverty, rather than relative poverty, was the only robust social determinant of ill health and that this effect was unidirectional, affecting those lower on the social ladder. The fact that health outcomes on those who live in inegalitarian societies are inferior to those who live in more egalitarian societies has led to the observation that some societies are indeed *unhealthy* (Kawachi and Kennedy, 2002; Wilkinson, 1996). Globalization, increasing evidence of heightened inequalities, increasing poverty, ill health in many parts of the world, and emerging transnational threats to health invite talk of an *unhealthy planet*, and have focused considerable attention on how health equity is to be achieved globally today (Whitehead et al., 2001). In 2001, the World Health Organization (WHO) Commission on Macroeconomics and Health turned much conventional wisdom on its head by demonstrating that health is not only a benefit of development, but also is indispensable to development. Illness all too often leads to *medical poverty traps*, creating a vicious circle of poor nutrition, forgone education, and still more illness—all of which undermine the economic growth that is necessary, although not sufficient, for widespread improvements in health status.

Geographical differences, leading to varying kinship patterns and sociocultural differences, also have varied status implications for women in different parts of the country (Dyson and Moore, 1983). In the North, marriage is exogamic and often employed as a means for intergroup alliances which leave women with very little choice and restricted social mobility. In the South, because of cross-cousin marriages and unions among persons in familiar households, women have greater social mobility and, therefore, better health opportunities. In addition to poverty and geographical location, another factor which influences the health of women is the caste that they belong to. Caste impinges on women's lives, intersecting with poverty and their autonomy (Deshpande, 2002; Dube, 1996). Lower-caste women are vulnerable due to their lower socioeconomic status and social exclusion, whereas high-caste women have lower autonomy and less control over their lives (Mohindra, 2009: 32).

Inequalities lead to discontent and, hence, to suffering. Several studies have shown the link between poverty and general health problems among women. According to the Canadian Research Institute for the Advancement of Women's (CRIAW) Women and Poverty fact sheet (2002), acute and chronic ill health, susceptibility to infectious and other diseases, increased risk of heart disease, arthritis, stomach ulcers, migraines, clinical depression, stress, breakdown, vulnerability to mental illness, and self-destructive coping behaviors are all linked to women's poverty. Women in developing countries are often in poor health and overburdened with work; they are tired, and many suffer from malnutrition, parasitism, and chronic ill health due to lack of personal attention and adequate health care, especially during pregnancy and childbirth. Early marriage, repeated childbearing, ignorance, poverty, and manual labor all have deleterious effects, as do lack of access to resources and lack of training opportunities. Women in rural areas are particularly badly affected and their special needs are often ignored by health planners. Further, discrimination against them in almost all social, economic, and political areas means that they have to bear a disproportionate share of unmet needs.

Low-income women report that financial limitations, stress, and isolation wear them down emotionally and physically. Poverty undermines self-confidence, making it more difficult to be healthy and to provide a positive environment for children. The challenges of living in poverty are manifold. They include finding work, locating better paid jobs, and finding adequate housing and subsidized child care to facilitate work or school involvement. With limited resources, women must meet the nutritional, clothing, and other needs of children and themselves, and get emotional support from others. Many are trapped in a cycle that opens few avenues. Low-income women struggle to meet minimal living standards, leaving them with limited resources for change (Morris, 2002). In India and other low-income countries, common mental disorders were about twice as high among the poor as among the non-poor, and there is a higher prevalence of these disorders among women, especially women with lower levels of autonomy (Patel et al., 1999). Patel and his colleagues recently examined women's mental health in the state of Goa. In a community study of 3,000 women aged 18–50 years, chronic fatigue (symptoms experienced for at least six months) was found among 12 percent of the sample (Patel et al., 2005). Chronic fatigue was associated with poor mental health, gender disadvantage, and poor socioeconomic conditions.

By now, there is evidence of greater prevalence of depression, somatoform, and dissociative disorders in hospital settings (Vindhya et al., 2001), of somatic, anxiety, and depression complaints among women in primary health care settings (Patel et al., 1999; Devi, 2003), and of a close association between reproductive illnesses, such as gynecological morbidity, and common mental disorders among urban poor women in particular (Jaswal, 2001). The greater prevalence of common mental disorders such as depression and somatoform disorders in women is linked to the impact of social circumstances on women's lives, a position that is at variance with the traditional intrapsychic approach to mental disorders. Thus, discrimination in education, economic resources, legal and health services, the disproportionate burden of caregiving functions, and different forms of physical, psychological, and sexual abuse across the life span are social factors that place women at greater risk of these disorders (Barnes, 1997; Davar, 1999). Men control almost all economic resources and are the major decision-makers in the household, especially on key matters, such as intra-household allocation of resources and contraceptive practices (Mohindra, 2009: 29). Das Gupta and Chen (1996) further argue that although women are the *biological* reproducers, men control *social reproduction*, that is, it is through males that children form their identity as members of society. Because males have a clearly defined role in their family and society and women are viewed in relation to their subordination to males, female well-being often takes a backseat to male well-being. Although males provide identity to the children, the sex of the child seems to be the responsibility of the woman. Producing a male child is often one of the biggest life stresses which women face, and inability to produce one might stigmatize them for life in their marital home. Thapan (2006), while interviewing women in an urban slum, describes the experience of a woman in her early thirties who has three daughters. Thapan writes:

> Phoolwati has a cheery exterior but starts looking unhappy once the conversation centers on child bearing. She says in anger, "No one is allowing

me to live. All my in-laws are after me because I have not had a boy. The name of the family cannot continue which is very important." She explains that daughters do not stay with their natal family forever, and therefore, it is important to have a son.

According to Thapan, Phoolwati, through her tears and internalized experience of an unbearable condition, clearly expresses her embodied incapacity to bear a male child, and, thus, being incapable of lending to the continuity of the family name, failing in her maintenance of family honor and social identity. From the narrative, the feelings of helplessness and hopelessness of Phoolwati are apparent, indicating her suffering. Women being a part of society internalize the negative messages and hold themselves responsible for things that are beyond their control. Addlakha (2001) in her study, relating to psychiatric disorder with constructions of femininity, depicted how patriarchal standards of femininity condition the illness experience, perception, articulation, and behavior of the individual patient and her significant others. Through her interviews with the women in a psychiatric hospital in Delhi, she found that the women themselves internalize the gender-based evaluations in the evaluation of abnormality both within the family and medical discourses. She also highlighted the fact that mental health professionals, often unconsciously, carry the gender and class biases that they have been socialized in into their practice. This in turn creates a vicious circle whereby women are judged through erroneous means.

The aforementioned literature presents how the position of women affects their mental health. This implies that a combination of factors related to place of living, globalized environment, caste, class, and kinship have a bearing on the choices available to women and ultimately on their mental health.

II

Psychosocial Disabilities: Pathways to Healing

The ways to improve mental health or to reduce psychosocial disability depended on the way madness[1] was understood over the ages. Foucault has pointed out that each age of civilization, from the medieval period to the modern times, has its own views of madness which reflects the general social and logical preoccupations of the time. According to him, increase in the number of mentally ill or in the number of people who were confined was related to the economic crisis in the Western world. These observations point to the fact that concepts of mental illness, mental health, and madness are largely embedded in the historical and socioeconomic position of a community at a particular point in time. For Foucault, mental illness was not an objective fact which remained the same in all historical periods and meant the same thing in all cultures. It was only within a definite discursive formation that the object *madness* could appear at all as a meaningful and intelligible construct. It was constituted by all that was said, in all the statements that named it, divided it up, described it, explained it, traced its development, indicated its various correlations, judged it and possibly gave it speech by articulating, in its name, discourses that were taken as its own (1972: 32). And it was only after a certain definition of *madness* was put into practice that the appropriate subject—the *madman* as current medical and psychiatric knowledge defined *him*—could appear.

In Foucault's work, understanding of mental illness can be largely seen as being determined by the society and the particular stage that it is in. But the concepts of mental illness and distress are not just determined by the structures present in society but are also mediated by the interaction between the structures and individuals. Bourdieu's work on the interaction between field and habitus offers explanatory potential. The concepts of field and habitus offer the possibility of exploring the significance of power relations in the details of ordinary lives and of understanding how the structural realities of the economic, cultural, and social are internalized over time to become habitualized, unconscious practices. According to him, social structures inculcate mental structures into individuals; these mental structures in turn reproduce or change social structures (Bourdieu, 1988, cited in Bourdieu and Wacuant, 1992). Therefore, it becomes important to understand the existing structures that affect the definitions of women's distress and women's agency in mediating this.

In the beginning, the medicalization thesis[2] was gender-neutral. During the first phase, Illich's (1976) book *Medical Nemesis* was widely cited by sociologists and used to point out the harmful effects of medicine and to the health care consumer's loss of autonomy. But this book did not have a gender agenda (Riska, 2003: 65).

It was in the mid-1970s that the feminist scholars started unraveling the history of modern medicine and suggested that "professionalism in medicine is nothing more than the institutionalization of a male upper class monopoly" (Ehrenreich and English, 1973: 42). These studies pointed out that during the 19th century, the traditional role of women as lay healers was supplanted by a new scientific knowledge promoted by a cadre of male physicians, establishing themselves as the profession of scientific medicine (Ehrenreich and English, 1973). Ehrenreich and English (1974) argued that persecution of witches was primarily a campaign against women and particularly against women healers. Biomedicine or allopathic paradigms have been given prominence which by their very nature of emphasizing trained expertise, knowledge which is acquired at institutions, keep women out of the system. They access it but that is not their preferred system; the faith lies elsewhere. Chesler (1972: 67–69) noted in her pioneering book *Women and Madness*, which reviewed theories on mental health, that "only men can be mentally healthy" because "the ethic of mental health is masculine in our culture." Women's ways of coping with distress were gradually included in the gambit of psychiatry and they became more and more *abnormal*. Their location in the society which was causing the distress was mostly ignored. Anything that is perceived to be an impediment to the subject, who is supposed to be fully in control of herself, is quickly categorized as a disorder, while the subject's inner turmoil and dilemmas with regard to social expectations quickly get named as anxieties (Salecl, 2004: 3).

In their quest to earn enough for the family's survival, men and women work beyond their perceived capacities, running out of energy, feeling fatigued, and vulnerable to illness. This leads to a state of non-health—a condition of liminality where one is neither healthy (because of loss of economic and emotional well-being) nor ill (as one is able to carry out everyday activities [Gaur and Patnaik, 2011]). In this state, threat from illness appears imminent from various sources related to the *three worlds*. While a healthy individual has ability to fight and successfully conquer these agents, a non-healthy individual lacks that strength. Because the body acts as a *microcosm of the universe*, its state of health is dependent on and vulnerable to feelings, wishes, and actions of others, including spirits and dead ancestors (Scheper-Hughes and Lock, 1987: 20). Women's experiences, such as pregnancy, menstruation, and menopause, have been medicalized and psychologized, which have created a series of paradoxes. The medicalization of menstruation, for instance, reinforces the idea that women are controlled by biology in general and their reproductive systems in particular. This has been used to legitimize the exclusion of women from positions of power because of supposed emotional instability and irrationality (Vindhya et al., 2001). Women's personal and social worlds are defined in terms of home, family, childhood, workplace, and life experiences at various times in their lives. In the process of articulating their lifeworlds, women traverse untrodden paths of revelation, strength, and surprise as well as the more frequented ones of abuse, dishonor, shame, and rejection. In these, they revert to memory, narrative, and voice as tools for reconstructing their emotions, thoughts, and experiences in making sense of their own constitution as embodied gendered beings (Thapan, 2006: 203). Habitus clearly constructs their experiences in many important and non-subversive ways, but their voices also reflect the call for challenging the structuring structures of the habitus through negotiation, contestation, and transformation (ibid.). Therefore, these concerns had to be addressed by the broader women's movement.

Women's Movements

The challenge to the medical model of psychosocial disability and the view that women's health was being viewed from a patriarchal lens did not come from the health sector as this was being taken over by men; instead, it came from the women's movements which recognized that health was being used as a means toward the goal of controlling women's actions. A common assumption shared by various women's movements on women's health was that it had been medicalized in the past, and the gender-biased medical knowledge and diagnoses and treatments decided by biased male physicians had resulted in the overtreatment of women documented in high surgery rates for hysterectomies and mastectomies, and overuse of drugs, especially psychotropics. Women's movements at that stage sought to halt the further medicalization of women's bodies by a redefinition of what is healthy. Many insiders are of the view that the women's movement in India itself is a mental health movement (Shatrughana, 1999; Uberoi et al., 1995).

During the 1970s, women's organizations directly challenged the patriarchal social order while rallying around issues of violence against women, such as dowry deaths and rape cases. The backdrop of this was constituted in a specific socioeconomic and political context. Civil rights, women's and students' movements in the West precipitated the situation (Mehrotra, 2002). The ways in which the women's movement was providing spaces for women can be seen when we look at the functioning of women's organizations through the case study of an organization. Saheli, a women's group, is strongly opposed to any hierarchical structure, and it encourages democracy and equal participation of its members in decision making, which, according to it, are the prerequisites for the independence of women (Mehrotra, 1993; see also Gandhi and Shah, 1992). It wants women to be treated as *persons* and as full individual beings with rights over their life, body, sexuality, and other major areas of society. It seeks to understand the roots of oppression by politicizing the personal issues, by sharing experiences with other women and linking this knowledge with wider social issues. For Saheli, empowering women is an important step in countering patriarchy. It subscribes to women's liberation theory and believes in a socialist–feminist framework of action. Being a part of such a system in itself was healing for women in many ways.

The open-ended non-hierarchical structures of autonomous women's groups provided outlet to the women in distress who could share their anguish with those having similar experiences. For many women, being a part of the movement has proved to be cathartic. It gave them self-confidence, the will to survive, and the space to express themselves. It was later feminist disability studies that gave new and alternative ways for theorizing mental illness from a feminist perspective (Donaldson, 2002). The women's movement gave *mad* women a chance to locate their lives within patriarchy, understand their powerlessness, and engage with re-scripting their identities from a political perspective. If we see personal struggles, loss of identities, and living amidst privations and violations as the causal factors for psychological and emotional distress, then the women's movement, supporting major values, such as social justice, equality, and empowerment, was in fact a mass-based intervention to cure and prevent mental problems and promote the emotional well-being of many women (Davar, 2008).

The women's movement's approach toward de-medicalization of mental health care was not without problems. First, this route was more accessible to educated and middle-class women and, therefore, many women were left out of its ambit. Secondly, in its engagement with psychiatry to find different ways of looking at psychosocial disability, it inadvertently created more spaces for it. One of the important developments during the 1990s was the location of women's miseries within the realm of *distress*, rather than *illness*. Common mental disorders appeared to provide a comfortable space in psychiatric science for talking about distress. The collaboration of psychiatry with movements of women and persons with disability had some worrying outcomes which included the use of a *social language* to prescribe medicine. Although there was recognition of the social causes, the treatment consisted mainly of prescription of medicine because constraints of resources and time made this most feasible. There was the de-recognition of traditional healing practices; women who were visiting traditional healing centers were considered as superstitious and backward, and forcibly driven by cultural norms into acceptable spaces, from where they would be pushed back into their feminine roles through the use of religious discourse and morality. A range of Western readings of cultural practices supported this interpretation (Skultans, 1991; Thompson, 1983). Women visiting traditional healing centers, and those who professed to be healers, trancers, or possessed, were seen as victims of patriarchy (Davar, 1999: 350). There was no engagement with the question whether spirituality (defined here simplistically as access to the emotions of the sacred) had a role to play in self-experience, healing, and recovery (Seligman, 2005). The role of spirituality in creating spaces for women has been explored in anthropology; the following section examines this role.

Cultural Ways of Healing

Anthropologists have looked at the concept of healing for psychiatric difficulties as they feel that this makes the suffering more real. This can be further understood by examining the concept of *spirit possession*. This is the idea that supernatural personalities can enter, own, and use people while they are in an *altered state of consciousness* or trance state. Frequently, women are associated with spirit possession. One theory talks of women trapped by the double standards of male–female relationships or by the socioeconomic conditions of colonialism. The use of spirit possession as a means of resistance shows that since woman's choices are located within their everyday experience, they speak from within the multiplicity of their experience and location. They use several and varying acts of resistance that need not necessarily fall into a universal pattern, but remain embedded in local acts or modalities of agency evolving from individual ways of perception and action (Thapan, 2006). These cults are seen as ways in which powerless people work out their anger of and fears about more powerful people. I. M. Lewis (1966) explains that they grow out of deprivation and circumstances in which women's aspirations and intelligence outstrip their opportunities for expressing them. He says that through this, women find release from and alternatives to male-dominated societies and husband-dominated marriages. He further notes that the possessing spirits typically visit marginal or peripheral people, lower-class or otherwise socially powerless women and men (Ward, 1996: 198).

Kapadia (1995) in her ethnographic study, carried out in South India, examines the marginalization of women even in terms of possession. She says that among all the castes in South India, mostly malign possession is experienced by women, which is why far more women than men are possessed by *pey* (evil ghosts). But even when this is the case, women who become possessed may legitimately behave in a manner that would be considered improper or even obscene in normal circumstances (Kapadia, 1995). Therefore, spirit possession and local explanations of mental illness can be seen as women organizing their agency to make space for themselves within the existing structures. This has been evident in our ongoing research in a resettlement colony in Delhi where women spoke about resorting to *madness* as a way of expressing their anguish. When they were asked about their understanding of the relationship between the problems women faced and madness, they replied, "*Jab pareshanian had se bad jati hain tun auratain chandi ban jatin hain*" (When problems cross a limit, then women become take on the role of *Chandi*). Becoming *Chandi* here implies taking on the characteristics of Goddess Kali, which are considered negative, such as excessive anger and aggression (seen as being possessed by the goddess). They said that women become *Chandi* and scream because of the problems that they are facing, but others just consider them mad. No one realizes what they are going through except other women who might be undergoing similar experiences.

Harper (1963) also found that 10–20 percent of the women in the Havik-Brahmin caste of Karnataka experience possession at some point of their lives, many of them while in the situation of the newly married woman. He elaborates that there are not many choices available to them and this is one viable option. Before the current wave of industrial employment for young, single women, spirit possession was mainly manifested by married women, given the particular stresses of being wives, mothers, widows, and divorcees (see, for example, Kessler, 1977; Maxwell, 1977 [1883]). With urbanization and industrialization, spirit possession became overnight the affliction of young, unmarried women placed in modern organizations, drawing the attention of the press and the scholarly community (see Chew, 1978; Jamilah, 1980; Lim, 1978; Ong, 1987; Teoh et al., 1975). Anthropologists studying the spirit possession phenomena have generally linked them to culturally specific forms of conflict management that disguise and yet resolve social tensions within indigenous societies (Crapanzano and Garrison, 1977; Firth, 1967; Lewis, 1971). In contrast, policy makers and professionals see spirit possession episodes as an intrusion of archaic beliefs into the modern setting (Chew, 1978; Phoon, 1982; Teoh et al., 1975). This kind of de-legitimization of alternative routes to healing mirrors the early stages of medicalization, when the work of traditional birth attendants and healers was de-recognized, and *doctors* became the last word on health and sickness.

Psychosocial disability or distress cannot be explained just as physiological illness or a reaction against patriarchy. The use of *medical* as well as *social* can be seen as varied mediums through which women exercise their agency and voice their distress. World over, women's health has come into prominence along with the broader women's movements (Leeson and Gray, 1978). Self-help movements which involve self-examination and self-education, original research into health issues, group support for specific problems, and attempts to analyze and change aspects of the health care system locally are most effective. Leeson and Gray describe how women's groups studied herbal medicines, yoga, and massage, and used them as alternatives (ibid.: 196). Chiu, Morrow, Ganesan, and Clark (2005) conducted research on spirituality and treatment choices of Southeast Asian women with mental illness. They found that many women were using conventional medicine—they went for astrological readings, and tried various traditional healing practices such as acupressure, acupuncture, diets, praying, and worshipping God which they found to be helpful. They also experienced spirituality by helping others. Examples included showing compassion for those who were suffering and being willing to help, learning that by helping others, one helped oneself, and by getting involved in volunteer work, and so on. These studies show how the cultural ways of healing that have been used by women over the ages are being incorporated within the women's movement as well.

***

In this chapter, we have tried to present an overview of how women's psychosocial distress has been understood and addressed. This involved first the recognition of women's health as being separate from men's health, their location in society, and how this affected their mental health. In many ways, women's movements have provided secular spaces for women—spaces which have enabled them to seek the support of other women, to help themselves and others, and to explore ways of coping which have enabled to feel empowered. It is important to recognize the role of both the women's movement and the cultural ways of healing as they complement each other. On their own, the cultural ways of healing provided a space for expression and negotiation but did not challenge existing gender hierarchies. Whereas, the women's movement while focusing on systems of equality created a new discourse on normality.

With its emphasis on strength and empowerment, it ignored the spaces required for vulnerability and healing. These spaces were termed as mere superstitions, or worse, were viewed as communal practices. The fact that they are much more than that is evident from the fact that they continue to hold an important place in people's lives and are continuously accessed in the hope of being healed.

Women's movements and medical pluralism both seem to provide choices for people who are suffering. Within the field of medicine, searching for different cures has often been called *doctor shopping*. While we are not advocating that people keep running from one place to another; there is a need to acknowledge that the ability to choose and utilize different systems together—allopathic, homeopathy, ayurveda, voluntary work, spirituality, and so on—in order to heal oneself, is empowering in itself. Issues of illness and health remain embedded in social decisions and actions, not only in medical decisions about transmission and cure. The complex nature of *madness* or *psychosocial disability* has to be addressed from a variety of perspectives as multiple factors influence it. Enacted policies on transportation, housing, energy, education, and agriculture have both direct and indirect consequences for health; yet, in most governments or administrations, health policies are only haphazardly integrated with those of other departments (Bowker, 1998). This shows that there is an effort to take attention away from the real issues, and problems are given names that can be referred for a cure instead of addressing the larger systemic problem. Meaning-making needs to be critically evaluated as a political tool that reworks experience so that it conforms to the demands of power. Therefore, it becomes even more important to carry out more research on women's movements as mental health movements and explore cultural ways of healing. This would give us the connections between theoretical understanding of madness and women's life practices.

Notes

1. The term *madness* has been reclaimed by the feminist movement to be used as a metaphor for feminist rebellion. In this chapter, it has been used to depict the divergent meanings that have been ascribed to it historically by different stakeholders.
2. "Medicalization consists of defining a problem in medical terms, using medical language to define a problem, adopting a medical framework to understand a problem, or using a medical intervention to 'treat it'" (Conrad, 1992).

Bibliography

Addlakha, R. 2001. "The Lay and Medical Diagnosis of Psychiatric Disorder and the Normative Construction of Femininity," in Bhargavi Davar (ed.), *Mental Health from a Gender Perspective*, pp. 313–333. New Delhi: SAGE Publications.

Barnes, B. L. 1997. "Mental Health Issues in Young Females: A Gender Perspective," *Bombay Psychologist*, 14 (2): 37–45.

Bourdieu, Pierre and L. W. D. Wacquant. 1992. *An Invitation to Reflexive Sociology*. Chicago: University of Chicago Press.

Bowker, J. W. 1998. "Religions, Society and Suffering," in Arthur Kleinman, Veena Das, and Margaret Lock (eds), *Social Suffering*, pp. 359–382. Delhi: Oxford University Press.

Chesler, P. 1972. *Women and Madness*. New York: Double Day.

Chew, P. K. 1978. "How to Handle Hysterical Factory Workers," *Occupational Health and Safety*, 47 (2): 50–53.

Chiu, Lyren, Marina Morrow, Soma Ganesan, and Nancy Clark. 2005. "Spirituality and Treatment Choices by South and East Asian Women with Serious Mental Illness," *Transcultural Psychiatry*, 42 (4): 630–656.

Conrad, P. August 1992. "Medicalization and Social Control," *Annual Review of Sociology*, 18: 209–232.

Crapanzano, V. and Vivian Garrison. 1977. "Introduction," in *Case Studies in Spirit Possession*. New York: John Wiley.

Dan, A. 1994. "Introduction," in Alice Dan (ed.), *Reframing Women's Health*, pp ix-xxii. New Delhi: Sage Publications.

Das Gupta, M., and L. Chen. 1996. "Introduction," in M. Das Gupta, L. Chen, and T. Krishnan (eds), *Health, Poverty and Development in India*, pp. 1–24. Delhi: Oxford University Press.

Davar, B. V. 1999. *Mental Health of Women: A Feminist Agenda*. New Delhi: SAGE Publications.

———. 2000. "Writing Phenomenology of Mental Illness: Extending the Universe of Ordinary Discourse," in A. Raghuramaraju (ed.), *Existence, Experience and Ethics*, pp. 51–82. New Delhi: DK Printworld.

———. 2008. "From Mental Illness to Disability: Choices for Women Users/Survivors of Psychiatry in Self and Identity Constructions," *Indian Journal of Gender Studies*, 15 (2): 261–290.

Deshpande, A. 2002. "Asset Versus Autonomy? The Changing Face of the Gender–Caste Overlap in India," *Feminist Economics*, 8 (2): 19–35.

Dhanda, A. 2000. *Legal Order and Mental Disorder*. New Delhi: SAGE Publications.

Donaldson, E. J. 2002. "The Corpus of the Madwoman: Toward a Feminist Disability Studies Theory of Embodiment and Mental Illness," *NWSA Journal*, 14 (3): 99–119.

Dube, L. 1996. "Caste and Women," in M. N. Srinivas (ed.), *Caste: Its Twentieth Century Avatar*, pp. 1–27. New Delhi: Viking.

Dyson, T. and M. Moore. 1983. "On Kinship Structures, Female Autonomy and Demographic Behaviour in India," *Population and Development Review*, 9 (1): 35–60.

Ehrenreich, B. and D. English. 1973. *Witches, Midwives and Nurses: A History of Women Healers*. Old Westbury: The Feminist Press.

———. 1974. *Complaints and Disorders: The Sexual Politics of Sickness* (Glass Mountain Pamphlet No. 2). London: Compendium.

Firth, R. 1967. "Ritual and Drama in Malay Spirit Mediumship," *Comparative Studies in Society and History*, 9(2): 190–207.

Foucault, M. 1972. *The Archaeology of Knowledge*. London: Tavistock.

Gandhi, N. and N. Shah. 1992. *Issues at Stake: Theory and Practice of Women's Movement in India*. New Delhi: Kali for Women.

Gaur, M. N. and S. M. Patnaik. 2011. "Who Is Healthy Among the Korwa? Liminality in the Experiential Health of the Displaced Korwa of Central India," *Medical Anthropology Quarterly*, 25 (1): 85–102.

Hamilton, J. A. 1994. "Feminist Theory and Health Psychology: Tools for Egalitarian, Women-Centered Approach to Women's Health," in Alice Dan (ed.), *Reframing Women's Health*, pp. 56–66. New Delhi: SAGE Publications.

Harper, E. B. 1963. "Spirit Possession and Social Structure," in B. Ratnam (ed.), *Anthropology on the March*, pp. 165–197. Madras: The Book Center.

Illich, I. 1976. *Medical Nemesis: The Expropriation of Health*. New York: Pantheon Books.

Jamilah, A. 1980. "Industrial Development in Peninsular Malaysia and Rural–Urban Migration of Women Workers: Impact and Implications," *Journal Ekonomi Malaysia*, 1(June): 41–59.

Jaswal, S. 2001. "Gynaecological Morbidity and Common Mental Disorders in Low-Income Urban Women in Mumbai," in B. V. Davar (ed.), *Mental Health from a Gender Perspective*, pp. 138–154. New Delhi: SAGE Publications.

Kapadia, K. 1995. *Siva and Her Sisters: Gender, Caste and Class in Rural South India*. Oxford: Westview Press.

Kawachi, I. and B. P. Kennedy. 2002. *The Health of Nations: Why Inequality is Harmful to your Health*. New York: NY Press.

Kessler, C. 1977. "Conflict and Sovereignty in Kelantan Malay Spirit Seances," in Vincent Crapanzano and Vivian Garrison (eds), *Case Studies in Spirit Possession*, pp. 295–333. New York: John Wiley.

Leeson, J. and Judith Gray. 1978. *Women and Medicine*. London: Tavistock Publications.

Lewis, I. 1966. "Spirit Possession and Deprivation Cults," *Man*, 1(3): 307–329.

Lewis, J. M. 1971. *Ecstatic Religion: An Anthropological Study of Spirit Possession and Shamanism*. Harmondsworth, England: Penguin.

Lim, Linda. 1978. *Women Workers in Multinational Corporations: The Case of the Electronics Industry in Malaysia and Singapore* (Michigan Occasional Papers in Women's Studies, No. 9). Ann Arbor: Women's Studies Program, University of Michigan.

Maxwell, W. E. 1977 [1883]. "Shamanism in Perak," in *The Centenary Volume, 1877–1977*, pp. 222–232. Singapore: The Council, Malaysian Branch of the Royal Asiatic Society, 1977/1978.

Mehrotra, N. 1993. "A Study of Women's Organisations and Women Activism in Delhi," unpublished Ph.D. thesis, University of Delhi.

———. 2002. "Perceiving Feminism: Some Local Responses," *Sociological Bulletin*, 51 (1): 57–79.

———. 2011. "Disability Rights Movements in India: Politics and Practice," *Economic and Political Weekly*, XLVI (6): 65–72.

Mohindra, K. S. 2009. *Women's Health and Poverty Alleviation in India*. New Delhi: Academic Foundation.

Morris, Marika. March 2002. "Women and Poverty: A Fact Sheet." Ottawa: Canadian Research Institute for the Advancement of Women.

Mukhopadhyay, M. 1998. *Legally Dispossessed: Gender, Identity and the Process of Law*. Kolkata: Stree.

Ong, A. 1987. *Spirits of Resistance and Capitalist Discipline: Factory Women in Malaysia*. Albany: State University of New York Press.

Patel, V., R. Araya, M. S. Lima, A. Ludermir, and C. Todd. 1999. "Women, Poverty and Common Mental Disorders in Four Restructuring Societies," *Social Science and Medicine*, 49(11): 1461–1471.

Patel, V. et al. 2005. "Chronic Fatigue in Developing Countries: Population Based Survey of Women in India," *BMJ*, 330(7501): 1190–1193.

Phoon, W. H. 1982. "Outbreaks of Mass Hysteria at Workplaces in Singapore: Some Patterns and Modes of Presentation," in Michael Colligan, James Penne-baker, and Lawrence Murphy (eds), *Mass Psychogenic Illness: A Social Psychological Analysis*, pp. 21–31. Hillsdale, NJ: Lawrence Erlbaum Associates.

Riska, E. 2003. "Gendering the Medicalisation Thesis," in M. T. Segal, V. Demos, and J. J. Kronenfeld (eds), *Gender Perspectives on Health and Medicine: Key Themes* (Advances in Gender Research, vol. 7), pp. 59–87. Amsterdam: Elsevier JAI.

Devi, R. Sachi. 2003. "Common Mental Disorders in Primary Health Care Settings: A Study of Socio Demographic Correlates," unpublished doctoral dissertation, Andhra University, Vishakhapatnam.

Salecl, R. 2004. *On Anxiety: Thinking in Action*. London: Routledge.

Scheper-Hughes, N. and M. M. Lock. 1987. "The Mindful Body: A Prolegomenon to Future Work in Medical Anthropology," *Medical Anthropology Quarterly*, 1: 6–41.

Seligman, R. 2005. "Distress, Dissociation and Embodied Experience: Reconsidering the Pathways to Mediumship and Mental Health," *Ethos*, 33 (1): 71–99.

Shatrughana, V. 1999. "Foreword," in B. V. Davar (ed.), *Mental Health of Indian Women: A Feminist Agenda*, pp. 11–17. New Delhi: SAGE Publications.

Skultans, V. 1991. "Women and Affliction in Maharashtra: A Hydraulic Model of Health and Illness," *Culture, Medicine and Psychiatry*, 15 (3): 321–359.

Sharpe, A. 2010. "Gender, Health, Peace and Security," in Betty A. Reardon and Asha Hans (ed.), *The Gender Imperative: Human Security vs State Security*, pp. 351–383. New Delhi: Routledge.

Teoh, Jin-Inn, Saesmalijah Soewondo, and Myra Sidharta. 1975. "Epidemic Hysteria in Malaysian Schools: An Illustrative Episode," *Psychiatry*, 38(3): 258–268.

Thapan, M. 2006. "Habitus, Performance and Women's Experience: Understanding Embodiment and Identity in Everyday Life," in Roland Lardinois and Meenakshi Thapan (eds), *Reading Pierre Bourdieu in a Dual Context: Essays from India and France*, pp. 199–228. New Delhi: Routledge.

Thompson, C. 1983. "The Power to Pollute and the Power to Preserve: Perceptions of Female Power in a Hindu Village," *Social Science and Medicine*, 21(6): 701–711.

Uberoi, H., K. Shirali, and M. Sadgopal. 1995. *Dance of Madness*. Shimla: Kishwar.

Vindhya, U., A. Kiranmayi and V. Vijayalakshmi. 2001. "Women in Psychological Distress: Evidence from a Hospital Based Study," *Economic and Political Weekly*. 36(43): 4081–4087.

Wagstaff, A. 2002. "Inequality Aversion, Health Inequalities and Health Achievement," *Journal of Health Economics*, 21(4): 627–641.

Ward, M. C. 1996. *A World Full of Women*. Boston: Allyn and Bacon.

Whitehead, M., G. Dahlgreen, and T. Evans. 2001. "Equity and Health Sector Reforms: Can Low Income Countries Escape the Medical Poverty Trap?" *Lancet*, 358 (9284): 833–836.

Wilkinson, R. 1996. *Unhealthy Societies: The Afflictions of Inequality*. London, UK: Routledge.

World Bank (WB). 1990. *World Development Report: Poverty*. New York: Oxford University Press.

———. 1998. "World Development Report 1997: The State in a Changing World: Overview," *IDS Bulletin*, 29: 14–31.

HUMAN EXPERIENCES AND AGENCY

SECTION TWO

4

I Feel Normal Inside. Outside, My Body Isn't!

Malini Chib

Tottenham Court Road is a busy London street and I am happily strutting about without help, alone on my wheelchair. Suddenly the chair gets stuck in a puddle. I struggle to free my wheelchair. I can't. I panic. Concerned people stop by and ask if they can help. But they don't. It's not their fault, because they can't understand a word of my speech. Now, I am paralyzed.

—Personal

About Me

My chapter is going to be on *disabled identity*. Times are changing; even disabled people's attitudes toward themselves are changing. The pendulum has shifted right toward the other side. Disabled people want their own identity. Previously, the traditional view of disability focused on the individual's impairment. This chapter is about my growth and development and my acceptance of disability, and above all, how I have adopted a disabled identity.

Let me first begin by explaining my disability. I was born disabled at birth. I have cerebral palsy.

My Physical Disability

I have two major physical areas which have affected me. cerebral palsy has handicapped the right side of my brain, impairing my physical movement and permanently blurring my speech.

Walking, and thus by extension legs, forms a large part of an individual's identity. Not so much for me. I cannot walk without aid. I can manage short distances slowly on a walker, but for long distances, I need to use both a manual and an electric wheelchair. The walker, more specifically my wheelchair, is what a pair of legs is to a *normal* person. They are an integral part of my identity. Today, I am quite comfortable with them.

Years of training has enabled me to *speak* to a large extent, but to clearly understand me takes time, perhaps weeks, if you listen carefully. I have severe dysarthria. I can speak, but it takes time for an ordinary stranger to understand me. To me, my lack of articulate speech affects me acutely and is the most disabling handicap.

To make life easier for the listener and myself, I use a voice synthesizer where I type what I want to say, and it speaks it out. In an emergency, even a minor emergency, I would need aid and have to use a voice synthesizer (a contraption a bit like the one used by Stephen Hawking).

Just like the wheelchair, initially, I wasn't keen to use one. I used to think that being seen with a communication aid would make me look even more disabled. However, these gadgets are crucial for my identity.

Then London happened, and my identity as a disabled person blossomed when we moved there in 1993.

London and India

My mother was doing PhD from the Institute of Education, London, on exclusion of disabled children in mainstream education (that would finally culminate into the seminal book *Invisible Children—A Study of Policy Exclusion* in 1998). I accompanied her to London, and my life and my identity underwent a drastic transformation. At that time, the disability movement in England was changing course. It shifted from the medical model where disabled people were meant to be fixed and fitted to the social model that saw disabled people as people first and said that it was the environment that handicaps a disabled individual further. Disabled people's voices were slowly being heard.

The United Kingdom (UK), with years of work in the field of disability, was light-years ahead in terms of people's perception to disability. Having spent a large amount of time in the country, my family had a lot of friends there. This circle of friends in London, I was amazed to find, were extremely aware about how to treat a disabled person. Unlike in India where I was perennially patronized, both physically and intellectually, for the first time in London I found myself being treated like an adult. I was made to be responsible for my own actions. People wanted to hear my voice and see if I had a mind and a voice of my own. The most striking point for me was when we went to a conference, where there were severely disabled people and each of them contributed to the society and had a voice of their own. I saw people in electric wheelchairs and with voice synthesizers mingling freely with the abled and other disabled people alike.

Finding peers that I had missed in India, I finally gave my full consent to using my electric wheelchair. I acquired a voice synthesizer. These two *gadgets* revolutionized my life and allowed me to function an independent adult life for myself.

The electric wheelchair gave me a new sense of independence of movement in my life. Before I started using it, I was accompanied everywhere by my parents. With the wheelchair and the streets of London being accessible and people noninstructive, as well as helpful when required, I soon felt confident of going out on the busy streets of London on my own. Mother, however, needed a lot of persuasion before she let me be on my own on London roads.

I remember the first time. I was out on my own on the streets of London and in the midst of the hustle and bustle of London's traffic. The feeling was wonderful and phenomenal to just be a part of the crowd. My spirits were high and a sense of adventure crept over me as I wandered down in my electric wheelchair. I could not believe my newfound freedom. For the first time, I could go wherever and whenever, without explaining to anyone why.

I was ecstatic to have the power to move on wheels. It didn't matter that I was in a wheelchair. As I walked around the crowded streets, I felt free and alive. On my electric wheelchair I felt, as I feel now, that I can do a lot more.

The mobility on roads, which everyone else takes for granted in the developed world, but which I did not have in India and found for the first time in London, gave a big boost to my identity. I did everything, from window shopping to exploring the city, on my own.

I had never before experienced this form of freedom in my life.

Thus, the environment has to be accepting of us for us to explore our own identity. Due to poor inaccessibility of the roads, disabled people are not seen, and, as a result, we don't go out of our houses. This has a detrimental effect on our growth and experience. While I was growing up, I had no experience of moving out. Murugami writes that:

> [i]f society was willing to adapt to impairment through the removal of architectonic hindrances while making laws that recognize human rights, then the

effects of disability would be greatly reduced. The solution could be attained through special education, law, and architectural considerations tailored to persons outside the norm of the able-bodied persons. (2009)

Going everywhere on my own empowered me. For the first time in my life, I went wherever I wanted to. Initially, I was scared to venture too far as I was afraid that people would ask me questions and I wouldn't be able to talk to them in a language they could understand. Indeed, once I went to a student's union canteen and two students eating there thought I had escaped from a care home because they could not understand my speech. "How could someone who couldn't communicate cogently to others be on her own?" they thought, and called the police. However, I made a quick getaway on my electric wheelchair before the police got there. Perhaps, the two students didn't expect me to do that either. It is only in rare times like these that people's prejudices do come in handy.

What a disabled person is, thus, striving for is perhaps not *normalcy*, but societal acceptance. If the society accepts us as we are, life becomes normal for us.

What was nice for me, though, was that this experience was rare in London. In my wanderings and expeditions, I discovered that most people accepted and welcomed me, and that helped my development and my acceptance of myself the way I am.

With my newfound freedom on the roads, I grew and evolved as a person. I went to cinema halls, attended seminars, looked at the latest exhibitions, attended plays..., and here and there and everywhere I went on my own, where my fancy, imagination, and information took me. This, in itself, became a nurturing environment where I felt free to be myself despite my disability.

I learnt to be proud of myself and value myself as a disabled woman. I realized that no matter how different I got, there was one essential way in which I was similar to and shared a common bond with all women with disabilities, which was that, more or less, we faced similar kind of discrimination and segregation across the world.

My Master's in Women's Studies in England focused me into thinking about my needs as a disabled woman, which I had ignored in the past. Through my studies, I learnt that it was alright to ask for help. I learnt to be proud to be disabled. In my Master's class, I met different types of women: women from Mexico, Africa, Argentina, women of different sexual orientations, women from different social and cultural backgrounds, women of different ages and idiosyncrasies. This helped me in changing my self-image of myself. Seeing these differences made me realize that everyone is unique, and the uniqueness of each individual must be valued. We all want to be valued for our uniqueness, and yet we want to assimilate with each other and with the society. This is a catch-22 situation which I learnt to live with eventually.

Eight years later, I came back to India, and my concept of independence changed drastically once again.

In India, if you are disabled, you are simply not welcome. Go to any city in India and the state of its roads varies from bad to worse. Often, a road is nothing but an ensemble of potholes, puddles, cracks, and fissures. The case is so even in Mumbai where I live, the financial capital of India. You'll be hard-pressed to find even one mile of road free of any fault in India.

Societal perceptions in India are as fractured and potholed as its infrastructure. Till today, I regularly catch people staring at me as if I were a monkey in a zoo. The polite amongst the masses whisper, pointing at me. The rude ones talk disparagingly and pityingly about me right when I am there, as if I don't exist or I exist only for their amusement and ill-informed judgment.

You can count on your fingertips the number of buildings that are disabled friendly in Mumbai, and where a person in an electric wheelchair can go without needing the help of anyone. Even very few government buildings, which have been mandated by law to be made disabled friendly, rarely follow the law.

The situation in the rest of the country is much worse.

India, thus, does not allow the kind of independence to disabled people that a developed country like the UK does. I cannot go out on my own in any city in the country. I have a disability, but India paralyzes me multiple times over and in multiple ways—social, cultural, political, and economical.

Yet, in India, one can, with some effort, lead a semi-independent life. But this is possible only if you can afford a staff, like I could.

In India, I found myself a job as an event manager at Oxford Bookstore. And there I found other things that would let me be independent in different ways. At first, I thought I wouldn't be able to do the job as it required speech and interaction. But that was the time when communication technologies had made sufficient strides. I found that if I used modes of communication, such as mobile, chat, and e-mail, I could do my job with the least amount of disturbance and interference.

Yet, while technology empowered me and made me feel like I could do more than I had previously thought possible, the antipathy of society and the system it created and the structural antipathy for disabled people it harbors did just the opposite.

While I had a car and a driver to take me to and from my job, I couldn't spend my entire day in the office because they didn't have accessible toilets. And that is a problem pan Mumbai, rather pan India. No matter how qualified a disabled person became, doesn't matter even if she/he were a genius like Stephen Hawking, yet, the one simple factor that will prevent them from utilizing their genius for the betterment of society, one small insignificant detail, is the lack of toilets for people with disability.

The problem becomes much more acute when one considers the same for disabled women. How are we disabled women to get employed and contribute and be a part of mainstream life if we cannot even find one toilet to go to for miles when we need to do the most basic of human acts which other people take for granted?

As Brinsenden says, "The most important factor is not the amount of physical tasks a person can perform, but the amount of control they have over their everyday routine" (1986: 178). And as Oliver argues, "Independence is about control and not about abilities" (1990: 252).

There is a stream of thought in India, as in the rest of the world, that one who is not naturally independent to do his own work does not deserve society's helping hand. The problem with this line of thought is that in reality no one is totally self-reliant. The very structure of modern society does not permit total independence. It grants an individual a certain level of interdependence. If a so-called nondisabled person can be dependent on cooks and drivers in our present society, what's the problem with disabled people being dependent on a driver to take them to and from work or a helper to help them with some everyday functions? Aren't the people who help us also dependent on us for their livelihood?

Despite the multiple challenges I faced while working as an event manager at Oxford Bookstore, I managed to organize events and functions using only short messaging service (SMS) and e-mail. The best reward often came unexpectedly, when a person or celebrity I had interacted with via e-mail or SMS finally saw me in real life… on a wheelchair and with impaired speech. Their *shock and awe* often compensated for many other difficulties I suffered.

Often, when I find myself introspecting about the difference between my life in the UK and the one here in India, I find that at the most fundamentally personal level, I can see that in India I am always surrounded with people, while I had my privacy in the UK; the bane of population? More like the bane of societal antipathy toward people with disability.

Modern Times, Modern Communication

As I mentioned earlier, technology was a great helper and leveler for a disabled person like me. The enablement that technology provided me turned me into a technocrat. If you look at my life and my identity from the technological point of view, you'll find that both have advanced and formed with the development and formation of newer forms of communication technology; the more it advanced, the more I was empowered.

Yet the extent and level of technology that I use today has had such a profound impact on my life was not even around when I was growing up.

Due to my source of personal distress—my garbled speech—I missed out on a lot of quick repartee. I was intellectually adept, but my speech did not follow the commands of my mind and did not form in clearly audible words, the words and ideas that formed in my head.

Yet being raised and educated in a special school, I was given the time to speak and people had the patience to understand. It was an environment that encouraged. Despite my disabilities, life was good. Hence, in mainstream college, where I encountered people of my age, but without my disabilities, I was in for the shock of my life.

My first mainstream educational institute was St Xavier's College. Nothing in the nurturing environment of my special school had prepared me for the shock I would feel here. Confronted with my peers, I suddenly lost my own sense of self and identity. I realized my speech was pathetic. Since I was not vocal, I felt that I had no personality.

When people without my speech impairment exchanged words in a quick flurry, I always felt left behind because I was not fast enough in my repartees. Some of the *do-gooders* in college helped me and pushed my wheelchair around. However, they never took time to listen to me. Some would even whisper about me, as if I was not there or could not understand what was being said about me.

At Xavier's, I did have a small Canon typewriter, where what I typed came out on strips of paper. That helped a bit. That small Canon typewriter was my first means of independent communication. However, when I look back, I see that it was an extremely tedious way of communicating. It required a lot of effort and time. Hence, my only friends were those who understood my speech a fair deal. Even with the Lightwriter, I had to think of intelligent topics to attract those people besides my close circle of friends.

When I was in London, when my mother was doing her PhD, I had the chance to learn something that was new then, but would soon revolutionize communication and information dissemination and reception forever—the Internet. The advantage was that in a university surrounding one had easy access to Internet which wasn't as ubiquitous in the 1990s as it is now. Thus, I learnt the art of using electronic mail, in short—e-mail. That one thing, that was changing the way the world was communicating, changed my life much more that it did others'.

For the first time, I found it easy to communicate with friends. And best of all, e-mails were instant. You could send and receive replies instantaneously. It was almost like I was communicating with them in real time, and instead of it being only me with a typing pad on my lap, even the person communicating with me was with his or her own keyboard. E-mails, thus, brought communication with people to a democratic level, a level playing field, if you can call it that.

Yes, in my excitement, I often pressed the send button without re-reading my e-mails and, thus, my mails were full of flaws, but that was a minor hindrance.

Soon, something better would emerge, the word-chat services of yesteryears, wherein two people via the Internet could type messages on a tiny window on the computer, and the person half way across the world would get the message in a similar tiny window on their screen instantly and respond. Thus, I did not need my audience to be within visible distance of my communicator. They could be anywhere in the world, and I could communicate quickly and back and forth with them. If I couldn't reach up to their speed of speech, the computer brought them up to my speed of typing, even though I typed only with one little finger.

Then came another technological revolution, which once again changed my life much more, and to much greater levels than it would other people's lives. The revolution was heralded with a device that would grow tinier with age and advancement—the mobile phone.

When mobile phones came out, most people thought that the gadget was not for me because it was too tiny, and not having control over my movements, that tiny device would be useless to me. Once again, it was my absolute pleasure to break their perception about me and about the technology in question.

After Internet, e-mail, and then chat, time had come for the next communication revolution—social media: first Orkut and now Facebook. On the Internet, they say, you can be anyone you want to be. Your limitations don't matter on Facebook, as long as you can strike up an intelligent, fun conversation. What's more, you could be updated on the lives of your friends, as they could be about your life, without bothering each other. And it combined the previous advancements of e-mail and chat as well.

The social Web, that is, the usage of the Web to support the social process, represents a space in which people have the possibility to express and expose their identity (Marcus et al., 2006) in a social context. For instance, people define explicitly their identity by creating user profiles in social network services, such as Facebook or LinkedIn, or in online dating services (Siibak, 2007), as well as by using blogs and expressing opinions. An online identity, Internet identity, or Internet persona is a social identity that an Internet user establishes in online communities and websites. Although some people prefer to use their real names online, some Internet users prefer to use another identity. My communication has increased immensely with the use of technology. I sincerely believe that without communication, one's identity does not flower, and we cannot reach our potential. I have a right to think differently from others around me. In this new era of disability activism, disabled people have the right to behave differently to express themselves. And e-mail, chat, social media, and mobile phones give us the means to express those behavior and opinions.

Today, most people are surprised at the speed with which I communicate via SMS with them. My mother takes my help in technological matters, those dealing with the computer, Internet, mobile phone, and social networking.

Text messages on the phone and chat facilities, be it on social media sites such as Facebook or on e-mail service providers such as Gmail, have revolutionized my life by giving me a sense of identity, by giving me a means to not only form, but also maintain relationships without the hindrance of my disability which hampers me in real life. Sitting in Mumbai today, I am connected to friends from across the globe.

Technology has, thus, become an intricate part of my identity, helping it form and develop into areas I had never thought possible or ever knew existed. Like a wheelchair and communicator, they have become for me both an appendage and extension of my being. I may not have fully functional legs, but technology gives me wings.

My Non-Technological Extensions

No matter how much technology helps in the normalization of a disabled person's identity, it can only go so far. In the end, we live in a physical dimension, and our physical being is the primary source of our identity formation. What determines the shape and size of a disabled person's identity, thus, is the amount of physical help she/he needs. Some of us need it on a daily basis, and others like me need it almost hourly.

As disabled adults, we view our bodies as extremely inadequate and helpless, and, hence, dependent on our helpers and carers. Our identities, by extension, are intertwined with them. And our helpers become a subject of internal strife and argument for us, and we wonder if those of us who take help of caregivers constantly can truly call ourselves independent no matter what or how much we achieve otherwise.

Are Independence and Disability Mutually Exclusive Concepts?

Yet beyond the low self-esteem that is formed by asking these questions of ourselves time and again lies a fundamental truth—in any society, no one is truly or entirely independent. Indeed, the very idea of society is that everyone is mutually interdependent or, as it is said, "[N]o man is an island." Thus, no matter who it is, even those who consider themselves completely free from impairment are dependent in some way or the other on others, a dependence that is sometimes visible and at other times invisible.

For a disabled person, a personal attendant plays the role of a helping hand, who guides them in their daily living. Depending on our type of disability, a person might need help in using the toilet, dressing, eating, etc.

But how different is this dependence from the dependence of a seemingly nondisabled person on a carpenter, plumber, or electrician? Just like they are dependent on these people so that they can function more efficiently and can focus on their core competencies, disabled people also need helpers, for exactly the same reasons. Yes, we may need one or two people more than usual. Maybe a disabled person will need exactly that many helpers as others do. For example, Indian houses that can afford it usually have a cook, a driver, and a maid. I do too. And most of the times, I have an additional person helping me, a personal caregiver or attendant who helps me in my daily functions and needs. Just as in the relationship between anyone with their helpers, these people also help me focus my energies on my core competencies, like writing. Would I have been able to write this article without their help? Definitely not.

My argument is that if nondisabled people are invisibly dependent on other people, why can't disabled people be *visibly* dependent, thus, without being judged by others as dependent disabled?

Therefore, for me, a personal attendant is like one's hands and legs in the form of another human being. The disabled person instructs his attendant about the ways and means she/he would like to be helped. She/he is taught how to train his own personal attendant, to hire as well as to fire. To me, this form of interdependence is essential if I am to contribute positively to society, and not always be treated as a second-class citizen. This concept really appealed to me, and I have used several personal attendants during my adult life.

Aids and personal attendants often literally become the limbs of those people who are physically disabled.

With the help of aids and personal attendants, I found that I could lead a fairly normal life. I do believe that the concept of normal is different for each individual. My concept of normal is making my own decisions instead of those being forced onto me by some allegedly benevolent entity. I believe there are several ways that a person can be independent. A disabled person can organize life through her caregivers. Although a disabled person may not physically be able to do things on her/his own. She/he can instruct her own caregivers to do things the way he/she wants.

I use several aids for me to be able to lead a *normal* life. Actually, come to think of it, I need a variety of aids and people to enable me to function independently. I need an electric wheelchair and a manual wheelchair. For my communication needs I need a personal computer, which I use to communicate to most people by e-mail, chat, and by writing articles. I also use a lightwriter, which I use when I am with people who don't understand my speech.

Thus, in my 45 years, I have used a number of people as well as aids to help me. In India, I have more people to help me in my day-to-day life. Yes, one can argue that I come from a privileged family and, therefore, I can afford it; but I do believe that all people have to survive with their existing resources. If I were born and lived in a developed country with easy accessibility and helpful attitude of people toward the disabled, I wouldn't need so many attendants in the first place. The lack of accessibility in India is, thus, slightly compensated by the easily and inexpensively available manual help in India. For a person with disability, manual help thus compensates quite a bit for the lack of physical infrastructure that we see in the country.

Manual help also help in other ways. Adults' disabled bodies can often be repulsive as we are often unkempt and not well maintained, as disabled adults do not get enough of exercise without physical infrastructure or accessible gyms. Manual help compensates a bit for these lacks.

Education and Identity

Reflecting back to my Master's in Women's Studies in London, I realize that it was the first time that I came out as a disabled person. Before the Master's, I felt that I had to prove myself doubly hard to be as normal as possible. In college, we were never taught to celebrate our differences. From my experience, I realize that disabled people have to first come to terms with their disability. This can be hard as the outside world has an aversion to disability. Confession of one's disability in an able world is great and worthwhile, and it is exceedingly painful for a disabled person to come to terms with their own disability. Their identities have been suppressed. Previously, people tended to not regard the body of the disabled person.

I found when I did my first Master's at the Institute of Education that my tutors and my peers encouraged my voice to be heard. They were eager to know my individual experiences as a disabled woman. I felt comfortable to talk about my experience. I became interested in focusing my attention on the experiences of disabled women as there has not been much written about it. My attention was diverted to a disabled feminist author and researcher, Jenny Morris. She really helped me relate to my life as a disabled person, and it helped influence and develop my identity.

Before Morris became disabled at the age of 21, she was actively involved in the women's movement and the labor movement. Trying to make sense of her new identity as a disabled woman, she put her own personal experience into a broader framework, thus, making it political in keeping with one of the central themes of feminism, that the *personal is political* (Morris, 1991: 4; 1996). By *personal is political*, I refer to how a disabled woman copes in her everyday life and the relationship of this with the outside world. A disabled woman might need help with personal care, housekeeping, support with child care, and a number of other responsibilities which a nondisabled woman would take for granted. For example, the amount of personal assistance could be cut down for a disabled woman who relies on the social services, thus, affecting her professional life.

What well-known feminists with disabilities have done is to publicize their own personal experiences and put them into a wider context. This wider context makes personal assistance a matter of social concern, a social issue rather than a private and individual one. Again, if there are no disabled-friendly toilets in a public place where disabled people visit, the issue becomes public, one of impingement and restriction to a disabled person's life. These issues concerning disabled people are not merely individual and personal; they are public issues, which need to be politicized. Stanley and Wise argue that "For us, the insistence on the deeply political nature of everyday life and on seeing political change as personal change, is quite simply, 'feminism'" (1983: 192).

Sex, Disability, and Identity

Sex is a fundamental human need. Society accepts it as an extremely important need for the psychological growth of a person. Yet when it comes to a disabled person, the same society considers it a taboo, as if your disability turns you asexual. And injected into this general inequality is gender politics. For example, you'll often find disabled men who have married a *normal* person. Yet you'll rarely find a disabled woman who's married.

Disabled women's personal and sexual needs are constantly hidden and ignored. First of all, a woman is at a double disadvantage because a woman is seen as an embodiment of sexuality, and to have a disabled, disfigured body is, thus, going absolutely against the norms established and enforced by media stereotypes. Disabled women, directly and tacitly, are taught to be ashamed of their bodies. And disabled women too shy away from the problem, thinking they are asexual, and usually hide behind a self-created brave front of denying that sex and their sexuality matters to them.

A moot point to be considered, thus, is: What are the hidden problems that disabled women face? Is it the treatment they get from men, or is it the way they are shaped by society? Why do disabled people consider themselves asexual? Despite our sexual desires remaining similar to other people, why does an insensitive society suppress them?

The truth about disabled people is that disability does not hamper a person's emotional need to be touched and loved on an emotional and physical plane just like everyone else. Our sexual organs are not damaged or affected, and hence we do long for and are able to enjoy pleasurable sexual experiences.

Disabled men are luckier than disabled women when it comes to partners. Disabled men get more able-bodied partners than do disabled women. An *able-bodied man who is a lover, partner, spouse or even a long-term friend with a disabled woman* is an extreme exception.

When I was doing women's studies, I concentrated on disabled women and was disgusted at the stereotypical way disabled women were perceived. Their bodies are considered rejected and undesirable. Competing for a perfect body is like asking for the moon from them. In this way, a very important part of a woman's being—her sexual identity—is cruelly denied to a disabled woman.

Empowering Myself

A so-called able-bodied person manages to slip into multiple identities. So can people with disabilities. My disability is one of the components that make up my identity. I am a disabled, heterosexual, and an Asian upper-middle-class woman. My disability is only one part of my identity, yet sadly, that is the only part that the society decides to see, or even acknowledge.

> Society needs to acknowledge that sometimes elusive boundaries exist between having impairment and being able-bodied. It should acknowledge that very few of us qualify as fully able-bodied along all dimensions of functioning throughout all of our lives. Hence, impairment should be seen as part of the human condition rather than a basis for setting someone apart, or a characteristic diminishing one's humanness. (Gwernan, 2008)

> Even when a disability is obvious and impossible to hide on an ongoing basis, families sometimes create magnifications that disabled people are forced to play along. Many people have told me that when family pictures were taken as they were growing up, they were removed from their wheelchairs, or they were shown only from the waist up, or they were excluded from pictures altogether. The messages are that this part of you, your disability or the symbol of disability, your wheelchair, is unacceptable, or, in the last case, you are not an acceptable member of the family. (Linton, 1998)

Positive attitudes play an important part in formulating a disabled person's identity. My empowerment and entry into adulthood began for the first time in London, at a conference where for the first time I saw and met adults with disability who could contribute as they were. These adults, I noticed, used communicators, wheelchairs, and helpers. They were articulate and empowered and had their sense of independence about them despite their disability. For the first time, I realized that there was no shame in using any of these.

This is the sense, the feeling of freedom that I got in London that led me to writing in my book *One Little Finger.*

> The electric wheelchair gave me a tremendous feeling of movement and space. With this, I did not feel as if I could not walk. I did not feel helpless.

I could slip into shops, chemists, bookshops, restaurants etcetera. Whatever the so called normal person does, I could do. I did this with ease and it did wonders for my self-confidence. I was whizzing round, with mother. With this new freedom I went everywhere. Independent means of movement added a new dimension to my growth and identity. I could go wherever I wanted for the first time in my life. (Chib, 2011)

This was unique as for 29 years I had not experienced any independent freedom of movement on roads anywhere. Thus, in London, to be able to move on one's own was a luxury. Having got this freedom, it left me with huge number of choices about what I wanted to do. If I wanted to, I could go down to the pub instead of sitting in the library and completing my Master's. This independence of choice, as I stated earlier, had a tremendous impact on my identity, my empowerment, and my enrichment.

The *Abled* Identity in a Disabled Body

No man is an island. All individuals must have social interaction. A human being is shaped and reshaped by social interactions. As we grow and our powers of developing our identity increase through social interaction or interpersonal identity development, it allows one to question and examine various personality elements, such as ideas, beliefs, and behaviors, consolidating their sense of self or identity. Majority of disabled people have poor social interaction; therefore, they don't get the same kind of feedback from people as the nondisabled do. This may be due to lack of exposure.

This exposure today can be provided by an *online identity*. Disabled people must be allowed to have help. In the medical model, disabled people were supposed to be completely independent. Now, disabled people have their own personal attendants. In my first extended visit abroad as an adult, what intrigued me the most was the ease with which disabled people function, unashamed of their disability and unembarrassed about their helpers.

Linton (1998) argues that disabled people also speak of *coming out* in the same way that members of the lesbian and gay community do. Linton talks about a woman that she met at a disability studies conference who in the course of a conversation about personal experience said, "I'm five years old." The woman went on to say that despite being significantly disabled for many years, she had only recently discovered the disabled community and allied with it. For her, *coming out* was a process that began when she recognized how her effort to *be like everyone else* was not satisfying her own needs and wishes.

The phrase *overcome disability* may also be a shorthand version of saying "someone with a disability overcame many obstacles" (Linton, 1998). My perception of this is that disabled people have to come to terms with their disability as being part of themselves and to be willing to accept help so that they can become contributing members of the society.

I feel that a disabled person need not live in denial of their disability. Instead, a disabled person should celebrate her/his difference. This is despite it being unduly challenging to come to terms with ones disability, confronted as we are in society with *perfect* bodies who seem to have no difficulty in living a normal life. For a disabled person to accept her/his disability enables her/him to reflect on capabilities and limitations and to find a balance between the two. Disabled people have to find a way to feel comfortable with themselves and their own bodies. And this is despite the general apathy of society that fails to accept anything different from the norm. The temptation to acquire a false identity because it makes one believe that their disability is removed is strong with a disabled person. Yet it needs to be resisted, for only in being true to oneself and one's abilities and limitations can one truly come alive and contribute the best that they can. This is as true for those without inhibiting disabilities as it is for disabled people.

The fact that I belong to an anglicized family which is essentially Indian and a mix of two cultures has shaped my thinking; the fact that I am a woman, single, and heterosexual will influence my thinking about sex and marriage. I am essentially disabled. This all has contributed to my identity formation.

While making sense of one's disability, one must, like Foucault, ask: Who is normal? What we mean by normal is uniformity. However, since no two individuals are the same, how can anyone be truly normal?

Hence, to ascertain a disabled identity is not an easy task in the *abled, normal* world. It is only when the concept of *identity* has become both debatable and a new area of research that we will truly be able to acknowledge a disabled identity. Yet it is the self that must enable us to reflect on *who we are, whom we choose to identify with, and what we choose to do as matters of choice.*

Formulating self-identity that will culminate in a healthy self-concept becomes an uphill task, and sometimes persons with disabilities swim with the current to unintended destinations.

A person without disability automatically assumes that a disabled person wants to be cured. As if there is a cure for disability. Is there a cure for disability? For the disabled persons who are proud of who they are, for whom their identity as disabled has been an important part of making meaning about themselves and the people and the world they have known, the refusal of *cure* can be the response to this societal quest of *treating* disabled people.

But I didn't know this when I was growing up. In a world where the medical model was still prevalent, where a disabled person had to adapt to the normal world, where she had to be fixed and fitted, I forced myself to become as normal as possible. At Xavier's, when surrounded with hordes of normal people, I craved to be normal. Being normal was the ultimate goal of a disabled person.

I was embarrassed to be helped. Because I wanted to be normal, I wanted to do everything on my own. But doing everything on my own would take a long time and it would take a toll on my energy. The only reason I let people help me was because doing anything on my own looked extremely awkward. It is quicker and easier for other people to help a disabled person. It has already been stated that

> The affirmative model directly challenges presumptions of personal tragedy and the determination of identity through the value-laden presumptions of nondisabled people. It signifies the rejections of presumptions of dependency and abnormality.... Embracing an affirmative model, disabled individuals assert a positive identity, not only in being disabled, but also in being impaired. In affirming a positive identity, disabled people are actively repudiating the dominant view of normality. The changes for individuals are not just transforming of consciousness as to the meaning of "disability," of the value and validity of life as a person with impairment. (Swain and French, 2000: 578)

Reflecting back to my life as I do in *One Little Finger*, a normal identity was ingrained in me. My conditioning was to become normal or perfect. As I grew older, I realized being normal wasn't going to happen in this lifetime. This I realized during my Master's in London. It was at a time when the disability movement in London was beginning. Disabled people were just starting to fight for their rights. By fighting for their rights, they were discovering their own inner capabilities and potential. Learning about the latest social model of disability and the changing approach to the treatment of disabled people helped me to accept my own challenging situation and my body.

Most people think that disabled people are a liability and a burden. What does a woman of forty do? The normal and ordinary things like traveling. Why am I so special? I can live and contribute in society. People often ask me … "Can you live alone?" "Can you have a relationship?" and basically "Can you manage life as an adult?" I am just another person. I want to be accepted for just being who I am, without too much of questioning and stares about my disability … also a part of me will always long to feel I want to contribute to be a citizen … if I am allowed to. (Chib, 2004)

These comments have had a skewed effect on my disability identity. Society keeps hurling unsolicited suggestions which I may never get accustomed to; but in my 45 years, I am proud of being what I am despite the indifferent attitude of society. I desperately hold on to disability identity as I think my essence of being is my disability and I have to celebrate it, rather than reject it. Despite all the battles fought, all the stones hurled at me, I am proud to be disabled.

Inside, I am normal; outside, my body isn't. My mind is capable, but my body is disabled. My mind can run and wander the recesses of the most ancient and modern parts of the world, but my body forces me to stay put. My mind forms thoughts and ideas that could perhaps change the world, but by the time I manage to make anyone understand them, they have lost their power, their time, their moment of immaculate creation.

In the polarity of these extreme opposites, one negative and one positive, one flying and the other denying, one real and the other surreal, I live… I exist. In this no man's land between two constantly warring nations of my mind and my body, I—as do millions of disabled people in the world—try to find my own self, try to find the truth that defines me and my identity. And though this battle of the opposites raging both within and outside me often devastates me, I live on, I breathe on… I fight on for my identity, for my right to be… me… to be accepted as I am, supremely able in some things, disabled in others.

I am paralyzed on Tottenham Court Road, my wheelchair stuck in a puddle. No one understands my speech and hence can't help me even though they want to. Finally a cute young man with blue eyes, a square jaw and two dimples, pauses a little longer than the others. He gets down on his knees and tries to understand me. In my panic my words rush out more incoherently. In desperation, I point to my bag hanging behind my wheelchair and say "bag" repeatedly. He understands and as he looks inside and sees my communicator he asks, "You want this gadget with a keyboard?" I repeat a vehement "yes, yes." He puts it on my lap, I switch it on and I type on it: "my wheelchair is stuck on a puddle, can you help get it out." He smiles the most enduring smile, examines the wheelchair and the puddle and stops another passerby. *Together they push and shove my wheelchair out of the puddle and I can be on my way. But I don't go. "Can I pay you back for your kindness with a coffee," I type on the communicator after a "thank you." He lets out a loud laugh. He's both intrigued and amused. With the same enduring smile he says, "why not." I feel like I am the queen of the world.*

Bibliography

Alur, Mithu. 1998. "Invisible Children: A Study of Policy Exclusion," PhD thesis, Institute of Education, University of London, London.

Brinsenden, S. 1986. "Independent Living and the Model of Disability," *Disability, Handicap and Society*, 1 (2): 173–178.

Chib, Malini. 2004. "A Woman Disabled in India", paper presented and published in-house, The Spastics Society of India (now ADAPT)/NRCI, Mumbai.

———. 2011. *One Little Finger*. New Delhi: SAGE Publications Pvt Ltd.

Gwernan-Jones, Ruth. December 2008. "Identity and Disability: A Review of the Current State and Developing Trends," School of Education and Lifelong Learning, University of Exeter. Available online at http://www.beyondcurrenthorizons.org.uk/identity-and-disability-a-review-of-the-current-state-and-developing-trends (downloaded on 13. 06.2013).

Linton, Simi. 1998. *Claiming Disability: Knowledge and Identity*. New York: New York University Press.

Marcus, B., Franz Machilek, and Astrid Schütz. 2006. "Personality in Cyberspace: Personal Websites and Media for Personality Expression and Impression," *Journal of Personality and Social Psychology*, 90 (6): 1014–1031. Available online at http://www.sakkyndig.com/psykologi/artvit/marcus2006.pdf (downloaded on 13. 06. 2013).

Morris, J. 1991. *Pride Against Prejudice: A Personal Politics of Disability*. London: The Women's Press.

———. 1996. *Encounters with Strangers: Feminism and Disability*. London: The Women's Press.

Murugami, Margaret Wangui. 2009. "Disability and Identity," *Disability Studies Quarterly*, 29 (4). Available online at http://dsq-sds.org/article/view/979/1173 (downloaded on 13.06.2013).

Oliver, M. 1990. *The Politics of Disablement: A Sociological Approach*. New York: St. Martin's Press.

Siibak, A. 2007. "Casanovas of the Virtual World. How Boys Present Themselves on Dating Websites," paper presented at Young People at the Crossroads: 5th International Conference on Youth Research in Karelia, Petrozavodsk,

Republic of Karelia, Russian Federation, September 1–5, 2006, (eds) M. Muukkonen and K. Sotkasiira, Joensuu University.

Stanley, L. and S. Wise. 1983. *Breaking Out Again: Feminist Ontology and Epistomology*. London, UK: Routledge and K. Paul.

Swain, J. and S. French. 2000. "Towards an Affirmative Model of Disability," *Disability and Society*, 15 (4): 569–582.

5

What Is the Intersection between Oppression of Women and Psychiatric Oppression?*

Tina Minkowitz

Girls and women face many contradictions in the ordinary course of life, navigating myriad oppressions that put women in the wrong, whether for attempting stereotypically feminine behavior or for rejecting the limitations of a feminine role. Sexual predation, discrimination in public life, lack of safety even at home, and inequitable access to resources deprive women and girls of the conditions needed for free development of the personality. Psychiatric oppression, and the underlying ostracism of *mad persons*, is a trap that polices the behavior of all girls and women with unpredictable physical, emotional, linguistic, and legal violence, labeling those who fall in as members of an inferior social caste.

By *psychiatric oppression* we mean diagnostic labeling, civil commitment, forced interventions with drugs and electroshock, restraint and solitary confinement, and all the associated abuses and discrimination. We also refer to this as *psychiatrizing*. *Pathologizing* means the labeling of mental, emotional, spiritual, and social distress or crisis as an illness, with psychiatric diagnoses. A *psychiatric survivor* is a person who identifies as having survived psychiatric oppression or abuse.

---

* This chapter first appeared as a submission on behalf of the Center for the Human Rights of Users and Survivors of Psychiatry to the Committee on the Rights of Persons with Disabilities for its half day of general discussion on women and girls with disabilities, April 17, 2013.

Psychiatric Oppression in the Lifespan of Girls and Women

Psychiatric oppression often comes at the transition from childhood to adulthood, complicating this already difficult transition for girls/women. In many respects, it can also be seen as a punitive response to women's difficulties accomplishing the transition. Some girls are expected to take on adult responsibilities when they are still children, caring for parents or younger siblings while denying their own needs. The needs do not go away, and when the girl reaches womanhood, she may experience a crisis that is labeled by the psychiatric system as psychosis or some other pathologizing diagnosis. Some girls are pathologized and put into the psychiatric system as children and are deprived of ordinary life and development, including education, for many years, which can hinder them in adult life. In many cases, girls and women are psychiatrized for reacting to rape or other sexual violence, or as part of a pattern of domestic violence.

> I was originally taken for electroshock at age 17 because I slept too much to suit my parents, and because I argued with my father who was drunk every night on 4 or more martinis. I had mononucleosis and was tired and sleepy, but even though everyone knew that I had mono, no one made the connection between my need for sleep and having mono. (This connection was known even in 1965.) My parents did not want me to participate in any talk therapy and did not want anyone to know about their drinking or about their marital problems (they were on the verge of divorce).
>
> The next year, I was abducted at the airport (by my parents) and put in a mental hospital because my mother had been drinking and did not remember that she had told me over the phone to come home from college. She thought I had just decided to come home out of the blue. No one believed me when I told them I had cleared my return with my parents before I flew home. In the records from the hospital repeatedly it is stated that I kept saying I had cleared my return with my parents, but because my parents did not remember the phone call, no one believed me, and I was thought to be making it up. This led to three more years of outpatient maintenance electroshock and major tranquilizers. Yes, families can scapegoat people and can use the mental health system to do so. I begged my parents to get a second opinion, and begged them to let me talk to a psychologist or counselor, but my mother's defensive response was "The insurance pays 80% for the psychiatrist and only 50% for a psychologist, and besides, psychologists always say it's all the mother's fault. (Anonymous)

In addition, the adult roles open to women have been in transition themselves for the last half-century or so, and adulthood for women is not as clear a status distinguished from childhood as it is for men. Women did not have equal legal capacity as men until comparatively recently, and do not enjoy full equality under the law in many countries including the United States. Derogatory expressions toward women, particularly those who assert leadership or boldly pursue personal ambitions (whether for personal satisfaction or social justice or both), still hinder women's full self-expression and contributions to humanity. Women are still at times referred to as *girls* even when they are past the age of maturity, while boys on the contrary can be referred to as *men* before they become adults. Asserting personal authority or social authority demands of women a skill and sensitivity that can be challenging, and this can lead to psychiatric labeling when the woman experiences personal crisis as a result or when she comes into conflict with others who both enact gender politics and deny the relevance of gender in the situation. Women who react to years of domestic violence by killing the abuser can be imprisoned for life in the psychiatric system following a verdict of *not guilty by reason of insanity*. As women age, there are additional challenges of reduced social respect, impoverishment and vulnerability to economic exploitation, and deprivation of legal capacity.

Psychiatric Oppression and the Feminist Account of Women's Lives

Feminists have criticized the pathologizing of women's resistance to oppression, and yet, by and large, have failed to appreciate the depth to which this is present in all psychiatric labeling, thus, perpetuating a distinction between *mad* and *sane* women and perpetuating the power of psychiatry to make this distinction. It is not only when a woman is actively rebelling against patriarchal gender roles requiring her to be meek and submissive to men that psychiatric labeling is inappropriate. When a woman is trying to conform to gender role expectations, she may be equally likely to be pathologized as *too* passive. Self-expression that not only violates social norms but also confronts others with a depth of pain and contradiction that is uncomfortable to face, like self-injury (cutting), or retreating into silence, or taking one's clothes off in public, does not need to be fully understandable as an expression of gender politics to matter as a reflection of women's and girls' experience that has meaning. This is true also of the self-expression of boys and men.

Psychiatric oppression removes women from many of the opportunities to struggle with gender politics and actively contribute to the social transition toward gender equality and equity. It is not so much that there is an intersection of oppressions based on different facets of personal identity, but that psychiatric oppression places a person into a social caste with inferior legal rights and inferior access to resources and to the means to defend oneself against violations. In that sense, psychiatric oppression is related to other intersecting oppressions, such as poverty, or women who are sex workers or who live in the streets. There is a qualitative difference in experience to that of other women who have never been segregated in that way, and it creates a gulf between women and an omission of aspects of women's experience from much of the feminist account of women's lives.

Psychiatric oppression is more than the fact of madness or alleged madness, and more than being institutionalized and forcibly drugged or electroshocked. It means that a woman might lose her home and job, and have difficulty getting work because of gaps in work history that cannot be explained without divulging information that can be used against the person for discriminatory reasons. It means that a woman might be living in congregate mental health housing, which can impose demeaning requirements such as taking unwanted psychiatric drugs and allowing staff to enter at any time, because she cannot afford her own apartment on a disability pension and there are no friends or family with whom she can share living space. It means that a woman might be living in the community under an outpatient commitment order, required to take drugs and attend psychiatric programs, even if she has her own apartment and would prefer to get a job or go to school. It means that a woman might be less self-confident, less assured of a welcome for the whole of who she is, having the memory of being treated as if she were nothing as a *mental patient* in an institution, which the society around her does not condemn but actually endorses as public policy.

It means that she might be a *childless mother* whose children were taken away due to prejudice and fear after she was institutionalized. She might experience cognitive disabilities resulting from electroshock or tardive dyskinesia and other health problems from psychiatric drugs.

Women in the Psychiatric Survivor Movement

In the psychiatric survivors movement, women often take leadership roles, but it is difficult to address gender politics aside from issues of rape (trauma particularly from childhood rape as a cause of distress and crisis that gets responded to by psychiatrizing, and also rape in institutions) and discrimination in child custody. The politics of women's liberation is not universally accepted in the psychiatric survivor movement, particularly reproductive freedoms and the choice to terminate a pregnancy, women's right to function as assertive leaders and to not present themselves as maternal, and rejection of sexist cultural materials. The contents of men's subjective experiences of trauma and injustice, as well as their religious and spiritual beliefs, often include sexist material, which can be difficult for women to confront when it arises in peer support. (The same is true for people of color dealing with white people's subjective experience and beliefs that include racist material.) Women may face judgment in peer support settings regarding expression of anger (still reacted to as a male prerogative) and articulation of politics of women's liberation, and may not be able to trust the group with their most meaningful experiences or beliefs. Lesbian experience beyond the mere fact of orientation toward same-sex partners is invisible in the psychiatric survivor movement, in particular, the richness of lesbian-feminist culture and spirituality.

Intersecting Oppression

Thus, in many ways, the intersection of psychiatric oppression and women's oppression resembles a gap, rather a fertile space. A female survivor of psychiatry, particularly if she is a lesbian (and/or a woman of color/cultural minority woman), and if her experience of women's oppression is not centered on sexuality and reproduction, may find no *home* in any social justice movement or in mainstream society, while at the same time she may well make significant contributions to the feminist movement, the user/survivors movement, the disability movement, and society as a whole. Since the user/survivors movement is both politically small and a matter of urgency for those of us whose priority is resisting psychiatric oppression, there has been little opportunity to develop a substantial political space of female users and survivors of psychiatry. In the United Nations Convention on the Rights of Persons with Disabilities (UNCRPD) drafting and negotiations, we participated actively in work on Article 6 and gender issues, particularly at the beginning of those discussions; but when the women's caucus was holding all-day meetings near the end of the process, we fell away because our priority had to be the articles on legal capacity, liberty, and integrity/free and informed consent that would secure our legal equality and freedom. Our contributions are seen in some of the earlier International Disability Caucus proposals for Article 6, which included references to women's autonomy.

Recommendations

State obligations toward female users and survivors of psychiatry under the CRPD remain centered on the articles that secure our legal equality and freedom. It is essential to do away with substituted decision making and disability-based defenses that preclude criminal responsibility,[1] and to abolish civil commitment and forced or coerced psychiatric interventions, which have been recognized as acts of torture and ill-treatment[2] and as acts of violence against women.[3] In implementing Article 6 and other gender-related provisions of the CRPD, it will be necessary for states to address these legal and practical obstacles to the advancement, empowerment and equality of women with psychosocial disabilities; otherwise, measures for the advancement of women will fail to achieve these aims for women with psychosocial disabilities, leaving us further behind.

Furthermore, states should take account of the ways in which social and legal oppression of women, and violence against women, contribute to the kinds of personal or social crisis for which women may seek mental health services, or during which they come to be incarcerated in the psychiatric system. These gender-based injustices need to be addressed at the root, rather than targeting women for mental health screening that perpetuates a pathologizing approach to women's lives and needs. States should recognize the ways in which psychiatric violence functions as an extension of domestic violence, and should support social transformations that promote women's equality with men as well as the elimination of medical/legal authority over women's and girls' lives, including women and girls whose reactions to trauma take the form of serious crisis and distress. Furthermore, in implementing a shift from the medical model to alternative services and supports, states need to ensure that such services and supports are able to identify with female-centered life perspectives.

In keeping with other treaty bodies that have invoked a right to remedy and reparations for violations following the issuance of United Nations guidelines on the subject, the CRPD Committee should call for immediate action to cease violations against the autonomy and integrity of women with disabilities and of all persons with disabilities, and to institute measures of remedy and reparation for victims. Articles 4 and 16 support such actions, and in the interpretation of Article 16, the Committee must include all forms of violence, including forced psychiatric interventions. Remedy and reparations need to be undertaken in a spirit of holistic and comprehensive commitment to reversing the measures that violate human rights and involving victims of violations as full partners in every step of the process, particularly in telling their individual stories and having opportunities to collectively develop a framework and particular suggestions for reparation measures. As part of these measures, a holistic open political space needs to be created for female users and survivors of psychiatry to consider in full the varied dimensions of their experiences.

Notes

1. Office of the High Commissioner for Human Rights, A/HRC/10/48, paragraphs 43–47.
2. Special Rapporteur on Torture, E/CN.4/1986/15, paras 118-119; A/63/175 (2008) paras 38, 40, 41, 44, 47, 61-65; A/HRC/22/53 (2013), especially paras 85(e) and 89 (and see clarifications made in Mr Mendez's statement to the Human Rights Council on March 4, 2013, that deprivation of liberty on mental health grounds is not justified by a motivation to protect the person or others).
3. See statement by Rashida Manjoo, Special Rapporteur on Violence Against Women, at side event on violence against women and girls with disabilities, October 12, 2012 (New York).

Bibliography

Burstow, Bonnie. 2006. "Electroshock as a Form of Violence Against Women," *Violence Against Women*, 12 (4): 372–392.

International Network of Women with Disabilities. 2011, March. "Violence Against Women with Disabilities," *Barbara Faye Waxman Fiduccia Paper on Violence Against Women with Disabilities*. Washington, D.C.: Center for Women Policy Studies. Available online at http://www.centerwomenpolicy.org/programs/waxmanfiduccia/2011OnlineSeriesBarbaraWaxmanFiduccia.asp (downloaded on 20.12.2013).

Kovary, Myra. 2012. "Interdependence: Including Women with Disabilities in the Agenda of the Women's Movement—Our Fears, Realities, Hopes, and Dreams," presented at the Fifth Session of the Conference of State Parties to the Convention of on the Rights of Persons with Disabilities, United Nations, New York, September 12–14. Available online at http://webtv.un.org/search/women-with-disabilities-5th-session-of-the-conference-of-states-parties-to-the-convention-on-the-rights-of-persons-with-disabilities/183908322800-1?term=Conference%20of%20States%20Parties (downloaded on 19.12. 2014).

Minkowitz, Tina. "Psychiatric Assault as Violence Against Women." Chestertown, NY: Center for the Human Rights of Users and Survivors of Psychiatry. Available online at www.chrusp.org/home/resources (downloaded on 10. 09. 2013).

Robb, A. 2010. "A Sentience Explored: A Journey into the Experiential Meanings of Middleclass South African Women Diagnosed with Bipolar Disorder," unpublished thesis, University of Western Cape, Cape Town.

World Network of Users and Survivors of Psychiatry and Bapu Trust. 2006. *First Person Stories on Forced Interventions and Being Deprived of Legal Capacity*. Pune: Mudra. Available online at http://www.scribd.com/doc/55987517/First-Person-Stories-on-Forced-Interventions-and-Being-Deprived-of-Legal-Capacity (downloaded on 20.12.2013).

————. 2011. "Recognizing Forced and Coerced Psychiatric Interventions Against Women, Men and Children as a Harmful Cultural Practice," submission for Joint CEDAW-CRC General Recommendation/General Comment on Harmful Practices.

6

Tale of Married Women with Disabilities: An Oxymoron Reality*

Santoshi Halder

After working on the various aspects of women with disabilities for the last 10 years, I still feel somewhere lacking in my capacity to touch some topics and write about women's experiences in terms of disability in the Indian context.[1] However, I have come to terms with this state of mind and challenge it by putting into words some aspects of our lives. The purpose of writing this chapter is twofold. One is the daily struggle of women in general and a compounded factor of torment, ostracism, pains, and mental anguish impinged on women with disabilities. The other goal is to observe and learn from women with disabilities experiences and, henceforth, to challenge the social conditioning and irrespective of any differences join hands in building an all-inclusive community and accessible world, a community where every individual can stand with dignity and live life with liberty and equality.

Women with disabilities—*the world's largest minority*—is one of the most marginalized sections (42 percent of the total disabled population) in Indian society who face triple jeopardy due to their gender, disability, and their birth in a developing nation. India has achieved an effective literacy rate of 74.04 percent in 2011 indicating a vast gender disparity, males 82.14 percent and females 65.46 percent, clearly indicating that a large

* The author would like to express deep gratitude and appreciation to all those challenged women whom she interviewed for believing and relying on her to share and reveal honestly their own personal experiences and life. The names of the women interviewed in the self-narratives throughout the chapter have been changed in order to safeguard their identity.

number of women in India are illiterate (Ministry of Human Resource Development, 2011). The combined impact of the barriers women face at every stage and their unequal status in society entail enormous losses to the global community. At any given time, the people with mobility needs suffer tremendous hindrances mainly due to the structural, psychological, and sociocultural barriers (Halder, 2008, 2009) imposed upon them due to the developing nation characteristics. According to Census 2011, there are 26.8 million people with disabilities in India, out of which 15 million are men and 11.8 million are women, which constitute females being 44.10 percent of the total population with disabilities. From the various documentations, it may be generalized that the population with disabilities especially women face a higher risk of discrimination, exploitation, violence, and abuse (Hassouneh-Phillips and Curry, 2002; Rosen, 2006).

Normality: A Relative Concept

The United Nations Convention on the Rights of Persons with Disabilities (UNCRPD) definition of disability clearly marks a paradigm shift by utilizing a *social model of disability* as an involving concept, resulting from the interaction between persons with impairments, and the attitudinal and environmental barriers that hinder full and effective participation in society on an equal basis with others. The significance of the environment and the cultural context is clearly evident from this definition of disability and, thus, disability is a relative concept varying throughout the world, not much because of the person's own functional limitation, but more due to the environmental barriers being imposed upon the individual which limits his/her mobility and the ability to work. As the various definitions of disability throughout the world vary from country to country, so goes the tagging criteria (Degener, 2006).

Let's see the common norm deciding normality prevalent in our society from time immemorial, and the criteria has been always with regard to *majority/most* of the people in society. In common practice, *abnormal* is defined (Ira and Wile, 1940) as something which deviates from the usual type, and *normal* means being approximately average or within certain limits, in other words a person who fits into mainstream society. Thus, abnormality may be explained on the basis of mainly four types of deviations, namely, statistical infrequency, deviation from social norms, failure to function adequately, and deviation from ideal mental health. Under this definition (ibid.), a person is considered abnormal if he/she is unable to cope with the demands of everyday life (for example, self-care, hold down a job, interact meaningfully with others, make themselves understood, etc.). Thus, a person's thinking or behavior is classified as abnormal if it violates the rules about what is expected or acceptable behavior in a particular social group: the degree to which a norm is violated, the importance of that norm, and the value attached by the social group to different sorts of violation. Usually, the phrase *not normal* is often used negatively in society. If we stick to the aforementioned definition or explanation of disability, then I believe we need to understand and be clear regarding the criteria before tagging a person as *disabled* in society as it may open up quite new interesting dimensions, and chances are that we may end up with altogether different criteria. Is tagging necessarily essential for leading a respectful and contended life? Moreover, is it *a life by choice or imposed?*

It's not a very rare sight to come across many women without disabilities being completely non responsive to many life situations or rather leading a life the way others want them to in spite of having full-fledged capacity to make their own life choices. On the other extreme, we are also witness to those women, though countable few, in society who irrespective of all odds still have emerged to lead a challenging life with their own struggle and determination. Do people with disability deserve to be tagged as *not normal* and, thus, discriminated in society and go on with their continuous struggle to lead a full-fledged and respectful life? Now how far we will go on deciding and accepting disability in the typical, usual way as a *deviation of normality?* It is indeed a very pertinent question when we deal with the topic of *disability* for the very reason that the normal visibility of the policy makers has been always to focus on *what is the need of the so-called majority of the people in society,* and everything seems to get carried over by this myth so much so that after so many years of liberation and development, we are still unable to create a barrier-free, inclusive environment which may be accessed by all in spite of the individual differences.

Henceforth, quite often I am bound to question myself on the very criteria for tagging a person as *disabled.* The question which we need to ponder over is whether the tag is necessary, and, if so, then who ought to be tagged so? As Sreelata (name changed), a 30-year-old married women without disability, says:

> I had so many aspirations, desire, dreams, but I could not achieve a single one of them, due to this, that and so many reason …. I am leading the life which others wanted, the way each of those members wanted me to. I never led the life I desired. Perhaps I have forgotten this is my life.

Women in society who are considered typically *able* in the sense that they are those privileged to be born what is understood as *perfect* in every respect, that is, having a functional brain, with all the senses intact, with a healthy physique, and mental well-being, but still leading a life where their capacity of normal physical, sensory functioning gets carried over by their own mental block and learned helplessness. On the verge of the 21st century, do we need to believe that women have still not set themselves free from their own gender stereotype *boxes*? Do we really need to blame others for their so-called *typical gender status*?

It is propitious that *women with disabilities* set themselves as role models despite their functional limitations and challenge life in the midst of all odds. Mithu Das (name changed), 32+, is a woman with a severe physical disability of both the lower limbs. She does her entire household chores, from washing, cooking, and mopping to going out for daily activities. With tremendous difficulty, she passed class 10, but due to the accessibility barriers that prevail all around, she could not continue further. She says:

> Moving from one class to another was very painful… my mother requested the teacher to conduct the classes in the ground floor but they could not, as there are no big classroom in the ground floor … I could not continue for long … it was so painful.

After dropping out from mainstream education, she did not give up and took admission in a tailoring course in an institute a mile away. Today, she earns her own livelihood, offers tailoring courses to the women in the village for a meager fee, and takes care of her ailing mother. Such challenging instances in society surely may put forth reasons to question ourselves who ought to be tagged as *disabled* and who as *abled*.

Marriage and Women with Disability

Various marriage practices have emerged and existed throughout the world which has undergone transformations. In recent decades, due to globalization, many new marriage practices have emerged which brought a dramatic departure from the conservatism and stereotyped gender roles, but we need to explore the underlying basis of these. We believe that in India, there is still a tendency to follow the traditional sex roles assigned to males and females in a marital relationship, with the husband being the dominant superior and the breadwinner, and the wife being the submissive and homebound one who is the caretaker of the family. However, when it comes to a woman with a disability, the scenario may be completely different and complex.

Research highlights that women with disability are significantly less likely to marry than women without disabilities (Nagata, 2003). In a study carried out by the author in 2010 in the Eastern part of India—West Bengal (see note 1), interestingly, we found contrasting evidences with more than half of the women in our sample population with disabilities who married very early (Halder, unpublished). Though the possible reasons may be very complex and critical, it is important to initiate a discourse. Nevertheless, there was also evidence to suggest that significantly more women with disabilities are likely to be divorced or separated as also depicted by many other researchers throughout the world (Chenoweth, 1997; Traustadottir, 1990). The data available on this issue on the national and international fronts are very limited due to difficulties encountered by the researchers related to the sensitivity of the topic and sociocultural issues.

Significantly, in our research (under review/unpublished work), we rarely came across married women with disabilities (MWDs) to be financially dependent upon their husbands; on the contrary, in most cases, they were the sole breadwinners of the entire family apart from following the traditional assigned role irrespective of their disabilities. Though there is scant data available nationally related to the front number of women with disabilities who are married and their life thereafter, it can be assumed based on reports and our (unpublished) research work, that most women with physical disabilities tend to get married very early; however, the consequences are interestingly complicated. Each of these women in our study narrates similar yet unique experiences of discrimination, oppression, stigma, and mental anguish, which clearly depict the status of *women with disabilities* in particular and *women* in general still prevailing in our society after so many years of advancement (Rosen, 2006; Young et al., 1997). The marriage of women with disabilities makes them even more vulnerable, susceptible, and prone to oppression and exploitation (Milberger et al., 2002; Powers et al., 2002).

The oppression and social exclusion faced by MWDs is critically complex and multidimensional. Universally, it has been established by various researchers that women with disabilities, irrespective of the nature of disability, are more prone to exploitation and violence (Milberger et al., 2002) than the women in general. Such incidences of violence, sexual, physical, and mental abuse of the women with disabilities is more rampant in society. Women with disabilities, due to their triple jeopardy, tend to remain unexpressive often due to their social conditioning since birth, and thus tend to remain silent even in midst of all odds. Due to dearth of data, research on MWDs remains scanty in the Indian and global context (Sullivan, 2006). The marital status of women with disabilities is one of their barriers faced though most of them agree upon considering marriage to be as significant and indispensable as other basic amenities in life, while the level of fear associated with it reasonably remains insurmountable.

In this particular study (see note 1), we found 35 percent of the women with physical disabilities to be married, out of which 23 percent had their own account to relate. Each of these women narrates their similar yet unique experience of discrimination, oppression, stigma, trauma, etc. The psychological abuse and exploitation in various forms in their married life is very rampant and can be put along a common line (Monahan and Lurie, 2003; Young et al., 1997). Due to the complexities and difficulties, research on MWDs remains scanty in the Indian context. However, the issues concerning sexual needs of women with disabilities have been prominent in few academic discourses, but due to the unavailability of data and sensitivity of the topic, facts regarding MWDs remain an oxymoron reality yet to be fragmented.

During the field interviews of the research on which this chapter is based, we spoke with Mithu, aged 32, with severe physical disability. She is afraid of getting married, unable to come out of the dilemma whether to get married to somebody like her or to a *perfect* man. Does she have the right to make choices for herself? She is independent and has a couple of vocational degrees to her credit, and teaches tailoring to the rural women apart from running a tailoring shop. She dreams of migrating someday to the urban cities to open up her own school and a tailoring shop with government aid.

However, the literature on disability studies have traditionally used a typical narrow approach in issues concerning marriage and related areas due to the orthodoxy attached to the topic itself, and, at the same time, due to the difficulty of exploring the magnitude of such facts and unavailability of data (Morris, 2005; Nosek, 2000; Sobsey and Doe, 1991). According to the National Health Interview Survey (National Center for Health Statistics, 2002), women with disabilities, compared to other women, are less likely to be married, more likely to be living alone, and less likely to be employed (Young et al., 1997).

Apporva (without a disability) married Lata although she had a severe physical disability. His purpose in marrying a woman with a disability surfaced three years later. He confronted Lata with her inability to get a job despite the reservation of 3 percent employment quota for persons with disabilities. His stand was that as he did not have a job and had no such entitlement, it was her responsibility to work. He made it clear that this was the reason why he had married her. His words were cruel: "I am not your care taker. I can't take care of you. Let the government take its responsibility."

Over the years, the transformation in terms of shifting sex roles in a marital relationship has taken on a new dimension as it remains not only limited to those without disabilities, but also extends to the marital life of the persons with disabilities, and it is quite interesting to note its different impact on both groups. We need to keep in perspective that although the rules, ramifications, and the very reasons for getting married have changed over time due to various societal changes, the significance of marriage in India still remains intact for the majority of its people. However, the new shift and trend that has emerged with respect to the reasons of persons with disabilities for getting married compels us to rethink about the policies and intervention measures that are framed for helping persons with disabilities and the way they are being used in our society, especially in the developing countries. This may seem like a contradiction as women with disabilities are typically seen as asexual (Ghai, 2001) and at a much greater risk of being sexually or physically abused and exploited than other women.

Himadri, a school teacher, married Mohua, with a severe physical disability, years ago. Mohua is a beautiful woman with minor burns in her upper limb and a little bit on the lower jaws and neck. She was hiding her neck and hands under her *pallo*/drape (saree). Mohua is not divorced but separated, and has to live with her father along with her four-year-old daughter after her husband refused to live with her. Himadri was initially happily married but eventually shunned social gatherings, neighbors, and started hiding Mohua from the people's gaze. They (people) used to say, "Didn't you get anyone else to get married but a witch?" (In Bengali as said: "*Kopal ta ki purechhilo na bhimroti hoichhile je omon ekta petni ke bie korli?*"). Finally, due to social pressure, he asked her to leave. This raises questions as to who is to be blamed for this situation: Himadri, the husband, or Mohua for not standing up for her rights, or the sociocultural environment which did not support her?

This episode takes us back to the way women were portrayed in Indian films in the 1960s where beauty was the center point. It was later that the movie *Satyam, Shivam, Sundaram* projected the socio-psychological trauma of the man who falls in love with a woman who he thinks is beautiful, but then finds out that she has a deep scar due to a burn on one side of her face which is kept hidden. His struggle is between the appreciation of her feminine identity based on societal norms of beauty and the confrontation with her disabled identity. The pertinent question today is: With regard to tremendous changes in scientific, economic, and technological global advancement, where do we stand? We believe that change is for all, but in reality it has kept women out.

In another interview, we spoke to Ramesh and his wife Meena. Meena, who met with an accident resulting in a disability, found her husband not being able to accept her new condition. He has asked her for a divorce, leaving her vulnerable and unable to cope with the situation at a time of high trauma. "I can't live with you anymore! You have become incapable below your waist. Your lower limb doesn't respond. Who is going to take care of my sexual needs? I can't feed you without any reasons. You are of no use. I want a divorce," said Ramesh to his wife at the hospital bed. The vulnerable status and oppression of women sometimes goes beyond any extremity and is unbelievable.

This and many such instances reflect a feeling of anxiety and fear among the young women and girls with disabilities. Despite the impediments, we found women with disabilities getting married, and most often to persons insensitive to disability. The dilemma itself reveals a complicated environment and consequences where women with disability exercise their choice to get married, but are faced with uncertainty and insecurity. The issue confronting us is that while choice is exercised, the aftermath leaves the women with disabilities facing extreme violence and exclusion in most cases.

People in society may respond differently, irrespective of whether they have a disability or not. From a psychological perspective, I think the theory of social conditioning may have an answer to this. Now why do we find few women behaving in a manner quite unexpected of them in a given situation? Such divergent responses can be understood on the basis of the behavioral psychology of *learned helplessness*. People may develop learned helplessness when they continue to lead a life not by choice, but by external control. Consequently, irrespective of their capabilities or incapability, once they start believing that whatever is happening in their lives cannot be controlled is not going to change, and that the cause is externally located, they just give up and start taking life as it comes (Weiner, 1986). Once a person develops learned helplessness, it effects their motivation, cognition, and also their affective domain, and they become incompetent, helpless, and reluctant to act and respond and, as a consequence, accept themselves, their lives, and the surrounding problematic environment The interesting part of it is that this phenomenon may equally operate in the lives of women both with disabilities and without disabilities. This emerges and develops because of sociocultural conditioning which women undergo right from birth in developing societies, such as India, though it is more or less universal throughout the globe.

In spite of the tremendous advancement in every sphere of women's lives and their extraordinary capabilities, there are still women who are not conscious of their own rights and are leading their life as dependents till mortality. Womanhood is not a composite whole as besides agency depicted by women, there are still some women who think they should not have a life of their own and that they are meant to take care of others' needs and expectations. Moreover, there are also some men who believe and reinforce such thinking and acts.

On the one hand, in general, the status of women has undergone a drastic change in society today. We see women come out of the age-old shackles of traditional homebound roles and making a mark in every sphere. They have successfully redefined their role, function, and identity in all walks of life. Be it business, corporate world, medicine, academics, researchers, politics, or administration, we witness women proving their skills and leadership capabilities in every sphere. There is no place which is not reachable by the women of today, with or without disability.

***

The most important determinant of a country's competitiveness is its human talent; the skills, education, and productivity of its workforce, and women account for one of the greatest potentials throughout the world. It has been repeatedly established that the nation's competitiveness depends significantly on whether and how it educates and utilizes its female talent to foster economic growth and enhance productivity, which can be attained by reducing gender inequality. The snapshot of the Gender Gap Index 2009 documenting India to hold one of the lowest positions in the world ranking (114 ranking in the world) is an issue of concern for the stakeholders. It is important that within those concerns women with disabilities are included. Investing in girls' education remains one of the highest return investments that a developing economy can make, and, in the current environment (economic recession), may be among the best use of limited funds, as pointed out by Amartya Sen (Sen, 1999) who said that more than anything else, what we need to focus on is to invest and take care of women through education and facilitate them to develop in every possible way (Herz and Sperling, 2004). The other areas of concern for a country can still wait, but if we delay the women issues, it may lead to exaggerating the already existing challenges of society and may add many new ones. Every year, a staggering figure of 200 million children under age of five suffer from stunted growth due to malnutrition of either the mother or the child, and those who survive have a higher risk of disease, disability, or high morbidity rate, which impairs their ability to work during adulthood (UNICEF, 2009). The infant mortality rate of India is 30.15 deaths/10,000 live births (CIA, 2009). Sick mothers give birth to sick children, and the relationship is an intergenerational and fearsome one, having long-lasting consequences not only on the individual but also on the society.

The discrimination persisting in the society is not just toward women, but rather, its boundaries have extended further toward women with disabilities. On the one hand, society has always been a witness to women's agency, and on the other hand, there are stories of oppression. The changes due to globalization and privatization have resulted in providing women with different platforms and roles in society far different from their traditionally assigned role. Today, women have proved their capabilities, talents, and skills in every spheres, be it the corporate world, academics, defense, modeling, or politics. Presently, women are empowered although the range is so diverse that to generalize the status of women in general and women with disabilities, particularly in India, would be a complicated one. There is every possible need to develop standards that would fit in the light of the new changes and circumstances. A paradigm shift from medical to human rights approach would need a constant effort to get rid of the deep-rooted social–cultural conditioning and understanding, which blinds the unique abilities of the women with disabilities in India.

Note

1. The two-year study on the women with physical disabilities in the eastern part of India—West Bengal—explored various barriers faced by the women with disabilities in the Indian context. The sample were 16 years and older who have completed their class 10, and they ranged from having mild to severe disabilities

as certified by the medical boards. The study identified many significant areas with respect to the cultural context of women in the developing world perspective and how these characteristics influence the basis survival of women with disabilities.

Bibliography

Central Intelligence Agency (CIA). 2009. *CIA World Factbook: India.* Available online at https://www.cia.gov/library/publications/the world-factbook/goes/in.html (downloaded on 05.01.2011).

Chenoweth, L. 1997. "Violence and Women with Disabilities: Silence and Paradox," in S. Cook and J. Bessant (eds), *Women's Encounters with Violence: Australian Experiences*, pp. 21–39. Thousand Oaks, CA: SAGE Publications.

Degener, T. 2006. "The Definition of Disability in German and Foreign Discrimination Law," *Disability Studies Quarterly*, 26 (2).

Gender Gap Index. 2009. "The Global Gender Gap Report 2009," in Hausmann, R., Tyson, L. D., Zahidi, S. (eds), *World Economic Forum*, Geneva, Switzerland, p. 4. Available online at http://www.weforum.org/reports/global-gender-gap-report-2009 (downloaded on 02.11.2009).

Ghai, A. 2001. "Mothering a child of disability," *The Journal Hyptia*, 2 (1): 20–22.

Hassouneh-Phillips, D. and M. A. Curry. 2002. "Abuse of Women with Disabilities: State of the Science," *Rehabilitation Counseling Bulletin*, 45 (2): 96–104.

Halder, S. Unpublished. "UGC Major Research Project, 2009-11."

———. 2008. "Rehabilitation of Women with Physical Disabilities in India: A Huge Gap," *Australian Journal of Rehabilitation Counseling*, 14 (1): 1–15.

———. 2009. "Prospects of Higher Education of the Challenged Women in India," *International Journal of Inclusive Education*, 13 (6): 633–646.

Herz, B. and G. B. Sperling. 2004. *What Works in Girls' Education*, pp. 1–20. United States: Council on Foreign Relations.

Ministry of Human Resource Development, Government of India. 2002. *Census 2002*. New Delhi: Government of India.

———. 2011. *Census 2011*. New Delhi: Government of India.

Ira, S. and M. D. Wile. 1940. "What Constitute Abnormality?" *American Journal of Orthopsychiatry*, 10 (2): 216–228.

Milberger, S., B. LeRoy, A. Martin, N. Israel, L. Potter, and P. Patchak-Schuster. 2002. "Michigan Study on Women with Physical Disabilities," Research Report, National Criminal Justice Reference Service. Available online at www.ncjrs.gov (downloaded on 22.10.2011).

Milberger, S. et al. 2003. "Violence Against Women with Physical Disabilities," *Violence and Victims*, 18: 581–590.

Monahan, K. and A. Lurie. 2003. "Disabled Women Sexually Abused in Childhood: Treatment Consideration," *Clinical Social Work Journal*, 31 (4): 407–418.

Morris, R. L. 2005. "Abuse of Women with Disabilities," *Dissertation Abstracts International*, 65: 3580-A.

Nagata, K. K. 2003. "Gender and Disability in the Arab Region: The Challenges in the New Millennium," *Asia Pacific Disability Rehabilitation Journal*, 14 (1): 10–17.

National Center for Health Statistics. 2002. "Healthy Women with Disabilities: Analysis of the 1994–1995 National Health Interview Survey: Series 10 Report." Atlanta: National Center for Health Statistics.

Nosek, M. A. 2000. "Overcoming the Odds: The Health of Women with Physical Disabilities in the United States," *Archives of Physical Medicine & Rehabilitation*, 81: 135–138.

Powers, L. E., M. A. Curry, M. Oschwald, S. Maley, M. Saxton, and K. Eckels. 2002. "Barriers and Strategies in Addressing Abuse: A Survey of Disabled Women's Experiences," *Journal of Rehabilitation*, 68 (1): 4–13.

Rosen, Daniel B. 2006. "Violence and Exploitation Against Women and Girls with Disability," *Annals of the New York Academy of Sciences*, 1087: 170–177.

Sen, A. 1999. *Development as Freedom*. Oxford: Oxford University Press.

Sobsey, D. and T. Doe. 1991. "Patterns of Sexual Abuse and Assault," *Sexuality and Disability*, 9 (3): 243–260.

Sullivan, P. M. 2006. "Children with Disabilities Exposed to Violence," in M. M. Feerick and G. B. Silverman (eds), *Children Exposed to Violence*, pp. 213–237. Thousand Oaks, CA: SAGE Publications.

Traustadottir, R. 1990. *Obstacles to Equality: The Double Discrimination of Women with Disabilities: Overview Article*. North Bay, ON: Disabled Women's Network Ontario.

United Nations International Children's Emergency Fund (UNICEF). 2009. "Urgent Efforts Needed to Tackle Under Nutrition," Press Release, UNICEF Report, November 11. Available online at http://www.unicef.org.u.k/Latest/News/Urgent-efforts-needed-to-tackle-undernutrition-says-UNICEF-report/ (downloaded on 05.01.2011).

Weiner, B. 1986. *An Attributional Theory of Motivation and Emotion*. New York: Springer-Verlag.

Young, M. E., M. A. Nosek, C. A. Howland, G. Chanpong, and D. H. Rintala. 1997. "Prevalence of Abuse of Women with Physical Disabilities," *Archives of Physical Medicine and Rehabilitation Special Issue*, 78 (12, Suppl. 5): S34–S38.

7

A Disabled Mother's Journey in Raising Her Child

Sandhya Limaye

Parenting is often perceived as a *normal* feature of independent adult life. When a woman without a disability decides to have a child, her friends, family, and doctor will often support her in her decision. But in case of a woman with a disability, it often is a different experience. Society, including professional organizations, and the family and friends of the parents with disabilities themselves, think that a woman with a disability cannot be a good mother. It is hard enough to deal with one's disability, but even harder to be a parent with disability and care for children while dealing with that disability. Even today, parents with disabilities are still sometimes met with discriminatory attitudes, inaccessible environments, and inappropriate support. The role of disabled parenting today, therefore, involves not only the usual challenges of raising children, but also the fight for adequate support services and preparing their children to face discriminatory attitudes.

Being a mother is hard enough; being a mother with disability can be an exceptionally difficult experience. The mothers with disabilities are largely invisible to researchers, mainstream parenting researchers, professionals, and organizations working for the disabled. In this chapter, mothers with disabilities share their parenting experiences of raising their children—the decision about having children, efforts in fulfilling their parental responsibilities, helping children in adjusting to having a *different* mother, and the kinds of barriers that mothers with disabilities faced while raising their children over time have been thoroughly discussed.

Parenting is often perceived as a *normal* feature of independent adult life. Parenting can be most rewarding as well as stressful, and is a nonstop 24-hour job in one's life. There are several books on pregnancy and tips for raising children for women without disabilities. It is believed that the to-be-mother has potential in developing parenting skills. She is also capable of performing roles and responsibilities in child rearing throughout the life cycle through learning, reading books, discussions with family, relatives, and friends, and their support and guidance, observation, and her own childhood experiences. Mothering involves the tasks of *protection, nurturance, and training*, and a readiness to respond to the needs of children with *care and respect*, qualities that are stereotyped as core attributes of hegemonic femininity (Ruddick, 1989). Similarly, Martha McMahon has argued that women undergo resocialization when they become mothers, in the process transforming themselves into women who are *loving, caring, and responsible* people, linking femininity and responsibility to female adulthood (McMahon, 1995: 130). But in the case of a woman with a disability, it often is a different experience.

Women are expected to aspire to norms of femininity that include ideal motherhood, where mothers are positioned as ever-available, ever-nurturing providers of active, involved, and expert mothering—indeed, being a caregiver is a main status for adult women in modernity. While this may be the case for all women, mothers with disabilities can have more a complicated relationship to ideal motherhood than others because they are perceived of either as asexual and inappropriate to the role of motherhood, or conversely because they are seen as sexually victimized and at risk. This also echoes the feminist perspective developed by Morris (1998) in identifying barriers to participation in parenting as particularly important for women with disabilities, given dominant social norms that see caring roles in general, and child-caring roles in particular, as an important element of adult, female identity. Restrictive environments control women with disabilities' access to public spaces, and hegemonic ideas about femininity, attractiveness, and dependence make women with disabilities vulnerable to social isolation or sexual and emotional exploitation (Malacrida, 2007). Women with disabilities are likely to marry less often, marry later in life, have fewer children, and divorce more frequently than women without disabilities (Asch and Fine, 1997; Asch et al., 2001). Just as women with disabilities have difficulties negotiating dependence and femininity, they face challenges in achieving idealized mothering.

While there are several books on raising children with disabilities, the literature is scant on experiences of women with disabilities who are raising children. Bringing together disability with mothering has the potential to challenge dominant narratives of both mothering and disability. How are women with disabilities discouraged from having children? How does the medical model of disability shape the meanings assigned to mothers with disabilities? Are mothers with disabilities healthy mothers? Are mothers with disabilities oppressed? How are pregnancy and birth experiences shaped by disability? How do children experience and understand a disabled mother? What support is needed and received by mothers with disabilities? How does the built environment, both public and private, shape the experiences of mothers with disabilities? What kinds of issues are there with children's schools, health professionals, and/or children's attitudes? Attention has not been yet paid adequately to such issues.

While parenting is a hard enough task by itself, it is even more difficult for mothers with disabilities to keep up with their children. Each individual faces different levels of difficulty and problems depending on the kind of disability they suffer from. It is hard enough to deal with one's disability, but even harder to be a parent with disability and care for children while dealing with that disability. All expectant parents want to be able to make choices about how they bring their child into the world and care for him/her, but it seems that in many cases there are still many barriers preventing disabled people from doing this. Even today, parents with disabilities are still sometimes met with discriminatory attitudes, inaccessible environments, and inappropriate support. The role of disabled parenting today, therefore, involves not only the usual challenges of raising children, but also the fight for adequate support services and preparing their children to face discriminatory attitudes.

It is worth noting that in spite of all the research on the lives of disabled parents, the number of disabled parents, for instance, in the United Kingdom, is entirely unknown at this point. In spite of the lack of specific, statistically based information, there is widespread agreement that there has been an increase in both the number of disabled parents and in their visibility as a subsection of the parenting population (Wates, 1997). The administrative *invisibility* of disabled parents has certainly contributed to the difficulty of planning and providing appropriate specialist information, and health and social services to disabled adults in their parenting role (Goodinge, 2000, cited in Olsen and Wates, 2003). In India, there are hardly any data sets on the number of disabled parents, especially mothers with disabilities, and there is a dearth of the research on the subject.

The Challenges

Women with disabilities can experience a fairly high level of prejudice. There is a common perception that a woman with a disability cannot be a good mother. I a woman with a disability and a child, and I am a proof of this insensitivity. Society feels that if a mother with disability cannot take care of herself without assistance or support, then she would not be able to help her child in growing up. It seems that she is depriving her own child of a healthy and normal childhood. As a result, doctors and counselors advise mothers to abort the child. The mother also faces pressure to test if the baby has any disability. Thus, the concern about the disabled women's parenting tends to be raised by other people, rather than the women themselves. Helping professionals and family members often discourage women with disabilities from becoming pregnant, expressing concerns that they will not be competent mothers and reflecting eugenic concerns that their disabilities will be passed on to their children (O'Toole and Doe, 2002). However, there is no evidence to support the view that having a disability will result in a reduced ability to parent. The fact is that society fails to meet the needs of women with disabilities as they have the right to life and rights to have a family.

For all new mothers, there come new challenges and responsibilities. Mothers with disabilities will be able to manage many of the new responsibilities themselves, even if it may take a bit longer than someone else. For those parenting tasks that are difficult, they will need extra support from partners, family members, and community service providers for either short or extended periods. If a mother with a disability has a partner without a disability, society tends to expect her husband to carry much of the additional workload to take care of the baby. In addition, society shows too much sympathy to male partners for carrying extra responsibilities and gives the impression that mothers with disability are still incompetent to take care of their children.

Mothers with disabilities face both physical and attitudinal barriers in addition to the daily challenge of raising children, for example, being unable to attend the baby health centre because it is not physically accessible to a woman in a wheelchair or with severe locomotor disability. Mothers with a hearing impairment may find it difficult to attend a parents' meeting. For women with cognitive disabilities, the stigmatization of their disabilities and social assumptions about their competency as parents leads to social isolation and surveillance (Olsen and Clarke, 2003). The assumption that disability is an individual characteristic (whether physical, sensory, cognitive, or related to mental health) that can be expected to have a negative impact on parenting is commonly believed.

Another important barrier faced by mothers with disabilities is discriminatory professional attitudes. A few years ago, the Maternity Alliance ran a conference for disabled parents, and they shared their experiences of assumptions that they could not be fit parents (Shackle, 1993, cited in Morris, 1998). Through the feedback received from parents with disabilities and health professionals, Olsen and Clarke (2003) in their study showed that these barriers include negative attitudes from some health professionals, a lack of knowledge and information available for parents and professionals, as well as poor communication between disabled parents and professionals. These factors, along with pressures of time and inaccessible environments, have led to inappropriate and inadequate care being given to physically disabled parents during pregnancy, childbirth, and early parenthood. Once women with disabilities become mothers, they face challenges in assuring the public of their appropriateness as parents and their capacity to mother adequately (Fitzmaurice, 2002; Grue and Lærum, 2002).

Grue and Lærum (2002) interviewed 30 women having multiple sclerosis, neuromuscular diseases, cerebral palsy, and spinal cord injury in the age group of 28–49 years. The women in this sample felt that they had to go to great lengths to *present* themselves and their children as managing *normally* in order to be accepted as *ordinary* mothers. Eventually, they feared that their children might be taken away from them if they did not live up to other people's expectations. One possible explanation for what they experienced as other people's skepticism might be that disabled people on the whole are primarily still looked upon as being dependent on other people's help and care. In short, they are often looked upon by professionals and lay people as receivers, and not as caregivers.

Wates (1997) explores parenting from the perspectives of 21 mothers with disabilities. She examines the tensions that exist for disabled parents, especially when balancing the recognition that there are additional barriers to against the desire to appear *normal* and to avoid stigmatizing intervention from welfare services. It seems that the mothers with disabilities are forced to accept the fixed or unwelcome intervention from the welfare department. She also discusses some of the key theoretical and empirical issues that ought to lie at the heart of parenting and disability research. Such attitudes the disabled parents are likely to face when it comes to having children. *To be disabled and a parent* counters the assumptions of emotional dependence and passivity, which are often made about disabled people.

Children depend on their mothers not only for compassion and care, but also for protection. Mothers with severe mobility impairments faced different challenges in caring for their children. Mothers with mild to moderate mobility impairments frequently spoke about how they managed to provide nurturance to their children despite their physical limitations. Nurturance includes not only qualities of warmth, tenderness, and compassion, but also providing comfort, feeding, soothing, cooking, cuddling, relationship building, tending to the sick, and providing small services, such as sewing on a broken button or tying a loose shoelace (Asch et al., 2001). Mothers are typically expected to provide their spouses and their children with such nurturance, yet this can be difficult for mothers with severe physical disabilities. Mothering comprises a wide range of activities, many of which occur outside the home. Mothers take children for walks, play with them in parks, take them to playgroups, schools, and lessons, volunteer in classrooms and clubs, and foster their children's public lives in myriad ways. These kinds of activities can be challenging or even impossible for mothers with physical impairments. Motherhood is an activity and a role that is highly policed for all women (Arnup, 1994). The women's experiences challenge the notion that good mothers must be physically active with their children, and instead focus on the personal relationships between mother and child as the important part of parenting (Kocher, 1994).

Overcoming Challenges

Many mothers with disabilities are able to adapt to and overcome the challenges of their disability to be successful, loving parents. Mary Hill (n.d.) writing from her perspective as a mother with a disability says, "Our message: We are parents first and foremost, and despite our disability, we have the same concerns as all mothers as we raise and nurture our children."

As we have observed attitudes toward disabled people who become parents, their access to facilities and resources, and the way in which services are planned and delivered, all have a more far-reaching impact upon parenting than impairment in and of itself (Oliver, 1992). To overcome these shortcomings, research shows that women adopt many methods.

Research carried out in many countries reflects a variety of experiences. The study undertaken by Malacrida (2009) examines the contradictions and tensions embedded in mothers with disabilities' performances of ideal motherhood, drawing on qualitative interviews with 43 Canadian mothers with cross-cutting disabilities. The article examined how women with disabilities reconcile the demands of ideal mothering against the realities of their disabilities. She asked how women deal with motherhood in ways that would undermine or challenge the perceptions of others. It also attended to the ways that normative orders relating to femininity and motherhood are embedded in mothers' social interactions with peers, helping professionals and structures, such as funding and care provision policies. Despite these barriers, however, women with disabilities go to creative and extraordinary lengths in order to be seen as complying with ideal motherhood, perhaps as a way to lay claim to a maternal and sexual identity that society frequently denies them. The experiences of mothers with disabilities as they negotiate the tensions of ideal motherhood permit us to see the challenges this construct poses for all women, and, thus, they call for a feminist politics that will challenge this ideal and work for change in the lived experiences of mothering.

In a study by Prilleltensky (2004), qualitative methodology has been used to analyze experiences of mothers with physical disabilities. Two focus groups were held for mothers with young children and mothers of older children. Eight mothers also participated in in-depth interviews. All had a physical impairment, and most were wheelchair users. The article focused on: (a) participants' attempts to ensure the physical and psychological well-being of their children, (b) their child-rearing philosophies and practices, and (c) the overall nature of the parent–child relationship. A range of parenting practices, experiences, and relationships were reported. The variability of experiences notwithstanding, participants' life stories demonstrate a strong commitment to children, actions to ensure their care and well-being, and attempts to shield them from any burden related to the maternal disability. Whilst challenges and barriers were candidly reported, by and large, they do not overshadow the joy and fulfillment that these women derive from motherhood.

Olsen and Clarke (2003) interviewed disabled parents and family members in 80 families and found the important role that professionals can play both in undermining and underpinning parenting roles. Olsen and Wates (2003) also found a mixed picture in terms of disabled parents' perceptions of professional support. Any one of a range of professionals, including family doctors, midwives, health visitors, occupational therapists, social workers, or teachers, may be picked out by one parent as having given excellent information, moral support, and useful referrals to other sources of help, while another parent will mention the same professional group as having been unhelpful. A number of parents indicated that their experience had varied from one encounter to another within the same professional group. Moreover, numerous disabled parents support organizations have been set up and are designed to assist various needs of such parents. Parents with disabilities share many experiences in common with other parents. They also need time out from parenting for themselves and to enjoy their own relationship. We believe that the best source of knowledge for parenting are parents themselves. The same holds true for parents with disabilities, and it is important to give parents an opportunity to share ideas and learn from each other.

There is already in existence a great deal of knowledge, information, and insight supplied by disabled parents themselves. However, alongside a general picture of support characterized by its patchiness, distinct patterns of response emerged in relation to different professional groups (Olsen and Wates, 2003). It is suggested that research, consistent with the social model of disability, directs attention to the social and economic contexts within which family life takes place. Mothers, as observed earlier, are invisible in our research and action. This invisibility is sustained and reinforced by the common assumption that parents are—or, at least, should be—nondisabled (Olsen and Clarke, 2003).

Approaches to Disability and Parenting

Mothers with disabilities are labeled as asexual, and society feels that they are not fit to be mothers. If women with disabilities decide to become mothers, then their children will be deprived of a normal and healthy childhood. Jenny Morris (1998), in her paper, discussed that society creates barriers for women with disabilities in participating in parenting roles as they are perceived as inappropriate roles. Her feminist disability theory explains how women with disabilities face social and attitudinal barriers that prevent them from their right to have a family.

The social model of disability enables us to identify the social barriers that influence disabled mothers' lives, and it is also important to understand the personal ways in which this is experienced. This model expects us to remove the barriers by encouraging mothers with disability in participating in familial roles, including parenting. Olsen and Clarke (2003) argue that the social model approach can highlight how disability not only has an impact on individuals who have impairments, but also on those with whom they have close relationships where disability is a central part of their life experiences.

The fact is that people who have a disability are capable and competent to raise their children, challenging the established assumptions that they are not fit as parents. Because of their disability and the way a family adapts, parents with disabilities can actually raise children who have a better insight into life and caring. Ecological approaches to parenting have their roots in broader theories of human, and especially child, development put forward by Bronfenbrenner (1979). With respect to parenting, the most influential work has been carried out by Jay Belsky and colleagues (Belsky et al., 1984; Vondra and Belsky, 1993). An ecological perspective views parenting as a set of activities influenced by three *domains*:

- The developmental needs of the child.
- The capacities and personal resources of parents in meeting those needs.
- The wider social and economic context in which parents operate.

This ecological perspective focuses on structural factors, environmental factors, as well as on the individual strengths of parents themselves. It, therefore, offers the opportunity for looking at the barriers and difficulties faced by parents, rather than automatically assuming that parenting deficits are the responsibility of parents themselves (Olsen and Clarke, 2003).

Belsky et al. (1984) argued that successful parenting depends not on any one factor but on the interaction of a range of factors, including the individual attributes of parents, the attributes of children, the nature of intra-family relationships, the sources of stress and support within and outside the family, as well as the broader socioeconomic context in which the family lives. The interaction of these factors is often placed within a life-course perspective which recognizes that parenting, and the stresses and supports influencing parenting, will change over time. Indeed, the authors go on to assert that while child attributes, social support, and personal capacity to parent are all important, it is the latter which is the most significant of all (ibid.).

The author has agreed to Belsky's argument about the factors that influence successful parenting as she has met many mothers with disabilities, who are open to learning parenting roles and exploring different practical strategies with the help of family members and friends while raising their children, and, thus, minimizing the impact of their impairment on their parenting roles.

Indian Context

In our situation, that is, in the Indian situation, the situation is not much different for mothers with disabilities. Mothers with disabilities, like Western mothers with disabilities, have the same issues: they face social stigma, become the victim of the concept of ideal motherhood, and are oppressed by their family members in various ways. There is a dearth of research on mothers with disabilities in India: it is important to ventilate the mothers to express their concerns while performing their role of mothers. It was decided to take an interview of some mothers with disabilities regarding their parenting experiences of raising their children—the responsibility of child rearing is not only a process that all mothers face, but it also has a second side to a coin where children have to adjust to a *different* mother. It does not imply that the experiences shared by mothers with disabilities are in any way representative of the entire population of mothers with disabilities. An attempt has been made to understand the mothers with disabilities' responses to various issues while fulfilling their mothering task.

Mothers with Disabilities

This chapter explores the issues and barriers faced by women with disabilities who already are mothers. Seven participants in the study are mothers with different disabilities living their lives and successfully raising their children who met the author from time to time, and much of the information comes straight from them. Three mothers are hearing impaired, two are visually impaired, and two are physically disabled. Some of the women have partners with disability, whereas others have partners without disability. The author uses the term *physically disabled* in the widest sense to include those with mobility problems and other physical impairments. In this chapter, the author uses the term *mothers (VI)* implying mothers with visual impairment, *mothers (HI)* meaning mothers with hearing impairment, and *mothers (PD)* meaning mothers who are physically disabled. The mothers' stories, regardless of the women's educational status, socioeconomic position, caste, or geographical location, inevitably spoke of how the structure of social life made the tasks of providing nurturance that much more difficult. It is also important to note that most of the women in this study were very creative and resourceful in negotiating ways to overcome barriers.

Decision about Having Children

When the mothers talked about their decision of having children first time, all six mothers, except one mother (VI), reported that their pregnancy was unplanned, but they decided to have another child based on the condition of their first child. A mother (HI) informed that once she came to know about her first pregnancy, her relatives' response was that she would bear a deaf child. They usually asked: "If your to-be child is deaf, then?" She was so upset with her relatives' strong, negative attitudeswhile her parents and family doctor tried to comfort her, she realized that her parents were tense about having a deaf child. Even her gynecologist wanted to check her to-be-child's hearing during pregnancy, but her parents strongly opposed the idea. They did not want to abort the child if the child was found to be deaf. She felt relieved when she found that her daughter is sound-sensitive.

Other mothers, (VI) and (PD), had different experiences. Their relatives, including their mothers, had doubt about their capabilities of being mothers. The mother of a (PD) mother said: "Poor your to-be-child! She/he will be deprived of having normal childhood." The voices of those who discriminate are usually one. The negative attitudes shattered their confidence, and they carried the tension throughout the pregnancy. Their friends who have similar disability gave strong support and became role models for these mothers as they had children without disability. It also shows that it is important for mothers with disabilities to produce perfect, healthy children as a part of ideal motherhood.

The mother (PD) was expected to walk, as an exercise during the pregnancy. Once the last trimester began, she found that she had increased mobility problems, but she was told by the doctor and the family that it is important to walk to be fit which created further tension. She strongly felt that nobody tried to understand her difficulty in mobility and was concerned about the adverse impact on her unborn child. After having experienced one safe pregnancy brought about by her own recognition of the body's needs, she felt more secure in her role as a parent and was not as concerned with conforming to society's standards.

In the same manner, they mean other mothers with hearing disability except one mother with a hearing disability. During the second pregnancy, the parents found that they were more comfortable compared to the first pregnancy, and they took better care of themselves. They also found a change in people's attitudes toward the pregnancy. Mother (VI) commented, "I did not like some people's comment as they admired my job as a mother." It seems that society looks at mothers with disabilities as *carereceivers*, rather than *caregivers*.

For one mother (HI), she was counseled by her gynecologist to undergo a tubectomy. Her mother-in-law had the fear of having the second child as deaf. She could not oppose their pressure. She informed that she had no problem if the second child was deaf, as there is nothing wrong in being deaf. She strongly felt that deaf people can understand each other and they are not disabled, they are only different in communication, that is, they use sign language. She was upset that her deaf husband did not play an active role in the decision-making process. She described him as a *mama's boy*. The management of impairment, the experience of disability, and the difficulties raised by the family members lead to frustration in her relationship with the family members.

In case of a mother (VI), she had planned for a pregnancy and discussed with the doctor to clarify whether she could have a child who had sight, but nobody could give her the assurance. She faced tremendous pressure throughout the pregnancy and spoke of her disappointment if she found her child to be blind. The daughter born was not blind. When she decided to take another chance, she had a lot of tension like her first pregnancy. She is the second sibling out of five, and she and her younger brother are blind. She stated that there is no genetic problem, but both the siblings have visual impairment. That made her fear that her second child might be blind like her. Fortunately for her, her son is sighted and she became more relaxed.

In case of other HI mothers, they were ready to accept their children if they are deaf. They felt that bringing their child with their own disability is a good thing because the family can share the culture that goes with that particular disability. However, genetic counselors, professionals, and the society at large may express that it is not acceptable to reproduce a child with that disability because they are unaware of the positive psychological and social aspects of a disability culture (Rogers, 1996). It was found that many women with disabilities were upset with the insensitive attitude, and they were anxious during their pregnancy as they did not know how to ventilate their tension. Rogers (1996) also found in her study that responding to the insensitivity of these professionals, the pregnant women with disabilities may become angry or anxious or both depending on their temperament.

It is important to remember that pregnancy issues are not only physical in nature; they include psychological concerns as well. Expectant mothers, especially physically disabled, received such advice as to not have a child due to the physical demands of (and risks to) pregnancy and childbirth (Olsen and Clarke, 2003) which created conflict in their mind: on the one hand, they felt guilty, and on the other, they felt frustrated due to social, attitudinal barriers. Increased level of distress was experienced. Olsen and Clarke (2003), as cited earler, had found in their study that decisions to add to the family were made despite any concerns about impairments and health problems.

Normalizing Birth

Once their pregnancy term was completed, all seven mothers were tense about delivery as they were confused about their actual role during delivery. They felt that doctors and relatives did not understand the importance of preparation for their delivery as they needed specific instructions due to their nature of disability. They wanted normal delivery if possible as they wanted to experience labor pain. They were afraid and wanted the doctor's advice, but they were told, "*Sab thik ho jayega, do not worry*" (Everything will be OK, do not worry). They strongly felt that doctors and nurses should understand their specific needs due to their disability so that they can prepare themselves in adjusting their delivery. As a mother (HI) commented:

> I had feared that I may not understand doctor/nurse's instruction at the time of delivery. Throughout the delivery, I had to tolerate the pain and at the same time I had to pay attention to the nurses to understand their instruction. It was a tough job for me.

Another mother (PD) had a different experience. Her nurses expected her to move her position at the time of delivery, but they failed to understand her difficulty to move quickly whenever required. She was tense during the labor pain as she was afraid that her difficulty to adjust her position would create a problem for the newborn child. She informed that her psychological tension created difficult and prolonged labor.

Mother (VI) had a different experience. She informed that nurses could understand her difficulty and her mother was with her in the labor room to support her. She felt that the doctor should have given her idea about the time that was required for delivery as she was not informed about the delivery process.

All of them had normal delivery, and they realized that they are like other women! It also gave emotional satisfaction to them due to their positive personal experience. It also became clear from their experiences that they have specific needs and problems due to their nature of impairment. Mothers noted that many professionals knew little about the specific needs arising from their disability. Lack of knowledge of how, for example, particular birth positions might impact on mothers with physical disabilities was also highlighted. They also faced a challenge in getting appropriate information and support to enable them to prepare for childbirth. Hidden disabilities such as hearing impairment were often overlooked, with assumptions being made that people had no access needs (DPPI, 2009).

After birth, mothers (HI) immediately made a sound by clapping and shouting to test their child's hearing condition. Once the children responded to the sound, they were happy and felt relaxed. The mother (VI) called an ophthalmologist to check her child's eye condition, whereas another mother (VI) decided to trust God. When her friend informed her that her child has normal eyesight, she felt that God had been kind to give her a wonderful gift. Mother (PD) checked her child's physical condition and asked the doctor to conduct a complete physical checkup of her child. All mothers were very anxious about possibilities of impairment in their children and they themselves checked again and again to confirm the *normalcy* in their children. The fact is that if woman cannot accept her own disability, she cannot accept the disability in her child. It may be because women with disabilities may have experienced society's negative and discriminatory attitude toward them and treated them as a burden, and those attitudes make it difficult for women with disabilities to accept their own disability in a natural way. Besides, if women with disabilities could not accept the disability in their children, society would not accept their children's disability. In Mumbai, the author found that many deaf young generations prefer to welcome their children's deafness as a part of the deaf culture, thereby challenging society to treat them as an unproductive member of the society.

Experiences as a Parent

The impact of their impairment began after having become a parent. Some mothers were less likely to see their impairment as central to their experiences as parenting.

After birth of their children, mothers (HI) had problem in hearing their children's cry at night. The family members and nurses helped them by waking them up. They felt so guilty about their inability to hear their children cry, they could not get adequate sleep, and this affected their health. Once a few months passed, they learnt to adjust with their children's demand for food and other needs. One mother (HI) informed that she has installed a bell with a bulb on her bed, and her mother-in-law in the next room rings the bell so that she can feel the vibration of sound and see the light. That strategy helped her to take care of her child. In case of other mother (HI), she used to keep her child between her and her husband so that the child's movement in the night would wake her up.

For mothers (VI) and (PD), they had family support in taking care of their children, whereas one mother (VI) who stayed with her VI husband only had to struggle to take care of her children. She took tips about childcaring from her friends who are visually impaired. She said, "[B]ecause of my blindness, I put a necklace with bell in my children's feet so that I can hear the sound and I could understand where my children are." The mother (PD) felt that her family helped her a lot but in certain situations, her family's lack of trust on her ability to handle her children made her upset and it shattered her confidence. Sometimes, they would not allow her to change the diapers, to lift the child into her arms. It shows that she is oppressed by her family members by their underestimating her nurturing skills.

When children are growing up, they are curious to know how their parents are different than others. Mother (VI) said that she touched her children's mouth while feeding them food and after a few days, she found that her children moved toward the food without her touch. She also took them out to the park or market with other family members. As the children usually go out with her in-laws, she does not get to know their problems. She said that her children never asked her about her blindness, and she had no idea how her children sensed that she is different. She felt that she is lucky to have mature children.

In case of the other mother (VI), it was not an easy job for her. She had to explain to her children that she cannot see, and so they should behave properly. She said, "Children are children. Sometimes they do not follow my instructions. Sometimes they go very far without informing me and I panic when I do not see them. Now as they are growing up, they are beginning to understand my limitation."

Another mother (PD) said, "Getting outside was difficult, so I couldn't play with the children in the garden as much as I'd have liked. I felt a lot of frustration and had a feeling of incompetence at that moment." A mother with a hearing impairment said:

> I could not hear my four year old daughter's crying and she came in front of me and asked me to pay attention to her as she was crying. Once she made sure that I am paying attention to her, she suddenly started crying loudly!

All of them had no idea how their children noticed their differences, but they felt that the children had learnt to adjust to these differences. Mothers with hearing impairment reported that their children communicate with them through sign language and their children had become a liaison between them and the hearing world.

In case of school admission, they have to take help from their family members and friends in securing admission for their children. A mother with a physical disability communicated that she had experienced people's disconnect when she went for the admission process. There was a long queue but nobody offered her a seat even though she uses a caliper which is very painful. A mother with a hearing impairment said she was not even consulted by her family. Her parents and in-laws did not ask her about her child's admission into a school, especially in relation to the medium of instruction for her children. Another mother reported a similar decision by in-laws who informed her that she was not capable to take any decision related to her child. She was faced with many arguments with her in-laws over her child's education. As a result, after so many years, she and her mother-in-law took a mutual decision about her child's education. It seems that her mother-in-law has learnt to recognize her right as a mother or may have learnt to handle her tactfully. This barrier prevented mothers with disabilities from doing whatever they wanted.

All of them except mother (PD) reported that they had difficulty in attending parents' meetings and school functions. The mother (HI) informed that she did not understand a single word in the parents' meeting, and, later on, the teacher in the school explained to her about the meeting by writing to her. Once her child grew up, the teachers gave instructions to her child who then communicated to her through sign language. She felt guilty that she could not help her children in their homework and many parents in the school advised her to take assistance through a tuition class. The mothers (VI) helped their children in their homework, except mathematics, but when they were asked by the school teacher to help their child to improve his/her handwriting, they strongly felt that the school teacher was being insensitive toward their difficulty. Another mother (HI) was asked by the teacher to get somebody's help in improving the pronunciation of her child's speech. She came to know from the teacher that her child talks with his classmates without voice very often. It is natural that the sign language becomes first language for such children, and they learn to communicate without voice. The children often forget that the hearing world find it difficult to understand speech without voice. The matter was explained to the teacher, and the teacher helped her child by paying attention in improving speech and in understanding subject matter by spending extra time.

Many mothers informed that their family members and their children's friends helped their children in selecting a vocation and a job, and they found that they did not have active roles in this process. They felt excluded from their children's lives, but felt that it was important to see their children to grow up with the skills needed for independence.

As time passed, all mothers became more comfortable with their parenting roles, and they felt that they can be competent enough to be efficient parents. Their impairment helped them to find different strategies to perform their role as a parent; it is society which they felt has problems regarding their parenting role.

Handling Children's Questions about Impairment

Children are curious to know about their parent's impairment as they are confused and want to know more their impairments. They also try to assist by finding solutions to these on their own. Adequate knowledge about the impairment can be a strategy to be adopted so that children can get help in coping with the situation.

A mother with a visual impairment said:

> My children asked me why I was not able to see. They did not understand the meaning of blindness. They asked me to open my eyes so that I would be able to see! They also tested my vision by showing their fingers and hands and asked me how many fingers they had.

Another mother with the same disability said, "My children asked me to cut a lot of onions so that water would clean my eyes and I would be able to see!"

Mothers (HI) informed that their children showed them how to open their mouth to talk! Even their children often asked the meaning of inability to hear but were confused. One mother (HI) reported that her children did not understand the relation between hearing loss and speech.

It was found that some mothers had difficulties explaining their impairment to their children. Some mothers tried to explain, but they were confused about how much information on their impairment should be given to their children. They took their own family's help for further explanation. One mother (VI) informed that her children never asked her about her visual impairment; perhaps, her sighted husband must have explained to their children. She did not feel the need to find out the reason as she felt that it is not important to discuss her blindness. One mother (PD) informed that the issue of disability came up in general conversation with her children but she felt that there was no real need to discuss her disability in detail.

One mother (HI) informed that her children asked her whether it is a genetic disorder and whether they have chances of suffering from hearing loss. She did not know how to answer and it upset her, and she was afraid of passing on her impairment to her children. She wanted to tell them that it is her fault but could not get the courage to say it.

Helping the Children in Adjusting with Their Mothers' Differences

Mother (HI) informed that she did not understand the price of goods that she bought and her children helped her through sign language. One shopkeeper, when confronted with this scene where her child was trying to explain to her, asked her whether her son was mute or had a disorder. This comment disturbed her, and she asked her son to communicate verbally so that people would know about his normalcy. Another mother (HI) was asked by her son not to use sign language in public places as it would confer the disability on him. They asked their son also to ignore public comments, as it was not their fault that she was deaf. The stigma against disability becomes a burden which even the children have to bear. A daughter who got angry at the public response about her mother's deafness and argued with the people explained that it was lucky that her mother could not hear the comments passed by the public about her. The burden of the mother falls on the child when there is lack of awareness of disability in the public domain. The mothers are sensitive about the invisible burden on their children due to their disability, and they reported that it is difficult to deal with their own emotion of being responsible for their children's suffering.

Children start to hide their mother's disability from public and even friends, and, consequently, some do not invite them home. This was not confined only to mothers with deafness, but those with a visual disability as well. They said that their children were upset with public comments and cried on hearing them. This mother found it difficult to handle their emotion, especially when it resulted in fights with neighbors. The neighbors criticized them by targeting them as children of *such* mothers, leaving bitterness in relationships. Her moot point was, "How many times can we ignore? We understand that we have limitations but we also have self-esteem." Some children coped with the help of friends and a mother (VI) said, "The kind of friend my son had really helped him to overcome this barrier."

Another mother with a physical disability also expressed a similar opinion. She was upset about the language people used to describe her condition. She learnt to ignore them, but had problems when faced with her children's pain consequent to the language used about her. She felt guilty about their lost childhood as they grew up early and faced the world like grown-ups. Some children withdrew from social contacts, while others had to fight regular battles with people.

Many mothers, on the other hand, overcame barriers and found that children helped them in various adverse situations, while their family members could be a great source of help in helping their children in coping with their mothers' impairment.

It seems that mothers with disability will accept their own disability and will adjust to live with stigma, but they cannot tolerate their children's suffering due to society's discriminatory attitudes. It is a tough task for mothers, but they learn to find their own way in dealing with such situations. In addition, the temperament of the children and availability of supports help their children to cope with the society's negative attitudes.

Parenting over Time

The mothers with disability discussed about their tensions and difficulties while parenting their younger children as they were parents for the first time, and were very conscious about their parenting roles. Despite the support of family, relatives, and friends, they felt it was an intricate problem but despite this, they enjoyed their parenting roles.

All mothers agreed that when their children were small, it was easy to convince them to ignore the public comments, but when they grew up, they became more self-conscious about their parents' impairment. This could be overtly linked to bullying experienced by children as they started secondary school and were meeting new children (Olsen and Clarke, 2003). Thus, it became a difficult job for mothers to help them cope with the difficult situation. Some mothers informed that their children discussed these issues with them and their family, whereas some mothers reported that their children preferred not to discuss this issue at home, and they had no idea how their children handled this tough situation. It is important to our understanding of disability to explore these children's personal experiences of their parents' impairment and their way of handling the situation.

Some mothers reported that once their children were out of their teens, they learnt to overlook these problems and accepted their mothers' disability as a part of their life without feeling guilty. It is not a very easy job for such mothers to perform the role of a mother, and, therefore, they get a great source of support from their own parents as well as their children. They strongly feel that their impairment did not affect their parenting roles, but it limited their roles in certain situations. In summing up, the experiences shared by mothers with disabilities show that society perceives women's disabilities as a barrier to ideal mothering as mothers with disabilities can face bodily challenges in performing ideal mothering roles—picking up a crying child, bathing her, or running after her in a public space, nurturing her child, and providing a safe and healthy childhood. They face many barriers, such as the negative attitude of society toward mothers with disabilities, lack of knowledge and information available on parenting, and family members' underestimation of mothers with disabilities' capabilities as mothers. Mothers with disabilities are well aware of public stigma and prefer to challenge the established concept of an ideal mother. The social model of disability has given them the language to describe their experiences of discrimination and prejudice. However, mothers with disabilities often found ways to work around these issues with the help of available sources of support, especially their own children, family members, and friends. Performing the role of a mother has meant, for mothers with disabilities, drawing on their own experiences of disability to provide the most positive learning environment. For most of the mothers with disabilities in this chapter, their perceptions of others, and their concerns about others' perceptions, resulted in a clear sense that although they saw themselves as good mothers, they realized that they did their performances of motherhood at their own best. Thus, the social model of disability is committed to the identification and removal of barriers constraining full participation in parenting roles.

This chapter, taken from the perspectives of mothers with their different impairments and varied life experiences, shows the different ways in which mothers with disabilities manage both their parenting roles and the disability they encounter. There are various factors that influence the parenting experiences, such as availability of supports, type of disability, and access to supports, nature of family environment and relationships, and the active role of children in shaping the parental experiences. It is also important to note that most of the women in this chapter were very creative and resourceful in negotiating ways to overcome barriers. Thus, disability is one of many factors that structure the experience of parenting for mothers with disabilities.

Unfortunately, many nongovernmental organizations working in the field of disability in India, especially for women with disabilities, overlook the importance of services and supports for mothers with disability. The fact is that most women with disabilities, especially in rural areas, lack proper support and medical assistance. They are considered a burden and often discouraged to marry or become mothers. There has been some change with the introduction of a scheme under the National Policy for Disabled where the Social Justice Ministry has proposed to pay a grant of ₹2,000 per month for a period of two years to each mother with a disability in rural areas to take care of her children. This is a step forward to help mothers with disabilities in rural areas, but clearly there is still a lot of work to be done in getting disabled parents onto mainstream parenting support agendas in relation to both research and practice.

Bibliography

Arnup, K. 1994. *Education for Motherhood: Advice for Mothers in Twentieth-Century Canada.* Toronto: University of Toronto Press.

Asch, A. and M. Fine. 1997. "Nurturance, Sexuality, and Women with Disabilities: The Example of Women and Literature," in L. Davis (ed.), *The Disability Studies Reader.* London: Routledge.

Asch, A., H. Rousso, and T. Jefferies. 2001. "Beyond Pedestals: The Lives of Girls and Women with Disabilities," in H. Rousso and M. Wehmeyer (eds), *Double Jeopardy: Addressing Gender Equity in Special Education*, pp. 13–48. New York: State University of New York Press.

Belsky, J., E. Robins, and W. Gamble. 1984. "The Determinants of Parental Competence: Towards a Contextual Theory," in M. Lewis (ed.), *Beyond the Dyad.* New York: Plenum Press.

Bronfenbrenner, U. 1979. *The Ecology of Human Development: Experiments by Nature and Design.* Harvard: Harvard University Press.

Disability, Pregnancy, and Parenthood International (DPPI). 2009. *Maternity Information Gap for Physically Disabled Parents.* London: DPPI, National Centre for Disabled Parents, www.dppi.org.uk

Fitzmaurice, S. 2002. "A Mother's Narrative: Reflections on Life with Disability," *Sexuality and Disability*, 20 (2): 117–123.

Grue, L. and K. Lærum. 2002. "Doing Motherhood: Some Experiences of Mothers with Physical Disabilities," *Disability & Society*, 17 (6): 671–683.

Hill, M. n.d. "Mothers with Disabilities," *BabyZone.com.* Available online at http://www.babyzone.com/features/content/display.asp?contentid=1537 (downloaded on 16.03.2005).

Kocher, M. 1994. "Mothers with Disabilities," *Sexuality and Disability*, 12 (2): 127–133.

Malacrida, C. 2007. "Negotiating the Dependency/Nurturance Tightrope: Dilemmas of Motherhood and Disability," *Canadian Review of Sociology and Anthropology*, 44 (4): 469–493.

154   SANDHYA LIMAYE

Malacrida, C. 2009. "Performing Motherhood in a Disablist World: Dilemmas of Motherhood, Femininity and Disability," *International Journal of Qualitative Studies in Education, Disability Arts, Culture and Politics: New Epistemologies for Qualitative Research* (special issue), 22 (1): 99–117.

McMahon, M. 1995. *Engendering Motherhood: Identity and Self-transformation in Women's Lives.* New York: The Guilford Press.

Morris, J. 1998. "Feminism, Gender and Disability," paper presented at a seminar in Sydney, Australia. Available online at http://www.leeds.ac.uk/disability-studies/archiveuk/morris/gender and disability.pdf (downloaded on 30.01.2012).

Oliver, M. 1992. "Changing the Social Relations of Research Production?" *Disability, Handicap and Society*, 7 (2): 101–114.

Olsen, R. and H. Clarke. 2003. *Parenting and Disability: Disabled Parents: Experiences of Raising Children.* Bristol, UK: The Policy Press.

Olsen, R. and M. Wates. 2003. *Disabled Parents—Examining Research Assumptions.* UK: Research in Practice. Available online at www.rip.org.uk (downloaded on 28.12.2014).

O'Toole, C. and T. Doe. 2002. "Sexuality and Disabled Parents with Disabled Children," *Sexuality and Disability*, 20 (1): 89–102.

Prilleltensky, O. 2004. "My Child Is Not My Carer: Mothers with Physical Disabilities and the Well-Being of Children," *Disability & Society*, 19 (3): 209–223.

Rogers, J. 1996. "Pregnancy and Physical Disabilities," in Krotoski, D.M., Nosek M.A., and Turk M.A. (eds), *Women with Physical Disabilities: Achieving and Maintaining Health and Well Being.* Baltimore: Paul H. Brooks Publishing Co.

Ruddick, S. 1989. *Maternal Thinking.* Boston: Beacon Press.

Vondra, J. and J. Belsky. 1993. "Developmental Origins of Parenting: Personality and Relationship Factors," in T. Luster and L. Okagaki (eds), *Parenting: An Ecological Perspective.* New Jersey: Lawrence Erlbaum Associates.

Wates, M. 1997. *Disabled Parent: Dispelling the Myths.* London: National Childbirth Trust and Radcliffe Medical Press.

8

Developmental Disability and the Family: Autism Spectrum Disorder in Urban India

Shubhangi Vaidya

Introduction

The experience of disability, be it physical, sensory, or intellectual, is not merely an individual one; its resonance is found across all the relationships and social institutions within which the individual is embedded. The family is the core social institution within which disability is managed, more so in non-Western contexts where institutionalization and incarceration of the disabled has not been a part of the society's precolonial history, as in the West. Much of the Western literature on the family and disability has focused on the parental responses to a child's disability in consonance with the medical model of disability. This perspective viewed the impact on the family as pathological, stressful, and inimical to the interests and well-being of other family members, especially siblings without disabilities. The practice of sending children with developmental disability to institutions or *homes* is part and parcel of the *disciplinary* charter of Western capitalist society so powerfully analyzed by Michel Foucault. The disavowal of the medical model in favor of the *social model*, the emerging of disability studies as a discipline, and the Disability Rights Movement in the 1970s in the United Kingdom and the United States signaled a change in the manner in which the family–disability relationship was viewed. Rather than exclusively emphasizing on emotions, marital role disruption, social withdrawal, and stigma, issues such as class, poverty, access to services and opportunities, participation in community life, etc. also were taken up for study. Family research changed its focus from family pathology to family adaptation, life course development and activity settings (see Ferguson, 2001 for a comprehensive mapping of research on disability and the family).

The introduction of disability rights legislation, inclusive social policy, educational and other provisions and the shift from institutional segregation to inclusion and participation in community life have considerably improved the life conditions and opportunities for persons with disability in the West. However, in countries like India where chronic poverty, malnutrition, lack of access to basic healthcare and education, and glaring social inequalities remain the major areas of concern for policy planners, disability is viewed as a marginal category despite the promulgation of progressive legislation such as the Persons with Disabilities Act, 1995, The National Trust Act, 1999, and ratification of the United Nations Convention on the Rights of Persons with Disabilities (UNCRPD) on disability rights. In India, the family and kin group continue to be the sole providers of care and lifelong sustenance, often, against the most daunting odds.

The arrival of a child with developmental disabilities in the family profoundly affects interfamilial relationships as well as interactions with the wider circle of kin, community, and society. Raising the child presents enormous challenges economically, socially, and emotionally. In case the child is a girl, the situation worsens (Ghai, 2002). The onus to obtain appropriate services and facilities falls entirely on the family; in many instances, children are either abandoned or subjected to fatal neglect. Families have to draw on whatever resources they can muster to manage the child and his/her difficulties.

The dominant cultural perspectives toward disability in India regard it as the consequence of *karma* (ibid.), which is to be accepted and borne stoically. In rural settings, disabilities or deficiencies of the mind are not pathologized if the individual is not impaired physically and can contribute to domestic and farm work. However, this becomes problematic in urban settings and middle-class families where intellectual attributes and academic performance become the currency by which individuals are valued (Mehrotra and Vaidya, 2008).In the wake of urbanization, expansion in educational opportunities, social mobility, and the spread of Western biomedicine, awareness of disabilities which were earlier neither *named* nor pathologized are increasing. The growing recognition and salience of conditions, such as learning disabilities, dyslexia, autism spectrum disorder, etc., are noteworthy and merit sociological attention.

This chapter focuses on the experiences of families of children diagnosed with Autism Spectrum Disorder (referred to as *autism* in this chapter). Specifically, it draws upon the findings of the author's doctoral research with families of children with autism in Delhi. Autism is a lifelong developmental disability that profoundly impacts the social, communicative, and imaginative capacities of an individual. *The Diagnostic and Statistical Manual of Mental Disorders* (DSM) of the American Psychiatric Association defines autism as follows:

> Pervasive Developmental Disorder (also called Autism Spectrum Disorders) are characterized by severe and pervasive impairment in several areas of development, reciprocal social interaction skills, communication skills, or the presence of stereotyped behavior, interests and activities. These disorders are evident in the first years of life and are often associated with some degree of Mental Retardation. (American Psychiatric Association, 2000: 70)

The latest edition of the DSM, which became operational in 2013, highlights social and communication difficulties, and repetitive and restrictive behaviors which impede the individual's functioning as the core diagnostic markers of autism.

In India, as in several other developing countries, knowledge about and awareness of the disorder is limited, even though it has increased in recent years, and persons presenting with its symptoms are often misdiagnosed as mentally retarded or mentally ill. Although no large-scale, community-based epidemiological studies have as yet been conducted to assess the incidence of the disorder, extrapolation from prevalence rates worldwide indicates that the figure could range from a conservative 2 million (Daley, 2004) to a staggering 10 million, according to the National Trust for the Welfare of Persons with Autism, Cerebral Palsy, Mental Retardation and Multiple Disabilities.[1]

Autism emerged as a distinct diagnostic label with the publication of the Austrian psychiatrist Leo Kanner's paper "Autistic Disturbances of Affective Contact", published in 1943. Based upon clinical reports of 11 children treated by him, the paper drew attention to a fundamental disorder present in them all, namely, their "*inability to relate themselves* in the ordinary way to people and situations from the beginning of life" (ibid.: 242, emphasis original). Just a year later, another Austrian, Hans Asperger, independently published a dissertation on *autistic psychopathy* in childhood (Asperger, [1944] 1991).

However, Asperger's patients, unlike Kanner's, were highly verbal and displayed advanced cognitive abilities. Yet they were socially impaired, awkward, and often the subjects of merciless bullying and teasing by their peers. The diagnostic label *Asperger's Syndrome* has become associated with this form of autism.[2]

In the 1950s and 1960s, autism was often referred to as *childhood schizophrenia* and considered to be an emotional or psychiatric disturbance. It was also speculated that it was the consequence of cold, disengaged parenting practices (the infamous *refrigerator mother theory*), a peculiarly *Western* affliction associated with the affluent, upwardly mobile sections of society, and the preponderance of the nuclear family (Sanua, 1984).

However, research over the past half century indicates that autism is a neurodevelopmental disorder found across cultures and socioeconomic strata. Interestingly, there is also a remarkable consistency of its symptoms cross-culturally; autism *looks* similar everywhere. Wing (1988) identifies a *triad of impairments* in the realms of socialization, communication, and imagination that appear to characterize much of the behavior that is found in persons with autism. However, the manner in which it is categorized and conceptualized varies across cultures, much like other intellectual disabilities which may be labeled and medicalized in Western contexts, but accommodated and contained within the ambit of kin and community in non-Western settings (see Nuttal, 1998; Whyte, 1998). The latest edition of the DSM (DSM-V) referred to earlier subsumes the various subtypes of autism under one umbrella category, *Autism Spectrum Disorder*.[3]

Anthropological accounts describe folk concepts of conditions similar to autism: the *nit-ku-bon* or *marvelous children* of Senegal (Ellenberger, 1968, cited by Daley, 2002: 534) and *Samqng Ulan* of rural Laos (Westermeyer, 1979, cited by Daley, 2004). Accounts of so-called *feral children* who supposedly lived with wild animals in the jungle also appear to be referring to children who fit the behavioral criteria for autism and the exotic stories surrounding them have been proved false (see Grinker, 2007). Daley (2002) cites a slew of cross-cultural studies (mostly unpublished dissertations) that indicate the prevalence of autism in settings as diverse as South Korea and Israel.

In the Indian context, Tamara Daley's (2004) study based on interviews with 95 families in four cities—Bangalore, Chennai, Calcutta, and New Delhi—provides rich data on symptom recognition, help seeking, and diagnosis of autism in urban India. R. Richard Grinker's (2007) mapping of the world of autism across cultures has a section on India and highlights the impact of globalization, Western biomedicine, and the information revolution in making autism a *recognizable* diagnostic category across the world.

Autism and the Family in Urban India

The doctoral dissertation which this chapter draws upon (Vaidya, 2008) is an ethnographic study of 20 families in Delhi having a child diagnosed with autism. The fieldwork was carried out during the period 2005–2007.

It attempts to chronicle the lived experiences of families negotiating with this complex, much misunderstood disorder and their attempts to *make sense* of the situation, and the unique subjectivity of their child. The study does not pathologize the individual and the family, but rather locates itself within the contemporary trend of family research which attempts a more nuanced understanding of the means by which families engage with society and culture in coping with a child's disability (Ferguson, 2001). While writing about the family, the issue of gender is critical; it is implicit in the ordering of familial relationships, division of labor (both material and emotional), and cultural understandings of the *good* mother, father, sister, or brother.

This chapter is located against the backdrop of structural and interactional transformations within the Indian family which impact child rearing, socialization, and, of course, the position of women. It uses disability as a lens through which to observe these transformations, as the breach in the fabric of the normal and everyday that enables the social scientist to map the shifting trajectories of family dynamics, gender, and power.

With regard to the care of the ill, aged, or members with disabilities in the family, it is invariably the women in the family who are expected to shoulder the burden: failure or refusal to do so causes discrediting both within and outside family circles. The *dirty work* of cleaning, washing, handling bodily wastes, and exudations which is part and parcel of the everyday reality of caring for a person with profound disabilities is conceptualized as *women's work*, more so if it involves the care of her own child. Hooyman and Gonyea (1995) point out that it is gender, more than kin ties, that determines the assumption of the *caring role*. In the rare instances where men are the *unsung heroes* and take up this role, it is usually because of the lack of availability of a female family member.

Some feminists assert that by portraying the family as the smallest unit of analysis, social scientists obscure the complex, gendered nature of caregiving, resulting in policies and programs which are not gender-sensitive (Traustadottir, 1991). The large and growing literature on caregiving and care work (both paid and unpaid), which draws heavily on feminist and Marxist conceptual frameworks, addresses the issues of devaluation of care work despite its contribution to public good and analyzes the manner in which women are made *prisoners of love* and exploited for their emotional labor (see England, 2005 for a review). Hooyman and Gonyea (1995) cite studies which capture the subjective, cognitive, and emotional dimensions of caregiving, underscoring the manner in which cultural ideologies and assumptions regarding gender-appropriate behavior translate into the manner in which men and women perceive and enact caregiving roles. Chakravarti (2008) forcefully brings out the manner in which poor-class, urban mothers of young people with cerebral palsy attempt to cope with the *burden of care*, especially when their children grow up and are no longer eligible to attend special schools.

At the same time, as this chapter indicates, the agency of the caregiver cannot be subsumed under an overarching model of the over-socialized victim; women also redefine their roles and convert the *burden* of care into windows of opportunity creating social spaces for themselves and their children. Of course, the class and caste dimensions must be accounted for as the opportunities and spaces available to the urban, predominantly middle-class families represented in this chapter (referred to by Shah, 1998 as the new *cosmopolitan class*) can certainly not be equated with those of the majority of disabled persons, and their families in the country's smaller towns and vast rural hinterland denied of even the most basic facilities of health care, sanitation, nutrition, and education.

In the following sections, the methodological underpinnings of the chapter will be discussed, with special reference to the author's location as the mother of a child with autism, and the challenges and opportunities this opened up. Next, the chapter elaborates upon some of the themes that emerges through the chapter. The section "Encounter with Autism" traces the processes of symptom recognition and diagnosis, and draws upon the metaphors used by the respondents to make sense of the child's disability. The section on family dynamics examines the manner in which families negotiate the challenges of living with a child with such a complex disability, bringing out both its difficulties and rewards. The chapter concludes with a discussion on the need for gender-sensitive support systems for families grappling with a child's disability and suggesting directions for the way forward.

Methodology

As mentioned earlier, the author's identity as the mother of a young boy with autism was instrumental in shaping an understanding of disability and the family. It proved to be a valuable resource in enabling access to informants, establishing rapport and probing sensitive, emotive issues. However, it also created several methodological and ethical challenges with regard to the issues of empathy and involvement, objectivity and distance (see Vaidya, 2010, for a detailed discussion). An engagement with feminist writings that critiqued *positivist* research methodologies challenged the hierarchical separation of the researcher and the researched (Wolf, 1996), and issued a call for *passionate scholarship* (DuBois, 1983) informed the chapter.

The deployment of a qualitative research methodology, namely, ethnography, was felt to be best suited for the aims and objectives of the research, which were to paint a nuanced picture of the everyday business of living with and caring for a child with a lifelong developmental disability.

The sample of 20 Delhi-based families, all having at least one child with autism, was selected through snowballing and personal contacts. The families belonged predominantly to the middle and upper classes, reflecting the class dimension in obtaining diagnosis and the onus placed on the family for seeking referrals and help. With the exception of two low-income families, the majority were financially well placed with access to the comforts and facilities that characterize the lifestyles of urban professionals. With regard to their educational profiles, the majority had studied beyond the higher secondary level. The sample included engineers, doctors, ICT professionals, government servants, a university teacher, and media professionals. Of the mothers, the majority were homemakers or worked *flextime* from home. Only three mothers were in fulltime paid employment outside the home.

With regard to family structure, 18 of the 20 families were nuclear and two had an extended structure. 13 families were first-generation residents of the city, having migrated from other places for professional reasons as well as, in some cases, in order to obtain better rehabilitative facilities for their child with a disability. At the time of the chapter, nine of the children were the only child in the family, while the rest had one or more typically developing siblings. In terms of ethnic and regional profile, the sample had a good mix of linguistic communities but was predominantly Hindu in terms of religious affiliation. The children in the sample ranged between age from 5 to 12 years and displayed various degrees of severity of their condition. All 14 boys and six girls were in receipt of some sort of educational intervention. While the process of diagnosis in the case of the youngest children in the sample was relatively quick, families of the older ones revealed experiences of long, confusing, and traumatic visits to a plethora of medical and other specialists. The next section details the *encounter* with autism narrated by parents.

Encounter with Autism

The narratives of families indicate their conceptualization of autism as a *rule-defying* condition that breaches cultural understandings and social expectations, and flies in the face of notions regarding competent personhood and received understandings of *normalcy*. Impacting as it does, the core *human* capacities of language, communication, and sociality, it confuses and confounds families whose babies seem *normal* in the physical sense, but fail to *relate* to people or appear dissociated from the world around them. Unlike more culturally recognizable conditions, such as mental retardation or sensory and locomotor impairments, autism is an unknown category, more closely resembling the cultural stereotype of *paagalpan* or *madness*. The stigma carries over to the family, and, this, along with the complexity of the disorder, puts them under greater pressure. Mothers are particularly blamed for faulty parenting and not teaching the child socially acceptable behavior (Gray, 1993).

Some of the metaphors or images culled from the narratives depict it as an enigma that is hard to understand or unravel, a curse that is a product of karma, a state of *permanent childhood*, and paradoxically, also a state of divinity. Cultural tropes of the *divine innocence* or lack of worldly wisdom of those with impaired intellectual capacities find space within the more Western biomedical notions of illness and impairment. The terms *bhola*, *seedha*, *bawla* (innocent, simple, guileless) (Mehrotra, 2004) are affectionately used to denote an absence of cunning and worldly wisdom and demonstrate how family members also deploy positive categories to depict their children's conditions. Grinker (2007) reports how some of the mothers he spoke to used the metaphor of Lord Shiva to describe their child indifferent to the niceties of social behavior and societal expectations! A mother described her son as *aghori baba* or ascetic sadhu who walks around naked with matted hair and bad hygiene!

As autism affects the faculties of language, communication, and social interaction, it is only around the second year of a child's life that parents become aware that something is *wrong* with their child. Volkmar (1987) notes how the social behavior of young autistic children is remarkable because of its sharp contrast with the irrepressible sociability of non-autistic toddlers. A mother remarked with the benefit of hindsight how her child appeared indifferent to other children, including the sibling.

> One day when I was waiting for my other child at the bus stop, I noticed another mother waiting for her child as well. Her toddler was so excited to

see her brother. She smiled and babbled. But my kid? He just did not seem to care!

Delayed speech is also an area of concern. Parents were concerned not just with the child's apparent inability to speak, but also the apparent inability to understand and respond to the speech of others as well as nonverbal cues.

> My sister in-law's child was the same age as mine (2 years) but the comparison ended there. I was amazed at the things she could do... her mother asked her to close the door and she actually did it! She would nod, shake her head, and make gestures... but my child was totally unresponsive—like a stone. I tried to convince myself that girls learn faster than boys but... I realized that he was not normal. (Narrative of a mother)

Erratic, uncontrolled behavior, tantrum-throwing, *dirty habits* (picking food from the floor or dustbin, eating mucus or feces, etc.), in other words, behavior that demonstrated acute social disconnect elicited much concern and also public disapproval. Mothers frequently bore the brunt of the *blame game* as the child's behavior was attributed to faulty mothering and overindulgence, as mentioned earlier. A mother recalled her mother-in-law's harsh comment, *"Bacche ko jaanwar bana diya hai"* (You have made the child an animal). The gradual unfolding realization that the child's development was atypical would then spur the long, painful process of obtaining a diagnosis, frequently at great financial, physical, and emotional cost.

A typical pattern of *diagnosis hunting* involved a visit to the family doctor who would assure the family that the problem would sort itself out, and usually blame the mother for not talking enough to her child and the lack of interaction with the extended family. The family would go away reassured, but soon the worries would resurface, and they would return to the doctor or seek the opinion of a specialist, usually a pediatrician, psychiatrist, or child psychologist. Only the youngest children in the sample received prompt and accurate diagnoses from the specialists, thanks to the growing awareness about the condition. The rest were subjected to multiple referrals and vague, confusing diagnoses that promoted further distress and unease. Through this entire phase of doubt and uncertainty, families had to carry on with the daily business of living: working, shopping, and attending to the needs of other children and aged parents.

Receiving the news that one's child has a lifelong incurable disability is devastating in itself. It is further compounded by the absence of accurate information, appropriate intervention, education, and training, and of course fear and uncertainty about the future. Some of the respondents reported extreme insensitivity of medical professionals in giving a diagnosis: "Your child will never be able to go to a school..." or "Put him in an institution and pray to God that He gives you another *normal* one..." were some of the most painful examples. Others complained that they were given vague hints and prognosis, adding to the feeling of uncertainty.

Psychological models of grieving identify various phases of grief through which families pass, for example, shock and numbness, longing, denial, anger, bargaining, sadness, and finally acceptance and reorganization (see Bowlby, 1979; Worden, 1991). However, scholars have pointed out that these models tend to be prescriptive and deterministic and do not take into account individual and cultural differences. Olshansky's (1962) concept of *chronic sorrow* emphasizes the ongoing nature of the grieving process which frequently resurfaces at various stages of the life course. The grieving process is also a gendered one; even though both fathers and mothers in the sample reported intense emotions, mothers due to their greater proximity with very young children were particularly badly hit. Their grief for the child was also accompanied by a feeling of entrapment at the enormity of the responsibility and a sense of guilt for their ambivalent feelings. A mother confided that she sometimes wished for the premature death of her child: "Not because I don't love him", she said, "but because I love him so much. What will happen to him after me? People will lock him up, beat him... only a mother can give this kind of love."

The reactions of the fathers, while no less intense, sometimes manifested in flight; some of them admitted that they would spend inordinately long periods at the workplace, or with colleagues, or drowning their sorrows in drink. Socially sanctioned avenues of *release* available to men were not available to women who frequently found themselves alone, isolated, and forced to deal with their sorrows on their own. The following case study demonstrates this pattern.

Voice of a Mother

S is the mother of a boy diagnosed with autism. Through his early childhood, both parents sensed that there was something amiss with his developmental pattern, but doctors were unable to put a finger on it. S recounted the days of uncertainty when she and her husband simply could not discuss their child's condition without her bursting into tears and him rushing out of the house.

She recalls the intense loneliness and depression she experienced when her son was finally diagnosed. She would weep silently in the bathroom or during her *puja* (worship/prayer). Her husband would stay out of the house until late at night and had started drinking heavily. He was prone to bouts of self-pity and did not extend her the emotional support she needed. Her own parents, though well meaning and supportive, would extend advice about *proper handling* of the child and tell her how she could do better.

S felt they were indirectly blaming her. She became hypersensitive to any comment or imagined criticism, and grew very possessive and protective toward her child. She withdrew into her shell and rejected social contacts with her friends and family. She wished that she had access to parent support organizations or counseling that would have enabled her to cope better. As time went by, S learnt to come to terms with her son's disability. She discovered his hidden potential, learned to accommodate his difficulties, and became less defensive. Her husband's road to acceptance was far harder; he now regards his son as a gift from God, but still has occasional bouts of anger and depression at his *fate*.

The encounter with autism narrated by families reveals an ongoing process of rewriting life-scripts, shattering of received notions of *normalcy* and personhood, and redefining parental roles and responsibilities. The following discussion brings out some of these issues and concerns.

Life with a Child with Autism

As has been mentioned earlier, the study is located against the backdrop of the changes taking place in the contemporary urban family. All but two of the families in the sample were nuclear in composition and represented a range of regional and linguistic communities. It, thus, exemplified a typical, upwardly mobile, urban middle-class profile where both parents were typically graduates and above, and where education and professional pursuits were highly valued. The arrival on the scene of a developmentally disabled child, thus, toppled the applecart and forced families to rethink their priorities, and revise their dreams and hopes about the future prospects of their offspring.

The lack of availability of reliable family and community networks and the anonymity of urban existence also put the conjugal unit at the center stage; in terms of management of the daily needs, routines, and care of the autistic child, it was the mother who assumed the greater responsibility. The majority of the mothers in the sample, including some with high professional qualifications, opted to stay home to look after their autistic child. In addition to the chores of feeding, cleaning, and toileting, they also had to assume the role of teacher, therapist, playmate, and constant companion. The valorized role of the Indian mother as the primary agent and moving force in the Indian child's life, which has been detailed by authors like Kakar (1978), assumes greater salience in relation to a child with disability. Pushed against a corner with few outlets or avenues for respite in an anonymous city, these mothers exemplified the persistence of a *mothering ideology* which glorifies sacrifice, self-denial, *seva* (service), and the cultural weight given to *mamta* or mothers' love. Reified or over-determined perceptions of the mothering role often resulted in women neglecting their own health and well-being, fitness, self-care, and emotional and sexual needs. One of the mothers reported that she felt guilty spending any time away from her child and had even stopped going to visit her friends or pampering herself with the occasional *facial* that she earlier used to enjoy.[4] Sara Ryan and Katherine Runswick-Cole (2008), both researchers and mothers of children with disability, highlight the marginal and liminal position of mothers of children with disability within the field of disability studies. While they themselves have no disability, they experience forms of disablism that mothers of nondisabled children do not. Yet the special competencies that they develop as a consequence of their experiences and intimate engagement with their children are largely overlooked and undervalued.

However, it would be a gross oversimplification to portray all these mothers as victims of circumstance. Some of them found opportunity in adversity and actively participated in voluntary and community work in the organizations and centers where their children were enrolled. Few of the mothers in the sample enrolled for training programs in special education and rehabilitation with a view to help their own child and others as well. The activism of mothers of children with disability has, in fact, acted as a catalyst for change in service provision, policy, and legislation. Several leading disability organizations in the country are headed by mothers of persons with disability. The names of Shyama Chona (Tamana and School of Hope, New Delhi), Merry Barua (Action for Autism, New Delhi), Shanti Auluck (Muskaan, New Delhi), and Poonam Natarajan (Vidya Sagar, Chennai, and the National Trust for the Welfare of Persons with Autism, Cerebral Palsy, Mental Retardation and Multiple Disabilities, Government of India) come readily to mind. These women are role models for many mothers who are then able to view their own lives not as *tragedies* but with the potential to bring about social transformation. As the mother of a little girl with autism put it, "Until she came into our lives I was just another ordinary housewife …. Because of her I have come to know how strong I am, that I can contribute to society." This mother underwent training as a special educator in Delhi and then moved back to her hometown in South India, where she now runs a school for children with autism.

With respect to the experiences of fathers, it was noted that while the majority of them did not actively participate in providing physical care (feeding, cleaning, toileting, etc.), they were deeply attached emotionally to their child and were struggling hard to meet professional expectations, succeed economically, and survive in a difficult, expensive city. Some of them had voluntarily moved from the relative security of extended family living in smaller towns and cities to the anonymity and impersonality of the metropolis so that their autistic child would have access to better services and opportunities. In the bargain, the quality of their own lives and time spent with family was compromised; this further accentuated the isolation and loneliness of the stay-at-home mother.

The breadwinner–caregiver dichotomy detailed earlier has serious implications for disability management and gender relations. Attributing inborn capacities of nurturance to mothers does a disservice to both parents, depriving fathers of the opportunity to bond deeply with their children, as the following case study will reveal. The overemphasis on the role of mothers in research as well as policy must, therefore, be addressed by factoring fathers into the family equation. This assumes greater salience when we consider that over 85 percent of children diagnosed with autism worldwide are male (www.autism-india.org) and, therefore, in need of same gender role models that will enable the formation of their own gender identities. Mehrotra and Vaidya (2008) note how the paucity of avenues for intellectually disabled males to form bonds of friendship with nondisabled male peers and their notional clubbing in the category of *women and children* has implications for the development of a *competent* male identity.

Gender Stereotypes and Parenting

P and M are the parents of a boy with autism. P, the father, has rapidly risen up the corporate ladder. He works hard and enjoys the *good things in life*: expensive clothes and gadgets, eating at high-end restaurants, driving a good car. His wife, M, stays at home to take care of their son. She gave up her job shortly after the birth of the child; now she fears that she will never be able to work again. P has a very busy schedule; he leaves home early and returns very late, after the child is asleep. M looks after the running of the house and does all the household chores. Their domestic help left the job, afraid of the *mad child* and his violent tantrums. M takes the child to his special needs center, brings him back home, and tries to keep him occupied at home. She is very sensitive about adverse comments about her son, so she hardly ever socializes with the other mothers and children in the colony. Her only solace is her daily telephone conversation with her mother who lives in another town. P and M's marital relations are strained; she feels he does not give her emotional support, and he thinks she is completely consumed by the needs of their son and has lost interest in him. He is secretive about his son and does not talk about him to peers and colleagues. This upsets M who accuses him of being ashamed of their child. His disengagement from his family life is intensifying as is her sense of frustration and entrapment. The father shared with the researcher that although he has deep love for his son, he feels excluded from the intimate dyad of mother and child, and, thus, cannot relate either to his wife or his child the way he wants to.

The task of parenting, which is not easy at the best of times, becomes even more challenging in the context of a disability like autism. The pressures of urban living and the stigma associated with the disability often result in families withdrawing from the supportive webs of kin and community networks so urgently needed to sustain them through difficult times. Supporting families is, therefore, a critical social responsibility.

Our discussion on family dynamics would not be complete without an examination of sibling relationship. Western studies on sibling-ship tend to focus on *sibling rivalry* which is seen as a critical aspect in the formation of an adult identity based on competition. However, Weisner (1993) points out that sibling life in South Asia is based on shared activity settings and is valorized as an ideal social bond.

In the context of disability and the family in urban India, the sibling is seen as the custodian and future guardian of the child with a disability, irrespective of age or gender differences. Parents whose first child was diagnosed as autistic revealed the familial and societal pressures upon them to *try* for a child who would hopefully be *normal* and assume the guardianship of the disabled one once the parents were gone. Despite individual decisions to not go in for another child (mostly on account of a fear that the second child might also have a disability), almost all the families emphasized the need for a typically developing child for the well-being of the family and to provide them demonstrative love and affection.

A sibling is *someone of one's own, someone who shares one's blood*, and the last reliable link with a disintegrating family support system. Older siblings would almost become surrogate parents; even younger ones soon learned to look out for and *protect* their autistic *bhaiyya* (older brother) or *didi* (older sister). Brothers were viewed as potential father figures, expected to provide home and shelter; sisters it was felt would be unable to do much once they went to their conjugal homes, even though they were the surrogate mothers who would provide unconditional nurture and love. The patriarchal ideology that sees the daughter as *paraaya dhan* (a stranger's wealth) operated with stark clarity and force.

Siblings shared their concerns and irritations and their resentment at sometimes having to play second fiddle and share their things without complaint. As one young boy succinctly put it, "Everything I have is his. But everything he has is also his!" Despite these minor irritants, siblings on the whole appeared more accepting of disability than several adults, a fact that humbled and made a profound impact on the researcher. The findings corroborated those of Raizada and Sharma (2003), and Saxena and Sharma (2000), who report positive relationships between those with a disability and typically developing siblings. The following aptly illustrates this.

K is a five-year-old girl with autism. She has profound difficulties and is not yet properly toilet-trained. Her parents are both in full-time employment and are out of the house all day. When K returns from school in the afternoon, she is attended to by her nine-year-old sister D. D feeds her lunch, changes her soiled clothes, and the two sisters watch TV and relax until their mother returns in the evening. D rushes off for her tuitions and then to play with her large group of friends. She appears a cheerful, well-adjusted child who loves her little sister and does not appear to find it burdensome that she has to perform care work for her sibling. Her mother, in the course of an interview, remarked that she was sure D would take good care of her little sister when the parents were gone. The father angrily snapped, "It is all very well to be so idealistic. But what will happen when she goes to her own home? Will her husband and in-laws allow her to bring a sister with a disability along?"

Siblings are seen as the last line of defense, the only *guarantee* that the disabled child will have someone to fall back on once the parents are gone. This belief sits uneasily with the realization that given their educational and professional compulsions, they are quite likely to migrate and set up independent households, much as their parents did. This nostalgic yearning for the old-style joint family of earlier times where family members unconditionally took care of those with disabilities came out sharply in the narratives as did the sense of fear and foreboding to that omnipresent question, "What will happen to this child when we are gone?" The concluding section looks at this question.

Supporting Families: The Way Forward

The decline of traditional support structures and the demands of urban existence forces families in difficult circumstances to seek alternative institutions and opportunities. Against this backdrop, the role of support groups becomes salient. Support groups enhance parental coping by providing information, opportunities for interaction with people in similar circumstances in a nonjudgmental environment, and hope and comfort through *success stories*. There is a particularly acute need for supporting mothers, who, as has been detailed earlier, suffer the most because of their virtual confinement within the four walls of the house and the constant, unending care work they must perforce render. Provision of respite care, special crèches for children with special needs, and day care centers can provide a much-needed break from routine and also provide the child with opportunities to socialize with peers. The anonymity of urban existence creates the need to forge bonds and networks that transcend the family, yet replicate some of its functions, viz., support, nurture, and guidance. Family-driven support groups and nongovernment organizations are beginning to play an important role in this regard. A case study of a pioneering organization, Action for Autism, was also conducted as part of the research. It amplifies the need for families in difficult circumstances to find spaces where they can come together and mobilize for the rights of their children and secure their future.

Action for Autism was set up in 1991 when its founder Merry Barua's son, Neeraj, was diagnosed with autism. The family was told that the condition was incurable, and worse, there were no educational or other facilities available for children with autism in India. Barua set about educating herself about the condition and set up a school with two children. She attempted to contact and establish links with other families, and over the years, the small group of parents has grown into an organization which has virtually become synonymous with the autism sector in India. Action for Autism screens children, offers diagnostic services, runs a model school and a work skills centre for adults, publishes a quarterly newsletter, and engages with the civil society and State through advocacy, awareness building, research, and policy formulation. Its extremely successful *Mother and Child Program*, now renamed the *Parent and Child Training Program*, where mothers (and the occasional father) come with their young children to the center and learn how to work one-on-one with their child and teach him/her basic skills, is an excellent example of parental empowerment. They not just learn skills but are also encouraged to imbibe the quality of acceptance and respect of difference. They get the opportunity to interact and form bonds with other parents, reinforcing the belief that they are not alone and that collective and community-based action ultimately yields better, more lasting results.

***

Family-driven support groups and organizations serve as a halfway house between the fast-declining extended family and the emergent welfare state. They play a significant role in lobbying for the rights of the developmentally disabled whose *voice* is unheard. Even though autism was not included as one of the disabilities listed in the Persons with Disabilities Act of 1995, is has found a place in the Rights of Persons with Disabilities Bill, 2014, which has been drafted in the light of the ratification of the UNCRPD by India and the need to make disability legislation more inclusive and rights-based. Similarly, parental activism played an important role in the enactment of the National Trust Act, 1999. The Act addresses the issues of protection, support, and guardianship of those categories of disabled persons who are likely to need lifelong care.

Family support organizations have also played critical roles in creation of services, dissemination of information, and mobilization of public opinion. However, despite the best efforts of these organizations, it is ultimately society and State that has to own responsibility for its marginalized citizens. Parmenter (2001) urges for the development of an *ethical community* whose central feature is the interdependence of all individuals. In the Indian context, Chaswal (2008) outlines a model for community care and support which utilizes local resources and members of the community and neighborhood. The need of the hour is the revitalization of our long tradition of communitarian care lodged within a human rights perspective. We argue in favor of revisiting cultural understandings of *difference* that do not isolate or stigmatize but rather emphasize our common humanity.

Notes

1. See http://www.autismresourcecenter.in/ (downloaded on 23.12.2014).
2. The character Rizwan Khan in the 2010 Hindi film *My Name is Khan* is depicted as a person with Asperger's syndrome.
3. See http://www.autismspeaks.org/what-autism/diagnosis/dsm-5-diagnostic-criteria (downloaded on 21.04.2014).
4. See Vaidya (2011) for a detailed discussion on mothering and disability.

Bibliography

Ferguson, P. Albrecht, Katherine, D. Seelman, and Michael Bury (eds). *Handbook of Disability Studies*, pp. 373–395. New Delhi: SAGE Publications.

American Psychiatric Association. 2000. *Diagnostic and Statistical Manual of Mental Disorders* (4th edn, revised, DSM-IV-TR). Washington, D.C.: American Psychiatric Association.

Asperger, Hans. [1944] 1991. "Autistic Psychopathy in Childhood," in Uta Frith (trans.), *Autism and Asperger Syndrome*, pp. 337–392. Cambridge: Cambridge University Press.

Bowlby, J. 1979. *The Making and Breaking of Affectional Bonds*. London: Tavistock.

Chakravarti, Upali. 2008. "Burden of Caring: Families of the Disabled in Urban India," *Indian Journal of Gender Studies*, 15 (2): 341–363.

Chaswal, Indu. 2008. "Building Community Support in India," paper presented at the South Asian Regional Conference on Autism, "Building Bridges," New Delhi, January 15–16, 2008.

Daley, T. C. 2002. "The Need for Cross-Cultural Research on Pervasive Developmental Disorder," *Transcultural Psychiatry*, 39 (4): 532–551.

———. 2004. "From Symptom Recognition to Diagnosis: Children with Autism in Urban India," *Social Science and Medicine*, 58 (7): 1323–1335.

DuBois, Barbara. 1983. "Passionate Scholarship: Notes on Values, Knowing and Method in Social Science," in Bowles Gloria and Renate Duelli Klein (eds), *Theories of Women's Studies*, pp. 105–116. London: Routledge.

Ellenberger, H. F. 1968. "Psychiatric Impressions from a Trip to Dakar," *Canadian Psychiatric Association Journal*, 13 (6): 539–545.

England, Paula. 2005. "Emerging Theories of Care Work," *Annual Review of Sociology*, 31: 381–399.

Ferguson, P. M. 2001. "Mapping the Family: Disability Studies and the Exploration of Parental Response to Disability," in Albrecht, Gary L. Ferguson, Katherine D. Seelman, and Michael Bury (eds), *Handbook of Disability Studies*, pp. 373–95. Thousand Oaks, CA: Sage Publications.

Ghai, Anita. 2002. "Disabled Women: An Excluded Agenda of Indian Feminism," *Hypatia*, 17 (3): 49–66.

Gray, D. E. 1993. "Perceptions of Stigma: The Parents of Autistic Children," *Sociology of Health and Illness*, 15 (1): 102–120.

Grinker, R. R. 2007. *Unstrange Minds: Remapping the World of Autism*. New York: Basic Books.

Hooyman, Nancy R. and Judith Gonyea. 1995. *Feminist Perspectives on Family Care: Policies for Gender Justice*. Thousand Oaks: SAGE Publications.

Kakar, S. 1978. *The Inner World: A Psycho-Analytic Study of Childhood and Society in India*. Delhi: Oxford University Press.

Kanner, L. 1943. "Autistic Disturbances of Affective Contact," *Nervous Child*, 2: 217–250.

Mehrotra, Nilika. 2004. "Understanding Cultural Conceptions of Disability in Rural India: A Case from Haryana," *Journal of Indian Anthropological Society*, 39 (1): 33–34.

Mehrotra, N, and S. Vaidya. 2008. "Exploring Constructions of Intellectual Disability and Personhood in Haryana and Delhi," *Indian Journal of Gender Studies*, 15 (2): 317–340.

Nuttal, Mark. 1998. "States and Categories: Indigenous Models of Personhood in Northwest Greenland," in R. Jenkins (ed.), *Questions of Competence: Culture, Classification and Intellectual Disability*, pp. 176–193. Cambridge, UK: Cambridge University Press.

Olshansky, S. 1962. "Chronic Sorrow: A Response to Having a Mentally Defective Child," *Social Casework*, 43: 190–193.

Parmenter, T. R. 2001. "Intellectual Disabilities—*Quo Vadis?*," in Gary L. Albrecht, Katherine D. Seelman, and Michael Bury (eds), *Handbook of Disability Studies*, pp. 267–296. Thousand Oaks: SAGE Publications.

Raizada, P. and N. Sharma. 2003. "Sibling Relationships of Adolescents with Intellectual Impairment," *Childhood Disability Update*, 3 (1): 20–25.

Ryan, Sara and Katherine Runswick-Cole. 2008. "Repositioning Mothers: Mothers, Disabled Children and Disability Studies," *Disability and Society*, 23 (3): 199–210.

Sanua, V. D. 1984. "Is Infantile Autism a Universal Phenomenon? An Open Question," *International Journal of Social Psychiatry*, 30 (3): 162–177.

Saxena, M. and N. Sharma. 2000. "Growing Up with a Mentally Retarded Child: A Study of Adolescent Siblings," *Journal of Psychiatry and Clinical Studies*, 16 (1): 16–23.

Shah, A. M. 1998. *The Family in India: Critical Essays*. New Delhi: Orient Longman.

Traustadottir, R. 1991. "Mothers Who Care," *Journal of Family Issues*, 12 (2): 211–228.

Vaidya, Shubhangi. 2008. Unpublished Ph.D. thesis. "A Sociological Study of Families of Autistic Children in Delhi," New Delhi: Jawaharlal Nehru University.

———. 2010. "Researcher as Insider: Opportunities and Challenges," *Indian Anthropologist*, 40 (2): 25–36.

———. 2011. "Mothering as Ideology and Practice: The Experiences of Mothers of Children with Autism Spectrum Disorder," in M. Walks and

N. MacPherson (eds), *The Anthropology of Mothering*. Bradford, Ontario, Canada: Demeter Press.

Volkmar, F. R. 1987. "Diagnostic Issues in the Pervasive Developmental Disorders," *Journal of Child Psychology and Psychiatry*, 28 (3): 365–369.

Weisner, T. S. 1993. "Overview: Sibling Similarity and Difference in Different Cultures," in C. W. Nuckolls (ed.), *Siblings in South Asia*, pp. 1–17. New York: The Guildford Press.

Westermeyer, J. 1979. "Folk Concepts of Mental Disorder Among the Lao: Continuities with Similar Concepts in Other Cultures and in Psychiatry," *Culture, Medicine & Psychiatry*, 3 (3): 301–312.

Whyte, S. R. 1998. "Slow Cookers and Madmen: Competence of Heart and Head in Rural Uganda," in R. Jenkins (ed.), *Questions of Competence: Culture, Classification and Intellectual Disability*, pp. 153–175. Cambridge: Cambridge University Press.

Wing, L. 1988. "The Continuum of Autistic Characteristics," in E. Schopler and G. B. Mesibov (eds), *Diagnosis and Assessment in Autism*, pp. 91–110. New York: Plenum Press.

Wolf, Diane L. (ed.). 1996. "Situating Feminist Dilemmas in Fieldwork," in *Feminist Dilemmas in Fieldwork*, pp. 1–55. Boulder, CO: Westview Press.

Worden, J. W. 1991. *Grief Counselling and Grief Therapy*, 2nd ed. New York: Springer.

TOWARD NONDISCRIMINATORY GENDERED STRATEGIES

SECTION THREE

9

Yes, Girls and Women with Disabilities Do Math!
An Intersectionality Analysis*

Stephanie Ortoleva

Introduction

The correlation between low educational outcomes and having a disability is often stronger than the correlations between low educational outcomes and other characteristics, such as gender, rural residence, or poverty.

Women and girls with disabilities have the lowest education participation rates of all groups. The knowledge of Science, Technology, Engineering, and Mathematics (STEM) subjects is especially deficient. Additionally, women with disabilities have low employment rates, as compared to men with and without disabilities and women without disabilities. Women and girls with disabilities often live in economic poverty and are recognized to be doubly disadvantaged, experiencing exclusion from the rest of society due to both their gender and disability.

Therefore, any discussion of gender and STEM must include women and girls with disabilities. Throughout the world, science and technology fields are dramatically expanding. This is true both in developed and developing countries; these skills and knowledge could provide

* The author would like to thank her partner, Frank Della-Penna, for his support of her work and patience as the research and writing proceeded. The author also thanks her colleague Marc Brenman for his editorial suggestions and sharing of valuable resources to this research. Finally, the author dedicates this chapter to current and future scientists, technology experts, engineers, and mathematicians who are women and girls with disabilities.

significant employment opportunities for women and girls with disabilities. Because of the important role that the knowledge of math, science, and technology play in everyday life, skills in these fields could create dramatic improvements in the daily lives and independence of women and girls with disabilities.

This chapter expands on a side event panel entitled "Expanding Access to Education and Employment Opportunities for Women and girls with Disabilities in STEM Strategy for Action!," held at the United Nations (UN) Commission on the Status of Women (CSW).[1] This chapter will begin with some background information on the economic and social situation of women and girls with disabilities, and their exclusion from education and employment opportunities. In this chapter, we will also discuss the synergy between the United Nations Convention on the Rights of Persons with Disabilities (UNCRPD), the Convention on the Elimination of All Forms of Discrimination Against Women (CEDAW), and the Convention on the Rights of the Child (CRC). In addition, this chapter will enumerate some of the barriers that limit the participation of women and girls with disabilities in education and employment in the STEM fields. Finally, it will conclude with some recommendations for change and strategies for action, and examples of effective programs already implementing change and increasing the participation of women and girls with disabilities in the STEM fields.

Background on the Exclusion of Women and Girls with Disabilities from Education and Employment Opportunities and the Necessity to Include Them in the STEM Fields

The World Health Organization (WHO) and the World Bank (WB) released a ground-breaking report on June 9, 2011 entitled "World Report on Disability." The report notes a dramatic increase in estimates of the number of persons with disabilities worldwide, stating:

> [A]bout 15% of the world's population [or one billion persons] lives with some form of disability, of whom 2–4% experience significant difficulties in functioning. The global disability prevalence is higher than previous WHO estimates, which date from the 1970s and suggested a figure of around 10%.

This global estimate for disability is on the rise due to population ageing and the rapid spread of chronic diseases, as well as improvements in the methodologies used to measure disability. (WB, 2011)

In addition, factors such as "population growth and war and conflict" also contribute to an increase in the number of persons with disabilities throughout the world (UN's Some Facts about Persons with Disabilities, CRPD). There are significant differences in the prevalence of disability (defined as "significant difficulties in their everyday lives") between men and women in both developing and more developed countries: male disability prevalence rate is 12 percent and female disability prevalence rate is 19.2 percent (ibid.). With such a dramatic increase in the percentage of persons with disabilities, and the high proportions of women and girls with disabilities, the urgent need to include women and girls with disabilities in the STEM fields in both education and employment is even more important.

Women and girls with disabilities are recognized to be doubly disadvantaged, experiencing exclusion from the rest of society due to both their gender and disability (Arnade and Haefner, 2006; David, 2004). Globally, women make up three-fourths of the number of persons with disabilities in low- and middle-income countries. Between 65 percent and 70 percent of these women live in rural areas (de Alwis, 2008).

Estimates of the percentage of children with disabilities not attending school are extremely variable. However, in general, children with disabilities are less likely to start school, and have lower rates of staying and being promoted in school than their peers without disabilities. The correlation between low educational outcomes and having a disability is often stronger than the correlations between low educational outcomes and other characteristics, such as gender, rural residence, or poverty. The limited statistics that are available indicate that although the literacy rate for adults with disabilities is 3 percent, only 1 percent of women with disabilities are literate (Rousso, 2003). These percentages are significantly lower than those for women in general.

In 2008, 796 million adults worldwide (15 years and older) reported not being able to read and write and two-thirds of them (64%) were women. The global adult literacy rate was 83%, with a male literacy rate of 88% and a female literacy rate of 79%. (UNESCO, 2010)

In 2010, this statistic improved marginally to a male literacy rate of 89 percent and a female literacy rate of 80 percent, with the percent differential between the genders remaining the same Huebler, Francis, 2012). The WB and WHO report, described earlier, states that out of the 51 countries included in the analysis, "50.6% of males with disability have completed primary school, compared with 61.3% of males without disability. Females with disability report 41.7% primary school completion compared with 52.9% of females without disability, a difference of 8.9% between males and females with disabilities" (World Bank, 2011). There is a direct correlation between poverty, being a child with disabilities and low education participation, with the girls with disabilities from lower socio-economic backgrounds rarely attending school (ibid.). One explanation for these discrepancies is that special education facilities are typically located in more urban settings and thus leave limited options for girls with disabilities in rural villages. Girls with disabilities have the lowest education participation rates of all groups and knowledge of (STEM) subjects is especially deficient (Fancasali, 2000). Furthermore, women and girls with disabilities have few opportunities for vocational training (de Alwis, 2008).

The education gaps, as outlined earler, also result in employment gaps for women with disabilities. Only 25 percent of women with disabilities are in the workforce worldwide (World Bank, 2009). Women with disabilities are twice as unlikely to find work as disabled men. Women with disabilities have low employment rates, as compared with men with and without disabilities and women without disabilities (Jans and Stoddard, 1999). Furthermore, WB and WHO report indicated, "employment rates of 52.8% for men with disability and 19.6% for women with disability, compared with 64.9% for non-disabled men, and 29.9% for non-disabled women" (World Bank, 2011).

The UN and the CSW, and Inclusion of Women and Girls with Disabilities in STEM Policies and Programs

The UN General Assembly resolutions, especially Resolution A/RES/65/186 as well as the Secretary-General's report A/65/173 (UN General Assembly, 2010a, 2010b), highlighted the importance of including women with disabilities and the gender perspective in mainstreaming disability in development as the missing link in the development agenda (UN General Assembly, 2010a, 2010b). The omission of the disability perspective in mainstreaming women and girls, and the gender perspective in development efforts not only affects women and girls with disabilities themselves, but also adversely affects the objectives of development for all individuals. The international community therefore called for priority attention and urgent action to mainstream disability, especially in the context of realization of the major internationally-agreed development goals, such as the Millennium Development Goals. Despite the implications for more than 500 million women and girls with disabilities and their families, issues concerning women with disabilities receive only limited, or even invisible, coverage in influential CSW Expert Group Meetings and preparatory papers. There is also the scant inclusion of issues concerning women with disabilities in side events at CSW sessions, other than those organized by women with disabilities themselves. The CSW can contribute to a more effective awareness of inclusion of all women in education and employment in the STEM fields by welcoming women with disabilities to these discussions

The priority theme for the 55th Session of the CSW in 2011 was "access and participation of women and girls to education, training, science and technology, including for the promotion of women's equal access to full employment and decent work" (UN Women, 2011a). In preparation for the CSW 55th Session, an Expert Group Meeting was held from September 28 to October 1, 2010 in Paris, France. In preparation for that meeting, a series of approximately 12 Expert Papers were prepared (UN Women, 2011b). Regrettably, references to women and girls with disabilities were rare and in the few instances where women and girls with disabilities were referenced, the comments were superficial and insufficient. For example, on page seven of the Secretary General's Report, having a disability as a barrier to education was lumped together with poverty, rural environments, minority groups and armed conflict zones. This grouping marginalizes the obstacles women and girls with disabilities confront in obtaining an education since simply listing women with disabilities with other groups does not afford an opportunity to enumerate and address the unique needs of and challenges facing women with disabilities nor does it encourage disability-specific solutions. On page 17 of this same report, it was noted that Greece is promoting women's entrepreneurship by allowing "persons with disabilities to claim their house as business property and other relevant expenses as business expense" (UN Secretary-General, 2012). Out of these 12 Expert Papers, only four included any mention of women with disabilities and such references were, like those mentioned earlier, superficial.

Due to the vigorous intervention of this author and other women with disabilities attending the CSW 55th Session, a few references to women and girls with disabilities were included in the Final Adopted Conclusions from the session. Conclusion number 2 referenced the CRPD in order to promote equality in education and employment. Conclusion *c* under "Strengthening National Legislation, Policies and Programmes" focused on the need to improve disability data collection in order to facilitate "legislative development and policymaking on education, training and science and technology." Conclusion 18 stated the need to improve policies to promote women's economic empowerment so that a disability is not an obstacle. However, references to women with disabilities in other parts of the Final Conclusions were necessary, but non-existent. For example, women and girls with disabilities should have been addressed in Conclusion 21 when barriers to education were discussed, but they were not (UN Women, 2011c).

In addition to the conclusions discussed earlier, the CSW 55 Session Report highlighted the need to focus on the increased susceptibility and prevalence of HIV/AIDS among women and girls with disabilities and the *serious and systemic* human rights violations against women and girls with disabilities, such as rape, torture, inhuman and degrading treatment and punishment, and the inability of the States to provide adequate protection and support (UN CSW, 2011: Doc./E/2011/27 and E/CN.6/2011/12). Regrettably, this CSW 55 Session Report made no mention of the need to include women and girls with disabilities as actively engaged in STEM education and employment opportunities, and seemed to only address their needs in terms of protection and support.

As is the usual practice of the CSW, the priority theme of a previous CSW session is reviewed, and for the CSW 58th Session, the review theme was "Access and participation of women and girls to education, training, science and technology, including for the promotion of women's equal access to full employment and decent work" (UN Women, 2014). The purpose of the CSW 58th Session review theme was to assess progress in the implementation of the Final Conclusions from the CSW 55th session, where the issue was the priority theme. To that end, at the CSW 58th Session, a side event entitled "Progress? Participation of Women and Girls with Disabilities in Education and Employment in Science, Technology, Engineering and Math," assessed progress and outlined positive strategies going forward.[2] The CSW 58th Session Review Theme Report highlighted some aspects of progress for women and girls, and also identified significant gaps in the progress. Regrettably, the report failed to mention women and girls with disabilities anywhere in the document, despite the specific provisions of the CSW 55th Session Final Conclusions which had several references to them, as discussed earlier. The 58th Session Report did reference *rural, indigenous and older women, having been excluded from STEM altogether* but did not take advantage of this opportunity to include women and girls with disabilities in the review of progress. Even when issues important to women and girls with disabilities were discussed, there was no mention of women and girls with disabilities, for example, the importance of ensuring that women and girls benefit from the development of new technologies and that they have access to new communication tools, to enhance safety, information, and entrepreneurship opportunities. This minimal attention to addressing the issues of concern to women and girls with disabilities at CSW seems to be a persistent process. Beijing + 20 Review at the CSW 59th Session presented another such opportunity for the civil society to engage with UN entities and governments at CSW (UN Women, Commission on the Status of Women [CSW], 2014).[3]

Intersectionality and Synergy—the CRPD, the CEDAW, and the CRC

Inclusion of women and girls with disabilities with respect to the theme of STEM are also provided for within the provisions of several major UN Conventions, including the CRPD (2006 GA Res. 61/611,UN Document A/RES/61/611, the Convention on the Elimination of All Forms of Discrimination Against Women (CEDAW, 1979), and the Convention on the Rights of the Child (CRC, 1990) among other international and regional treaties, and including the pronouncements of these convention's treaty bodies, as well as the Beijing Declaration (Beijing Declaration and Platform for Action, 1995).

A careful analysis of the intersection between the provisions of the CRPD, the CEDAW, and the CRC along with various UN Security Council Resolutions and other reports on women and persons with disabilities, demonstrates the synergy that exists to promote changes in law, policy, and practice to ensure the inclusion of women and girls with disabilities in education and employment in STEM. In its General Recommendation No. 18, the CEDAW Committee recommended that States:

> provide information on disabled women in their periodic reports, and on measures taken to deal with their particular situation, including special measures to ensure that they have equal access to education and employment,

health services and social security, and to ensure that they can participate in all areas of social and cultural life. (UN Committee on the Elimination of Discrimination Against Women [CEDAW], 1991)

The analysis, as follows, focuses on provisions in the CRPD, the CEDAW, and the CRC that have specific implications for inclusion of women and girls with disabilities in practices and policies concerning STEM.

The Gender Lens

The CRPD has adopted a gender lens in its terms and provisions, as shown in the Preamble, Article 3, Article 6 (Blanck, 2007) and also throughout the CRPD provisions specifically concerning women, such as Article 8 on awareness–raising, Article 16 on freedom from exploitation, violence and abuse, Article 24 on Education, Article 25 on health, and Article 27 on Work and Employment (CRPD, Articles 8.16 and 25). Since the CEDAW exclusively focuses on women, the entire document can be said to be written under a gender lens. In the CRC, Article 29(1) (d) references understanding the equality of the sexes (UNCRC, 1990).

General Obligations and Temporary Special Measures

Additionally, the CRPD, the CEDAW and the CRC share many common principles such as the overall obligations required of states under Article 4 of the CRPD, Article 2 of the CEDAW and the Preamble and Article 2 of the CRC. Each Convention requires states to enact legislative and legal protections for women, persons with disabilities and/or children, respectively. To alleviate the effect that stereotypes have on emphasizing notions of inequality toward women and persons with disabilities, Article 5 of the CRPD and Article 4 of the CEDAW include provisions authorizing the use of special measures to expedite and ensure the achievement of equality between the sexes and those with disabilities. The CEDAW states that temporary special measures "aimed at accelerating de facto equality between men and women shall not be considered discrimination and the CRPD has a similar provision, providing for such measures (UNHRC, 2009). Article 29 (1)(d) of the CRC calls for "[t] he preparation of the child for responsible life in a free society, in the spirit of understanding, peace, tolerance, equality of sexes, and friendship among all peoples, ethnic, national and religious groups and persons of indigenous origin" (UNCRC, 1990).

Stereotyping

Article 8 of the CRPD and Article 5 of the CEDAW emphasize the negative role that stereotypes can play in the lives of persons with disabilities, including women with disabilities and women in general. Article 8 of the CRPD lists ways in which a state may combat stereotypes against women and persons with disabilities. Article 8 of the CRPD recommends that States employ programs "to raise awareness throughout society, including at the family level... and to foster respect for the rights and dignity of persons with disabilities...including those based on sex and age..." Similarly, underthe CEDAW, States hold the responsibility to "[t]o combat stereotypes, prejudices and harmful practices" and to eliminate "prejudices and customary and all other practices" (UN CEDAW). The CRPD takes the CEDAW stereotype provisions further by recognizing that gender and disability stereotypes coincide to have a compound effect on women with disabilities (CRPD).

The CRC does not address the issue of stereotyping explicitly in its provisions, however General Comment Numbers 4, 10, 11, 12, and 13 do address this issue. To highlight a few of these comments which are most salient to the topic of this chapter, General Comment Number 4 calls for "effective measures to eliminate all acts and activities which threaten the right to life of adolescents, including honour killings" and the development of "awareness-raising campaigns, education programmes and legislation aimed at changing prevailing attitudes, and address gender roles and stereotypes that contribute to harmful traditional practices" (UN CRC, 33rd Session). In addition, General Comment Number 13, on Violence in the Mass Media, states that "[m]ass media, especially tabloids and the yellow press, tend to highlight shocking occurrences and as a result create a biased and stereotyped image of children, in particular of disadvantaged children or adolescents, who are often portrayed as violent or delinquent just because they may behave or dress in a different way. Such stirred-up stereotypes pave the way for State policies based on a punitive approach, which may include violence as a reaction to assumed or factual misdemeanours of children and young persons." General Comment Number 13 also calls on the need to address:

> gender-based stereotypes, power imbalances, inequalities and discrimination which support and perpetuate the use of violence and coercion in the home, in school and educational settings, in communities, in the workplace, in institutions and in society more broadly. Men and boys must be actively encouraged as strategic partners and allies, and along with women

and girls, must be provided with opportunities to increase their respect for one another and their understanding of how to stop gender discrimination and its violent manifestations. (UNCRC, G.C.13)

Legal Capacity and Access to Justice

Two crucial elements of human rights, legal capacity and access to justice, are incorporated in both the CRPD and the CEDAW. In the CRPD, Articles 12 and 13 address these issues, and in the CEDAW Article 15 addresses equality before the law for both men and women (CEDAW, para 1–4 and 13). The CRPD draws heavily on the approach taken in the CEDAW and rejects the narrower approach taken in the International Covenant on Civil and Political Rights.[4]

Interestingly, interpretations of Article 16 of the International Covenant on Civil and Political Rights make it abundantly clear that this provision only contemplates one aspect of this right—that every person is a subject, and not an object, of the law (UN High Commissioner for Human Rights [UNHRC], 2005). This provision does not guarantee that a person has the legal capacity to act. On the other hand, the approach used in the CRPD utilizes wording similar to that used in the second paragraph of Article 15 of the CEDAW.

Article 15 of the CEDAW asserts 4 provisions with respect to this topic. First, it requires States to grant women equality with men before the law. Second, it requires States, in civil matters, to accord women a legal capacity identical to that of men, as well as the same opportunities to exercise that capacity. More specifically, States must give women equal rights to conclude contracts and to administer property, and they must also treat women equally in all stages of court and tribunal procedure. Third, States must agree that all contracts and other private legal instruments directed at restricting the legal capacity of women are deemed null and void. Fourth, Article 15 requires States to accord men and women with the same rights regarding the law relating to the movement of persons, and the freedom to choose their residence and domicile (CEDAW). Furthermore, Article 15 of the CEDAW focuses on ensuring women's legal autonomy. It confirms women's equality with men before the law, and also requires States to guarantee equal rights in areas of civil law where women have traditionally suffered discrimination (CEDAW, 1994, 13th Session). Comparably, Articles 3 and 5 of the CRPD emphasize and assure the legal rights of persons with disabilities and of men and women (CRPD). Article 15 of the CEDAW guarantees women equal "legal capacity" with men and the same opportunities to "exercise that capacity," drawing from the principle of autonomy or self-determination (CEDAW). Each individual is presumed to be able to make life choices and to act independently (UN High Commissioner for Human Rights [UNHRC], 2005). Thus, the CRPD clearly incorporates both concepts of "capacity to be a person before the law" and "legal capacity to act," drawing on the approach taken in the CEDAW.

Article 37 of the CRC discusses prompt legal action if a child is deprived of basic rights, Article 12 of the CRC states the right of the child "to be heard in any judicial and administrative proceedings affecting the child.

Right to Education

The Right to Education is also guaranteed in Article 24 of the CRPD, Article 10 of the CEDAW, and Article 28 of the CRC. Each Article asserts the importance of an equal education and that States should work toward eliminating discrimination. The CRPD recognizes the right of persons with disabilities to an inclusive education without discrimination on the basis of equal opportunity. The CRPD also encourages States "to employ teachers, including teachers with disabilities, who are qualified in sign language and/or Braille, and to train professionals and staff who work at all levels of education (CRPD)." Similarly, the CEDAW education provision advocates for "the elimination of any stereotyped concept of the roles of men and women at all levels and in all forms of education... by the revision of textbooks and school programmes and the adaptation of teaching methods (CEDAW)." The CRC discusses each child's right to education and the duty of the State to prevent interference with this right to education, including accommodations for children with disabilities, affordable education for all, and to keep children free of economic and other exploitation that may prevent them from receiving an education.

Right to Work

The Right to Work and Participate in the Same E,conomy is also mentioned in Article 11 of the CEDAW, Article 27 of the CRPD and Article 32 of the CRC. All three conventions advocate for an inclusive work-force that will in turn advance the economy, human rights and development of the state (CEDAW). The CRPD maintains that "the rights of persons with disabilities...[include] equal opportunities and equal remuneration for work of equal value, safe and healthy working conditions... [and] protection from harassment, and the redress of grievances," as well as the right to reasonable accommodation (CRPD).

Article 11 of the CEDAW discusses the right to work as an inalienable right of all human beings (CEDAW). Article 11 also addresses the right to free choice of profession, the same employment opportunities, and the right to equal remuneration. In an effort to prevent discrimination against women who marry and have families, the CEDAW also calls for the right to have maternity leave and to prohibit a woman from losing her job due solely to pregnancy.

The CRC highlights:

> the right of the child to be protected from economic exploitation and from performing any work that is likely to be hazardous or to interfere with the child's education, or to be harmful to the child's health or physical, mental, spiritual, moral or social development."

Right to Health

Even before the CRPD came into force, the CEDAW Committee began to recognize that issues concerning women with disabilities played an important role in its work. For example, in its General Recommendation No. 24, the CEDAW Committee stated:

> [W]omen with disabilities, of all ages, often have difficulty with physical access to health services. Women with mental disabilities are particularly vulnerable, while there is limited understanding, in general, of the broad range of risk to mental health to which women are disproportionately susceptible as a result of gender discrimination, violence, poverty, armed conflict, dislocation and other forms of social deprivation. States parties should take appropriate measures to ensure that health services are sensitive to the needs of women with disabilities and are respectful of their human rights and dignity. (CEDAW, 20th Session, 1999)

The CEDAW Committee also referenced other issues of concern in another of its General Recommendations. For instance, the CEDAW Committee recognized that societal factors may be determinative of health status, and that special attention should be given to the health needs of women with disabilities, among other vulnerable groups.[5]

Additionally, Article 12 of the CEDAW and Article 25 of the CRPD specifically address the right to health among women and persons with disabilities, respectively. The CEDAW stresses the importance of access to healthcare for women, especially in the areas of reproduction and family planning (CEDAW). Also, the CRPD asserts "States Parties shall take all appropriate measures to ensure access for persons with disabilities to health services, including sexual and reproductive health, that are gender-sensitive, including health-related rehabilitation (CRPD).

Interestingly, note that Article 17 in the CRC addresses the need to provide for a child's mental health and avoid extensive exposure to the sensationalism in the media. Rather, Article 17 calls on States to encourage exposure to a broad array of cultures and information to promote a well rounded child. Article 23 recognizes the health needs of a disabled child and calls upon States to provide effective access to health care services. Article 24 calls on States to provide access to medical care, especially primary care and adequate treatment, and rehabilitative facilities for injured children (CRC).

The CRPD, the CEDAW, and the CRC provide a significant roadmap for the inclusion of women and girls with disabilities into education and employment in STEM fields and the UN development agenda framework. The failure to include women and girls with disabilities in such actions at the international and national levels runs contrary to the gender sensitive and disability inclusive approach and other principles found in these three treaties.

Barriers to Inclusion[6]

Various factors constitute barriers to inclusion of women and girls with disabilities in both education and employment in the fields of STEM. They are structural, attitudinal, societal, political, cultural, familial, economic, and stereotypical, and also flow from systems of patriarchy and paternalism, and the law and the legal system.

Following are brief discussions of some of the most significant factors which constitute barriers to the inclusion of and participation of women and girls with disabilities in education and employment in the STEM fields.

- *Cultural Bias*: In cultures where women are expected to become wives and mothers, rather than breadwinners, resources and education are allocated primarily to male children. Women and girls with disabilities are often viewed as unable to contribute to the family unit and thus are the last family members to receive resources (WB, 2011). On the other hand, for some girls with disabilities from economically advantaged families, they are assumed to be unfit to fulfil the traditional female roles of wife and mother, and thus may have greater freedom to explore other life options (Rousso, 2003).

- *Double Discrimination*: Women and girls with disabilities face double or intersectional discrimination based on both gender and disability (as well as other identities such as race, sexuality, indigenous status, etc.). Stereotypical attitudes toward women in general and persons with disabilities contribute to misconceptions and derogations of the abilities and potential of women and girls with disabilities, re-enforcing patriarchal attitudes and assumptions (Arnade, Haefner, 2006; David, 2004).

- *Invisibility*: Girls with disabilities are often kept in the home and their births may not be registered, making them invisible to the education system, either because of assumptions about their abilities or embarrassment on the part of the family (UNICEF, 2007). Sometimes, even if the girls are attending school, they may be invisible in the classroom, especially if most students are boys (Manwaring, 2008).

- *Discriminatory, Paternalistic, and Over-protective Laws*: In several nations there are laws that explicitly discriminate against women, and more specifically women with disabilities, especially through paternalistic and over-protective provisions. In several countries, in Eastern Europe and Central Asia, laws, policies and programs prohibit women from work underground, and work above ground that is perceived to be hazardous or a reproductive health risk (*The Economist*, 2010). Such laws recreate, reinforce, and perpetuate stereotypes that women and especially women with disabilities lack the capacity to engage in biotechnology, marine biology, industrial and chemical industries, and engineering, aerospace, etc., thus depriving society of talents and skills that could improve the world (de Alwis, 2010, 2011).

- *Violence Against Women and Girls with Disabilities*: Because they are erroneously perceived as sick, helpless, asexual, and powerless, they are seen as easy targets for sexual and gender-based violence (Ortoleva and Lewis, 2012). Because they lack both general education and sexual health education, they may not recognize nor know how to respond to such violence, where to go for assistance and support, or officials may dismiss their complaints simply because of their disability (Kett and Twigg, 2007). Women and girls with disabilities are more likely to experience gender-based violence than their non-disabled sisters (Corbett et al., 1987). Often the risk of violence is heightened in residential education facilities, and violence often results in parental over-protectiveness and reluctance to send their daughters to school (Baylor College of Medicine, 2009; Marit and Hellum, 2006).

• *Pregnancy, HIV infection, and Other Results of Sexual Assault and Rape*: As a result of sexual violence and rape, girls with disabilities may become pregnant and thus drop out of school (UN General Assembly, 2006). The myth that having sex with a virgin disabled girl will cure HIV/AIDS and the risk of disabled girls being sold into prostitution also occurs because it is thought that their disabilities may limit the chances of them being able to escape or to reach out to authorities or social services for those who are trafficked. In addition, the insular mindset present in certain nations with regard to sexual assaults of children with disabilities is particularly alarming. For example, in some African nations, many individuals who were interviewed reported that although they believe that sexual violence against any child is wrong, sexual violence against a child with a disability is not that serious of an offense since that encounter would make the child feel wanted and lucky to have any sexual contact at all, and if a girl with a disability were to become pregnant she should consider herself *fortunate*, since then she would have someone to take care of her in her old age (Groce and Trasi, 2004; Yale Center for Interdisciplinary Research on AIDS, 2004; Rousso, 2003: 7).

• *Bullying and Teasing*: Disabled girls are sometimes subjected to bullying and teasing by their peers based on their disability and gender. Bullying negatively impacts a child's emotional and cognitive development. Bullying can also cause low self-esteem and latent aggressiveness or hostility that can erupt at any time. Bullying occurs in both the Global South and also is prevalent in more developed countries, such as the United States (Young et al., 2011).

• *Economic Resources for Education*: Male education is prioritized as it is believed that a male child can contribute financially to the family, and women and girls with disabilities are not viewed as worthy of an education since many assume their disabilities will preclude them from being successful (ibid.).

• *Schools in Inaccessible Locations and/or Lack of Transportation*: Schools that provide special education and/or education for children with disabilities in integrated settings are often located in cities and because families are reluctant to have their daughters go to the city from the rural home community or because accessible transportation is not available, girls with disabilities are kept at home (World

Disability Report). Boys are often seen as more independent and encouraged to engage in problem-solving skills to overcome these barriers (Burgstahler and Chang, 2007).

- *Access to Assistive Technology and Rehabilitation*: Another manifestation of the preference for males is that boys with disabilities have greater access to assistive technology, rehabilitation programs, and prosthetic and orthotic devices than girls.

- *Accessibility of School Facilities*: The inaccessibility of school facilities is often a greater barrier for girls with disabilities, as boys with disabilities are more likely to ask for assistance from other boys and are more likely to take risks. Often accessibility plans do not take gender as well as disability into account when designed and implemented (ibid.; Opini, 2008).

- *Accessible Toilet Facilities and Assistance in Toileting*: Concerns of both families and school personnel regarding provision of toileting assistance place a particular burden on girls, especially with respect to menstruation which is often a taboo topic for discussion in many countries, and access to appropriate hygiene products is nonexistent or in very short supply, resulting in increased isolation for women and girls with disabilities and further impairs their ability to attend school or work during those times of the month (Burgstahler and Chang, 2007; Mollins, 2013).

- *Availability of Special Education*: Girls with disabilities are less likely to receive special education, in some instances, because teachers expect more from boys than girls and sometimes because girls, who may be less likely to act out due to cultural control pressures, are not referred for services because of a perceived learning or other disability. In addition, many special education classes for disabled girls have limited career counselling and prepare girls for very gender-distinctive roles, such as being a receptionist, secretary, seamstress, or sheltered workshop worker. Also, many special education classes tend to have more boys than girls which results in the boys tending to bully the girls more and therefore form a more threatening environment, making it difficult for a girl with disabilities to thrive in these special education classrooms. Given that boys outnumber girls almost two to one in disability classroom settings, there is the notion that many girls may not be appropriately identified or recognized as having a disability, and therefore may not receive the specialized services they may need (Arms et al., 2008).

- *Competitive Classroom Climate and Teaching Strategies*: Competitive educational approaches are challenging for some girls with disabilities, mainly for the same reasons discussed throughout this chapter, such as bullying, being outnumbered by males in the classroom, and low self esteem. In addition, many teachers are trained to teach more life skills to students with disabilities, rather than focus on challenging them with STEM subjects (Fancasali 2000; Hammrich, Price, and Slesaransky).

- *Digital Divide*: The digital divide refers to the gap created by lack of access to and the manner and use of technology by members of various social-identity groups, including both the access to equipment, as well as the cultural issues related to economic status, race/ethnicity, gender, and disability. For example, access to mobile technology, such as a cellular telephone, can provide an increased sense of security and well-being by making it easier to contact others in a moment of distress, to better stay in touch with family and friends, to access important internet resources or to engage in economic activity. Lower participation in advanced technology programs for girls and the digital divide, results in intersectional adverse effects for girls with disabilities in STEM (Gorski, 2005; McClan-Nhlapo, 2010; Thurston, 2011).[7]

- *Belief that Girls Do Not Do Math and Science*: Women and girls with disabilities are subjected to the erroneous assumption that *girls don't do math*, and thus they are presumed not to have aptitude in these subjects and are steered into gender stereotypical subjects, as well as the *talent myth* which is based on the erroneous assumption that skills in STEM fields are an innate talent and cannot be learned (Hill et al., 2010).

- *Girls with and without Disabilities Have Limited Interaction*: Girls with disabilities have limited interaction with nondisabled girls. Both groups would benefit from such interactions, as they contribute to networking and peer support, and reduction of fear and stigma (Burgstahler and Chang, 2007; Rousso, 2003).

- *Counselling Based on Stereotypical Roles for Women and Girls*: Girls with disabilities are steered toward gender-stereotyped jobs and are less likely to be afforded vocational education than others; many counsellors hold the incorrect societal perception that girls lack the ability to do well in math and science (de Alwis, 2008).

- *Absence of Women with Disabilities as Role Models*: The invisibility of women with disabilities in educational materials, as educators and in the media creates a dearth of positive role models for girls with disabilities. However, when children with disabilities attend school, they become role models to other children with disabilities and enable them to follow suit. Similarly, their parents serve as role models for other parents who have children with disabilities, since it is often difficult for the first family in a community to enroll their child with a disability in school (Rousso, 2003; Boston Women's Health Collective, 2005).

- *Shortage of women with disabilities as mentors.* A study on the effectiveness of a mentoring relationship disclosed that women in male-dominated programs had lower academic self-esteem and career commitment than their male counterparts. The study also discovered that having the support of a mentor enhanced both of these factors. Also interesting to note is that the gender of the mentor did not matter, only that a mentor was there to support the woman (Burgstahler and Doyle, 2005);

- *The medical model of disability.* The medical model of disability evokes pity and views disabilities as a tragedy which requires the individual to be "fixed" or "rehabilitated." Rather the social model of disability has replaced the medical model under the CRPD. It is now recognized that society should instead modify and lower the external barriers in society that create unnecessary obstacles for disabled individuals. Therefore, the social model of disability should be emphasized instead of the medical model (Lord and Stein, 2008);

- *The social model of disability.* An analysis of the inclusion of women and girls with disabilities in the STEM fields must be informed by and reflective of a social model understanding of disability, in keeping with the CRPD. The preamble of the CRPD together with Article 1, introduces the social model of disability by describing disability as a condition arising from "interaction with various barriers [that] may hinder [disabled peoples'] full and effective participation in society on an equal basis with others" (CRPD, U.N. Doc/A/Res/61/106, 2006). This social model perspective does not deny the reality of impairment or its impact on an individual. It does, however, challenge the physical and social environments—and legal frameworks—to accommodate impairment as an anticipated incident of human diversity. This perspective also emphasizes, as underscored in the preamble to the CRPD, that the isolation experienced by persons with disabilities inhibits their meaningful contribution to the society, thereby undermining community cohesion and development (CRPD, U.N. Doc/A/Res/61/106, 2006, para e.).

Many policies operate on the assumption that disabling conditions are pathological and a defect and not, as a social model perspective understands, a *socially ascribed* so-called deficit. The impact of such a perspective is clear: persons with disabilities are to be avoided and/or excluded, as opposed to accommodated and included in the community (Lord, 2012; Pillay, 2010).[8] Societal responses to disability are, qua the CRPD, accommodation, inclusion and support—including for families of persons with disabilities. Policies concerning the inclusion of women and girls in STEM education and employment are required to pitch toward these ascribed principles and not, toward isolation and exclusion.

To facilitate and encourage greater participation of women and girls with disabilities in the STEM fields, the stereotypes, barriers and challenges outlined above must be addressed. This is not only necessary to advance the rights and economic status of women and girls with disabilities, but also to advance society as a whole.

Future Developments

To ensure that women and girls with disabilities benefit from and enjoy the opportunities presented by education and employment in the STEM fields, and to ensure that the digital divide and other forms of marginalization and economic poverty experienced by women and girls with disabilities are reduced, action should be taken on the international and national level by international organizations and national governments, by business and educational institutions, by non-government organizations focusing on women's rights, disability rights, technology, development and other issues, and by researchers and scholars. Some possible future developments are outlined below, but these are only some of the many steps that might be taken.

- The UN system, the International Labor Organization (ILO), the UN Educational, Scientific, and Cultural Organization (UNESCO), UN Development Program (UNDP), governments and those institutions involved in development, health (including sexual and reproductive health) (WHO, 2009) and education, employment, etc., must address the rights and needs of women and girls with disabilities in their programs and reporting (CRPD, Articles 11 and 13).

- Inclusion of women and girls with disabilities in all UN research and programs on STEM, including The CSW, UN Women, the WB, the Special Rapporteurs on Violence Against Women, on the Right to Education (Special Rapporteurs on Right to Education),[9] on Disability (UN Special Rapporteurs on Disability), on the Right of Everyone to the Enjoyment of the Highest Attainable Standard of Physical and Mental Health (Special Rapporteurs on Right of Everyone to the Enjoyment of the Highest Attainable Standard of Physical and Mental Health).[10]
- Coordination between and among the Special Rapporteur on Disability of the Commission on Social Development, and other UN special mandate holders, especially the Special Rapporteur on the Right to Education,[11] and UN entities such as the CRPD Committee, the CEDAW Committee, the CRC Committee, etc.
- Collaboration with the UNICEF Senior Advisor on children with disabilities to include girls with disabilities in education (Bieler, 2011).
- Expanded research on enrollment, outcomes and barriers to education for disabled women and girls, with collection and analysis of disaggregated data on persons with disabilities by gender, and disaggregated data on women and girls by disability status (The Washington Group on Disability Statistics).[12] For example, the Program for International Student Assessment (PISA), an international study that was launched by the OECD in 1997. It aims to evaluate education systems worldwide every three years by assessing 15-year-olds' competencies in the key subjects: reading, mathematics and science. Regrettably, PISA misses an important opportunity to consider disability in its data collection and analysis (OECD PISA).
- More research on employment, advancement in employment and barriers to employment in STEM fields for women with disabilities, with disaggregated data by gender, and disaggregated data by disability status (ibid).
- Discriminatory laws prohibiting women and persons with disabilities from engaging in the so-called "dangerous" or "non-feminine" occupations should be repealed. One law in China states that women must meet certain aesthetic requirements where men are required to meet none. For example, height and weight requirements and that women should have fully developed female characteristics and both breasts be developed and symmetrical.

• Targeted scholarships and internships for disabled women and girls should be established by governments and the private sector.

• Explicit inclusion of disabled girls in all policies and programs for girls and in all policies and programs for disabled children on the local, national and international levels.

• Comprehensive approach to violence prevention and response for disabled women and girls, including widespread sex education and accessible sexual and gender-based violence assistance facilities and programs.

• Training on bullying and teasing of girls and persons with disabilities for teachers, counselors, school administrators, students and parents, with anti-bullying policies and appropriate enforcement mechanisms.

• Targeted outreach to parents to ensure that disabled girls have access to education, so that parents are aware of education opportunities for their daughters and incorporating awareness-raising to address negative stereotypical views of the abilities and appropriate areas of study for girls with disabilities.

• Expanded development and funding of science and math camps and other informal education programs focusing on girls with disabilities.

• Teacher and counselor education that includes training on gender and disability (including human rights) and the negative impacts of stereotyping.

• Programs specifically designed for disabled girls that include mentoring programs and access to role models and self-advocacy skills, and having a focus on assets and parent involvement.

• Temporary special measures and policies. The CEDAW and the CRPD require that such special measures be expanded to STEM areas for women and girls with disabilities.

   a. Quotas—One significant tactic would be a specific legal requirement of beneficial quotas for persons with disabilities. In India, the law compels government posts to be identified and reserved for persons with disabilities and the government must reserve not less than three percent of vacancies for persons with disabilities. However rarely is this extended to STEM-related positions, especially for women with disabilities. When applied to schools, research shows that teachers with disabilities are concentrated in music teacher positions. Generally government positions which persons with disabilities hold are low-level, semi-skilled occupations with limited opportunity for advancement. For example, in China, women who work in government or managerial positions are required to retire at 55, while men can retire at 65.

b. Affirmative action—Affirmative action and incentives would help to address the legacy of discrimination against women and girls with disabilities. A Spanish Legislative Decree reduces by 50 percent the social security contribution for employers who provide training contracts for workers with disabilities. Companies that employ persons with disabilities also can submit preferential bids for government contracts.

c. Equalization levies—Such levies must be paid in cases where the obligation to hire persons with disabilities is not met. The funds raised through the levies are used to develop structural measures in favor of persons with disabilities. For example, a New Zealand law relating to Employment and Promotion of persons with disabilities calls for levies to be paid by employers employing fewer persons with disabilities than the standard employment quota rate, and this levy is paid to the Minister of Labour.

d. Tax reductions—Under Thailand's law on the Rehabilitation of Persons with Disabilities, private enterprises are entitled to a 50 percent tax reduction for training expenses connected with persons with disabilities (Thailand Vocation Training Promotion Act, 1996).

e. Public-private partnerships—Public-private partnerships should be employed to advance women and girls with disabilities in education and employment in STEM fields. UN Women has emphasized the importance of such partnerships in advancing the rights of women, including women and girls with disabilities (Bachelet, 2011).

Such temporary special measures for women and girls with disabilities in both education and employment in STEM fields would contribute to greater opportunities and reduce discrimination. Greater employment leads to greater independence, less social dependence and reduces poverty. Temporary special measures such as government tax incentives for business entities that hire persons with disabilities should require that these jobs are dispersed among various occupations, thereby assuring that women with disabilities are not only employed in low-paying stereotypical occupations, thus affording greater opportunities for employment in the STEM fields. Similar approaches should also be taken with mandatory quotas for hiring of persons with disabilities in government (Chiafalo, 2011).

Examples of Programs and Projects that Encourage and Facilitate Participation

Several programs and projects encourage and facilitate participation in STEM fields in both education and employment for women and girls in general and women and girls with disabilities in particular. Harilyn Rousso began one of the first mentoring programs focusing on women and girls with disabilities with her Networking Project for Disabled Women and Girls, which was based out of a YWCA in New York City in the United States. Over the years, several programs have been created to increase the involvement of women and girls with disabilities in the STEM fields, but many of these programs are in developed countries and thus do not reach the most disadvantaged women and girls with disabilities. Regrettably, some development programs on women's empowerment in the STEM fields fail to include women and girls with disabilities, an opportunity lost.

Armenia

Agate (Center for Women with Special Needs)[13]

The *Agate* center for women with special needs was founded by Karine Grigoryan, a disabled woman herself, in November of 2006. The mission of the Agate is to assist and improve the lives of disabled girls and women so that they become self-reliant and self-confident, and remove the negative attitudes of society toward women with disabilities. In addition, Agate focuses on psycho-social integration by organizing leadership and human rights education trainings for women with disabilities. Furthermore, Agate facilitates computer, English and handicraft trainings for these women so that they may improve their chances of finding gainful employment.

India

Girls Institute for Technology[14]

The Girls Institute for Technology (GIFT) is designed to provide an academic environment for disadvantaged and disabled girls in northern India, regardless of religion or caste. The goal of the GIFT is to teach these girls useful computer and business skills so that they can one day support themselves. The GIFT provides free scholarships, living accommodations and a familial environment to these girls, who are typically marginalized in Indian society.

Shanta Memorial Rehabilitation Centre in India[15]

This center has launched an economic empowerment campaign for women with disabilities. The focus of this program is to train women with disabilities in information and communications technology and also to increase their access to health care. In addition, a two-year project aimed at building the capacity of women with disabilities in India while promoting the rights to health and employment is currently underway. This project seeks to facilitate the economic empowerment of women with disabilities in India through skills training in information and communications technology and the use of micro credit loans under the Indian Government's Self-Help Program. The project also aims to increase access to health care services by providing opportunities for women with disabilities to learn about and advocate for health issues and services and to influence national health policies as they pertain to women with disabilities by training them in advocacy.

Pakistan

Nawabshah Disability Forum[16]

Nawabshah Disability Forum (NDF) was established in 2002 by a group of young disabled individuals who sought to advocate for the rights of those with disabilities so that they may have safe and dignified access toward basic human needs (like food, shelter, healthcare, education and employment). In addition, through the "Empowerment Center for Women with Disabilities," which is funded by the ABILIS Foundation of Finland, NDF focuses on improving the capacity of women and girls with disabilities through skill development courses in information technology, English language coaching and handicrafts. This training is all provided free of cost and the goal is to make these women and girls with disabilities self-sufficient so they do not need to depend on others for a livelihood.

United States of America

Access STEM[17]

The Alliance for Students with Disabilities in STEM (Access STEM) is a program affiliated with the University of Washington and funded by the National Science Foundation. Access STEM began in 2002 with the intent to increase the number of individuals with disabilities in STEM career fields. This program advocates for universal design principles in instruction which will allow for better educational environments not only for students with disabilities but also for all students. Access STEM focuses on exposure to and support for students with disabilities to enter STEM fields through mentoring and through collaborative resources.

ADVANCE[18]

The National Science Foundation created the ADVANCE program with the intent to increase the representation and advancement of women in academic science and engineering careers, thereby contributing to the development of a more diverse science and engineering workforce. ADVANCE encourages institutions of higher education and the broader STEM community, including professional societies and other STEM-related not-for-profit organizations, to address various aspects of STEM academic culture and institutional structure that may differentially affect women faculty and academic administrators.

Entry Point![19]

Entry Point! is a program of the American Association for the Advancement of Science that opens doors and launches women into STEM education programs and careers by offering a wide variety of internships for individuals with disabilities. For example, since 1996, this program has placed students with disabilities at summer internships with NASA, IBM, Merck, Dow Chemical, Lockheed Martin, Ball Aerospace, L'Oreal and many university research programs. Entry Point! Screens students with disabilities and matches them with a suitable internship based on their skills and needs. Entry Point! is a dynamic program in that mentoring is championed and assistive technology is readily available, but most importantly, it promotes the development of individuals with disabilities studying in the STEM fields to make them better suited for the job market.

E.X.I.T.E.[20]

Exploring Interests in Technology and Engineering (E.X.I.T.E.) is a program specifically designed to increase the number of females with disabilities in the STEM career fields through interactive exposure to science and technology. The Pacer Center, the Minnesota Parent Training and Information Center, which is funded by the U.S. Department of Education, began the E.X.I.T.E. program in 2002 with its E.X.I.T.E. Camp. The E.X.I.T.E. Camp is a five day summer camp that targets middle school age girls with disabilities and exposes them to science, math and engineering, through hands-on learning experiences that allow each girl to use all of her senses to discover how science and technology are present all around her. In 2008, E.X.I.T.E. Technology for Girls was added, which is a series of workshops during the school year to keep girls interested in science and technology after their experiences with the E.X.I.T.E. Camp by conducting hands-on and interactive experiments. Given the age of the girls targeted for these programs, there is no conclusive data yet on what percentage of the girls who attended the E.X.I.T.E. camp entered a STEM career field.

Project KITE[21]

Similar to E.X.I.T.E, Project KITE is supported by the Pacer Center. Project KITE is designed as a training curriculum for parents and teachers of young children with disabilities. Project KITE teaches these individuals how to promote the inclusion of children with disabilities through the use of technology in classrooms and in the home.

Research in Disabilities Education[22]

RDE is a program funded by the National Science Foundation which aims to broaden the participation and achievement of people with disabilities in all fields of STEM education and associated professional careers. The RDE program has been funding this objective since 1994. Projects also investigate effective practices for transitioning students with disabilities across critical academic junctures, retaining students in undergraduate and graduate STEM degree programs, and graduating students with STEM associate, baccalaureate and graduate degrees. Research project results inform the delivery of innovative, transformative and successful practices employed by the Alliances for Students with Disabilities in STEM to increase the number of students with disabilities completing associate, undergraduate and graduate degrees in STEM and to increase the number of students with disabilities entering the United States science and engineering workforce. Additionally, RDE funds a virtual space for high school and college students with disabilities to enter for virtual tutoring, mentoring, and social networking. Their teachers and professors can enter the same space for training, professional development, and resources. K-12 schools and universities are using Universal Design for Learning in math and science classes to accommodate education for students with disabilities.

Research on Gender in Science and Engineering (GSE)[23]

The GSE program is another National Science Foundation program that supports efforts to understand and address gender-based differences in STEM education and workforce participation through research, the diffusion of research-based innovations, and extension services in education that will lead to a larger and more diverse domestic science and engineering workforce. Typical projects will contribute to the knowledge base addressing gender-related differences in learning and in the educational experiences that affect student interest, performance, and choice of careers; how pedagogical approaches and teaching styles, curriculum, student services, and institutional culture contribute to causing or closing gender gaps that persist in certain fields.

Science Camp for Interested Visually Impaired Students[24]

Science Camp for Interested Visually Impaired Students (SCI-VIS) makes science camp accessible to students with visual impairments. The camp is one week long and takes place at the United States Space and Rocket Center in Huntsville, Alabama. The camp has four separate programs: Space Camp, Space Academy, Advanced Academy focus on space travel and Aviation Challenge. These programs target students from grade 4 to grade 12.

Techgirlz[25]

Techgirlz is an organization based in Philadelphia, Pennsylvania in the United States that uses hands-on STEM activities to engage young girls who are deaf or hard-of-hearing to encourage these girls to enter technology based fields.

Zambia

Women Connect! of the Zambia National Association of Disabled Women[26]

Women Connect! of the Zambia National Association of Disabled Women focuses on teaching women and girls with disabilities how to use e-mail and the Internet, in particular how to conduct health and medical research. Women Connect! reaches out to women and girls with disabilities through seminars, workshops, education and employment training. Women Connect! has made significant strides in informing women with disabilities living with HIV/AIDS in Zambia about their treatment options and how to better care for themselves and avoid infecting others.

Although a few of the programs described above are focused specifically on women and girls with disabilities, most are focused on women generally and appear to have no disability-inclusive elements, or the programs are focused on persons with disabilities generally. If these types of programs would make the effort to incorporate a gender-sensitive, disability-inclusive approach, they would do well to address some of the many concerns outlined in this chapter. Additionally, the innovative projects that have a gender-sensitive, disability-inclusive approach can serve as best practice models that can be implemented in a variety of situations, all with the objective of advancing the economic empowerment of women and girls with disabilities.

***

This chapter has discussed numerous factors that constitute barriers to the inclusion of women and girls with disabilities in both education and employment in the fields of STEM. Efforts to reduce and eliminate these barriers must focus on numerous aspects: structural, attitudinal, societal, political, cultural, familial, economic, stereotypical, as well as the legal system and institutions of patriarchy and paternalism. Reforms must be undertaken on numerous levels from the local, national, regional and international levels and reforms must be addressed in various spheres, ranging from the education system, families, media, government, private businesses, and must also engage Disabled Peoples Organizations, women's rights organizations and the entire community. The result would be of benefit to all, especially to women and girls with disabilities who would have increased educational opportunities, greater employment, improved self-confidence, reduced likelihood of experiencing gender-based violence, economic empowerment and increased ability to provide for their families, as well as engage in the political system. The community as a whole would benefit from the contributions of women scientists, technology experts, engineers and mathematicians and families would benefit from mothers who have more skills to provide for their families and perform daily household tasks. This is a win–win situation for all.

Notes

1. For more information, please visit: http://www.un.org/disabilities/default. asp?navid=47&pid=1556 and http://www.WomenEnabled.org/science. html (downloaded on 22.12.2014; the side event was organized by this author and co-sponsored by the Governments of Argentina, the Philippines, South Africa and the Secretariat for the UNCRPD. This side event took place on February, 23, 2011 during the 55th Session of the CSW, from 1:15–2:45 pm in the United Nations North Lawn Building, Conference Room 4 located in New York City.)
2. The side event was organized by Women Enabled, Inc., and co-sponsored by the India Network of Women with Disabilities and the UN Women's

Report Network. This side event took place on March 14, 2014 during the 58th Session of the CSW from 12:30 to 2:00 p.m. in the United Nations Church Center, Boss Room located in New York city. For more information, photographs, panelists statements and biographies, see http://www. WomenEnabled.org/science.html (downloaded on 23.12.2014).

3. Comm. on the Status of Women, Econ. and Soc. Council, Moderator's Rep. on its 58th Sess. Review Theme Panel, Mar. 21, 2014, Mar. 10 to 21 2014, U.N. Doc. Available online at. http://www.un.org/ga/search/view_doc. asp?symbol=E/CN.6/2014/INF/5 (downloaded on 26.12.2014).

4. See UN General Assembly (1996); see also UNHRC (2000) stating:

> The right of everyone under article 16 to be recognized everywhere as a person before the law is particularly pertinent for women, who often see it curtailed by reason of sex or marital status. This right implies . . . that women may not be treated as objects to be given, together with the property of the deceased husband, to his family. States must provide information on laws or practices that prevent women from being treated or from functioning as full legal persons and the measures taken to eradicate laws or practices that allow such treatment.

5.   While biological differences between women and men may lead to differences in health status, there are societal factors which are determinative of the health status of women and men and which can vary among women themselves. For that reason, special attention should be given to the health needs and rights of women belonging to vulnerable and disadvantaged groups, such as migrant women, refugee and internally displaced women, the girl child and older women, women in prostitution, indigenous women and women with physical or mental disabilities.

6. The factors discussed in Section IV, which constitute barriers to the inclusion of and participation of women and girls with disabilities in education and employment in the STEM fields are inspired by the research and writings of prominent scholars in the field of women and girls with disabilities, education, employment and STEM, including Harilyn Rousso, Donna M. Mertens and Jolene Kay Jesse, as well as the contributions of those on the CSW STEM 55th Session panel. Akiko Ito, Harilyn Rousso, Ivonne Mosquera, Linda Thurston and Rangita de Silva de Alwis as well as other resources on women and girls with disabilities referenced herein. Akiko Ito is Chief of the Secretariat for the CRPD and UN Focal Point on Disability. She is also a Departmental Focal Point for Women of the Department of Economic and Social Affairs of the United Nations. Ms Ito has lectured and published extensively on issues concerning disabilities and human rights at the United Nations. Harilyn Rousso is an educator, psychotherapist, writer, filmmaker and advocate for disability rights. She is the founder of the Networking Project for

Disabled Women and Girls of the YWCA of New York City and the author of Double Jeopardy and Producer of Positive Images: Portraits of Women with Disabilities. Ivonne Mosquera is a Program Manager for Information Systems, Dow Chemical, a former U.S. National Science Foundation Fellow and the U.S. National Visually Impaired Female Triathlon Champion. Her personal website is http://www.iminmotion.net/index.html (downloaded on 28.01.2015). Rangita de Silva de Alwis is a director of human rights programs, and a Wellesley Centers for Women Susan McGee Bailey Research Scholar. She has published widely on gender, human rights and law reform in United Nations publications and law review journals. Her most recent work includes China's New Gender and Law Developments: Opportunities and Challenges to be published by the Yale Journal of Law and Feminism and A Review of Women's Human Rights Lawmaking in Eastern Europe and Central Asia to be published by the UNFPA. Dr de Alwis has a doctorate in law (SJD) from Harvard Law School. Linda Thurston is a project manager for Education and Careers in STEM for People with Disabilities a program of the National Science Foundation and on leave from her position as Assistant Dean of the School of Education at Kansas State University.

7. See Charlotte McClain-Nhlapo. July 1, 2010. "Talking Points for the ministerial Round Table: Accessibility ICT: a tool for empowering Women with Disabilities," *The Global Initiative for Inclusive ICTs*. Available online at http://g3ict.com/events/schedule/event_overview/p/eventId_198/id_537 (downloaded on 28.12.2014); stating "there is an increased concern about the impact on those left on the other side of the digital divide—the division between the information 'haves' and 'have nots'." Most women with disabilities living in developing countries are on the side of the divide—that is very distant from the information age. If access to and use of these technologies is directly linked to social and economic development, then it is imperative to ensure that women with disabilities in developing countries understand the significance of these technologies and use them... Therefore, 'engendering ICTs' is the process of identifying and removing gender disparities in the access to and use of ICTs, as well as of adapting ICTs to the special needs, constraints, and opportunities of women including women with disabilities" (February 23, 2011) available online at http://www.WomenEnabled.org under "Our Issues" and "Science, Technology, Engineering and Math", Women with Disabilities Australia, Bridging the Digital Divide'—A Resource Manual of Initiatives Enabling People in Disadvantaged Groups to Gain Access to the Internet. Available online at http://www.wwda.org.au/digital.htm (downloaded on 27.12.2014).

8. Janet E. Lord, "The Convention on the Rights of Persons with Disabilities and Antenatal Screening for Disability," Expert Opinion developed for Savings Downs, New Zealand, 2012 (on file with authors).
   This is summed up by the United Nations High Commissioner for Human Rights as follows: "The focus is no longer on a perceived "wrongness" of

the person, with the impairment seen as a matter of deficiency or disease. On the contrary, the Convention views disability as a 'pathology of society,' that is, as the result of the failure of societies to be inclusive and to accommodate individual differences. Societies need to change, not the individual, and the Convention provides a road map for such change." High Commissioner for Human Rights, NavanethemPillay, Foreword, *Monitoring the Convention on the Rights of Persons with Disabilities: Guidance for Human Rights Monitors* 5 (2010 [hereinafter Monitoring Handbook]). Policies and programs to address gender-based violence are subject to review under the UNCRPD for States Parties to the UNCRPD and must conform also to its purpose which is "to promote, protect and ensure the full and equal enjoyment of all human rights and fundamental freedoms by all women with disabilities, and to promote respect for their inherent dignity."

9. For information on the mandate of the Special Rapporteur on the Right to Education, see: http://www2.ohchr.org/english/issues/education/rapporteur/index.htm (downloaded on 28.01.2015). For information on Special Rapporteur on Violence against women its causes and consequences, see http://www2.ohchr.org/english/issues/women/rapporteur (downloaded on 23.12.2014).

10. For information on the Special Rapporteur on the Right of Everyone to the Enjoyment of the Highest Attainable Standard of Physical and Mental Health, see: http://www2.ohchr.org/english/issues/health/right/ (downloaded on 20.03.2011). For information on Special Rapporteur on Disability, see www.srdisability.org (downloaded on 26.12.2014).

11. For more information on the mandate of the Special Rapporteur on Disability, see "UN Special Rapporteur on Disability." Available online at http://www.srdisability.org/en/aboutus.html (downloaded on 28.01.2015).

12. *See generally* The Washington Group on Disability Statistics, which is charged with promoting and coordinating international cooperation by developing sets of general disability measures, suitable for use in censuses, sample based national surveys, or other statistical formats. Available online at http://unstats.un.org/unsd/methods/citygroup/washington.htm (downloaded on 27.12.2014) and http://www.cdc.gov/nchs/citygroup.htm (downloaded on 27.12.2014).

13. For more information, please visit: www.agatengo.com/ (downloaded on 28.01.2015).

14. For more information, please visit: http://www.mcdeanfoundation.org/docs/GIFT_Info.pdf (downloaded on 28.01.2015).

15. For more information, please visit: http://www.smrcorissa.org/content.php?id=64 (downloaded on 23.12.2014).

16. For more information, please visit: http://www.ndfpakistan.org/ (downloaded on 23.12.2014).

17. For more information, please visit: http://www.washington.edu/doit/programs/accessstem/overview (downloaded on 28.01.2015).

18. For more information, please visit: http://www.nsf.gov/funding/pgm_summ.jsp?pims_id=5383 (downloaded on 25.12.2014).
19. For more information, please visit: http://ehrweb.aaas.org/entrypoint/ (downloaded on 28.12.2014).
20. For more information, please visit: http://www.pacer.org/stc/exite/ (downloaded on 28.12.2014).
21. For more information, please visit: http://www.pacer.org/stc/kite/ (downloaded on 28.12.2014).
22. For more information, please visit: http://www.nsf.gov/funding/pgm_summ.jsp?pims_id=5482 (downloaded on 28.12.2014).
23. For more information, please visit: http://www.nsf.gov/funding/pgm_summ.jsp?pims_id=5475 (downloaded on 28.12.2014).
24. For more information, please visit: http://www.tsbvi.edu/space/ (downloaded on 27.12.2014).
25. For more information, please visit: http://techgirlz.org/ (downloaded on 28.12.2014).
26. For more information, please visit: http://www.un.org/disabilities/default.asp?id=1516 (downloaded on 04.02.2015).

Bibliography

Primary Sources

Arms, Emily, Jill Bickett, and Victoria Graf. 2008. "Gender Bias and Imbalance: Girls in US Special Education Programmes," Gender & Education, 20 (4): 349–359.

Bachelet, Michelle. 2011. "Statement to the First Regular Session of the Executive Board, United Nations Entity for Gender Equality and the Empowerment of Women." Available online at http://www.unwomen.org/en/news/stories/2011/1/statement-to-the-first-regular-session-of-the-executive-board-united-nations-entity-for-gender-equa (downloaded on 04.02.2015).

Baylor College of Medicine. 2009. "Violence Against Women with Disabilities—Prevalence." Available online at http://www.bcm.edu/crowd/?pmid=1338 (downloaded on 30.12.2014).

Beijing Declaration and Platform for Action. September 15, 1995. Fourth World Conference on Women, A/CONF/177/20. Available online at http://www.un.org/womenwatch/daw/beijing/platform/declar.htm (downloaded on 28.12.2014).

Berman-Bieler, Rosanglea. February 17, 2011. Letter of the Senior Advisor on Children with Disabilities, UNICEF. Available online at http://www.usicd.org/index.cfm/news_unicef-senior-adviser-on-children-with-disabilities-rosangela-berman-bieler (downloaded on 27.12.2014).

Blanck, Peter. 2007. "Defying Double Discrimination," Georgetown Journal of International Affairs, 8 (1): 95–104.

Boston Women's Health Collective. 2005. "Our Bodies, Ourselves: A New Edition for a New Era." Available online at http://www.ourbodiesourselves.org/book/excerpt.asp?id=2 (downloaded on 29.12.2014).

Burgstahler, Sheryl and Andrea Doyle. 2005. "Gender Differences in Computer-Mediated Communication Among Adolescents with Disabilities: A Case Study," *Disability Studies Quarterly*, 25 (2). Available online at http://www.dsq-sds.org/article/view/552/729 (downloaded on 13.05.2013).

Burgstahler, Sheryl and Chuan Chang. 2007. "Gender Differences in Perceived Value of a Program to Promote Academic and Career Success for Students with Disabilities," *Journal of Science Education for Students with Disability*, 12 (1). Available online at https://library.rit.edu/oajournals/index.php/jsesd/article/viewFile/135/103 (downloaded on 24.06.2013).

CEDAW. December 18, 1979. G.A. Res. 34/180, U.N. Doc. A/RES/34/180. Available online at http://www.un.org/womenwatch/daw/cedaw/text/econvention.htm (downloaded on 29.12.2014).

———. 1991. General Recommendation 18. 10th session. Available online at http://www.un.org/womenwatch/daw/cedaw/recommendations/recomm.htm (downloaded on 27.12.2014).

———. 1994. Report on its 13th session, April 12, Para 26. UN Doc. A/49/38.

———. 1999. General Recommendation No. 24, para. 25, 20th session. Available online at http://www.un.org/womenwatch/daw/cedaw/recommendations/recomm.htm (downloaded on 27.12.2014).

Chiafalo, Samantha. March 21, 2011. "What's Your QQ (Quota Quotient)? Managing Disability Employment Obligations Worldwide," *ORC Networks*. Available online at http://www.orcnetworks.com/networks/breakthrough-diversity-network/news/whats-your-qq-quota-quotient-managing-disability-employ (downloaded on 29.12.2014).

Corbett, Katherine, Susan Shurberg Klein, and Jennifer Luna Bregante. 1987. "The Role of Sexuality and Sex Equity in the Education of Disabled Women," *Peabody Journal of Education*, 64 (4): 198–205.

CSW. 2011. Report of the Economic and Social Council on its 55th session, U.N. Doc. E/2011/27, E/CN.6/2011/12.

———. 2014. Moderator's Report on the Economic and Social Council's 58th Session, Review Theme Panel, March 21, 2014, March 10–21, 2014, U.N. Doc. Available online at http://www.un.org/ga/search/view_doc.asp?symbol=E/CN.6/2014/INF/5 (downloaded on 28.12.2014).

David, Natacha. 2004. "Women with Disabilities—Dual Discrimination," in Jim Baker (ed.), *Trade Unions and Workers with Disabilities: Promoting Decent Work, Combating Discrimination. In Labour Education.* 2004/4 No. 137: 17–21.

de Alwis, Rangita de Silva. 2008. "Disability Rights, Gender, and Development: A Resource Tool for Action," Report of the Secretariat, United Nations Population Fund and Wellesley Center for Women. Available online at http://www.un.org/disabilities/documents/Publication/UNWCW%20MANUAL.pdf (downloaded on 28.12.2014).

de Alwis, Rangita de Silva. 2010. "Opportunities and Challenges for Gender-Based Legal Reform in China," *East Asia Law Review*, 5 (2): 197–301.

———. 2011. "Examining Gender Stereotype in New Work/Family Reconcilliation Policy: The Creation of a New Paradigm for Egalitarian Legislation," *Duke Journal of Gender Law and Policy*, 18 (Spring): 305–334. Available online at: http://scholarship.law.duke.edu/djglp/vol18/iss2/3 (downloaded on 14.06.2013).

Fancasali, Cheri. 2000. "What We Know About Girls, STEM, and After School Programs," Education Equity Concepts Summary Report. Available online at http://www.jhuapl.edu/mesa/resources/docs/whatweknow.pdf (downloaded on 30.12.2014).

Gorski, P. 2005. "Education Equity and the Digital Divide," *AACE Journal*, 13 (1): 3–45.

Groce, Nora Ellen and Reshma Trasi. 2004. "Rape of Individuals with Disability: AIDS and the Folk Belief of 'Virgin Cleansing'," Global Health Division, Yale School of Public Health. Available online at http://aidslex.org/site_documents/DB-0021E.pdf (downloaded on 26. 03.2011).

Hammrich, Penny Lynda Price and Grace Slesaransky-Poe. 2001. "'Daughters with Disabilities: Breaking Down Barriers," *Electronic Journal of Special Education*, 5 (4). Available online at http://ejse.southwestern.edu/article/view/7666/5433 (downloaded on 01.04.2013).

Hoem, Kvam Marit and Braathen Stine Hellum. 2006. "Violence and Abuse Against Women with Disabilities in Malawi," SINTEF Research Report A576. Available online at http://www.sintef.no/upload/Helse/Levek%C3%A5r%20og%20tjenester/AbuseMalawi.pdf (downloaded on 29.12.2014).

Hill, Catherine, Christianne Corbett, and Andresse St. Rose. 2010. "Why So Few? Women in Science, Technology, Engineering and Math," AAUW. Available online at http://www.aauw.org/resource/why-so-few-women-in-science-technology-engineering-mathematics/ (downloaded on 28.01.2015).

Huebler, Francis. 2012. "Adult and Youth Literacy in 2010," *International Education Statistics*. Available online at http://huebler.blogspot.com/2012/05/literacy.html (downloaded on 30.12.2014).

Jans, Lita and Susan Stoddard. 1999. "Chartbook on Women and Disability in the United States," Report of the US National Institute on Disability and Rehabilitation Research. Available online at http://www.infouse.com/disabilitydata/womendisability/ (downloaded on 29.12.2014).

Kett, Maria and J. Twigg. 2007. "Disability and Disasters: Towards an Inclusive Approach," *International Federation of Red Cross & Red Crescent Societies*. Available online at http://www.ifrc.org/Docs/pubs/disasters/wdr2007/WDR2007-English-4.pdf (downloaded on 26.03.2011).

Lord, Janet E. 2012. "The Convention on the Rights of Persons with Disabilities and Antenatal Screening for Disability," Expert Opinion developed for Savings Downs, New Zealand.

Lord, Janet E. and Michael Ashley Stein. 2008. "The Domestic Incorporation of Human Rights Law and the United Nations Convention on the Rights of

Persons with Disabilities," *Washington University Law Review Association*, 83: 449, 460.

Manwaring, Joanne S. 2008. "Wendy or Tinkerbell? How the Underrepresentation of Girls Impacts Gender Roles in Preschool Education," *Teaching Exceptional Children*, 40 (5): 60–65.

Mertens, Donna M., Amy Wilson, and Judith Mounty. 2007. "Gender Equity for People with Disabilities," in Susan S. Klein (ed.), *Handbook for Achieving Gender Equity through Education*, pp. 583–604.

McClanNhlapo, Charlotte. 2010. "Talking Points for the Ministerial Round Table: Accessibility ICT: A Tool for Empowering Women with Disabilities," *The Global Initiative for Inclusive ICTs*. Available online at http://g3ict.com/events/schedule/event_overview/p/eventId_198/id_537 (downloaded on 28.12.2014).

Mollins, Julie. 2013. "Menstruation Taboo Puts 300 Million Women in India at Risk." Available online at http://www.trust.org/alertnet/news/menstruation-taboo-puts-300-mln-women-in-india-at-risk-experts/ (downloaded on 30.12.2014).

Mosquera, Ivonne. February 23, 2011. "Expanding Access to Education and Employment Opportunities for Girls and Women with Disabilities in Science, Technology, Engineering and Math (STEM) Strategy for Action!," panel presentation at the 55th session of the UNCSW panel [under "Our Issues" and "Science, Technology, Engineering and Math (STEM) Strategy for Action].

Ortoleva, Stephanie and Hope Lewis. 2012. "Forgotten Sisters—A Report on Violence Against Women with Disabilities: An Overview of its Nature, Scope, Causes and Consequences," Northeastern University School of Law Research Paper No. 104-2012. Available online at http://ssrn.com/abstract=2133332 (downloaded on 30.12.2014).

OECD PISA. http://www.oecd.org/pisa/ (downloaded on 30.12.2014).

Opini, Bathseba M. 2008. "Strengths and Limitations of Ontario Post-Secondary Education Accessibility Plans: A Review of One University Accessibility Plan," *International Journal of Inclusive Education*, 12 (2): 127–149.

Pillay, Navanethem. 2010. "Foreword," in Monitoring the Convention on the Rights of Persons with Disabilities: Guidance for Human Rights Monitors, p. 5. New York: Office of the United Nations High Commissioner for Human Rights.

Rousso, Harilyn. 2003. "Education for All: A Gender and Disability Perspective." Available online at http://unesdoc.unesco.org/images/0014/001469/146931e.pdf (downloaded on 28.01.2015).

———. 2003. "Gender and Education for All: The Leap to Equality," *UNESCO, Education for All Global Monitoring Report*, Background Paper. Available online at http://unesdoc.unesco.org/images/0014/001469/146931e.pdf (downloaded on 28.12.2014).

Sigrid, Arnade and Sabine Haefner. 2006. "Gendering the Comprehensive and Integral Int'l Convention on the Protection and Promotion of the Rights and Dignity of Persons with Disabilities." Berlin: Disabled Peoples' International.

The Economist. June 17, 2010. "Women's Economic Opportunity." Available online at http://graphics.eiu.com/upload/weo_report_June_2010.pdf (downloaded on 28.01.2015).

The Washington Group on Disability Statistics. Available online at http://unstats.un.org/unsd/methods/citygroup/washington.htm and http://www.cdc.gov/nchs/citygroup.htm (downloaded on 30.12.2014).

Thailand. 1996. Vocation Training Promotion Act.

Thurston, Linda P. February 23, 2011. "Expanding Access to Education and Employment Opportunities for Girls and Women with Disabilities in Science, Technology, Engineering and Math (STEM) Strategy for Action!, National Science Foundation Panel Presentation at the 55th Session of the UN CSW panel, "Expanding Access to Education and Employment Opportunities for Girls and Women with Disabilities in Science, Technology, Engineering and Math (STEM) Strategy for Action!" Available online at http://www.women-enabled.org/pdfs/SummaryNotesSideEventonScience,Technology&MathW omenwithDisabilitiesFebruary23,201155thSessionUNCommissionontheStatu sofWomenpanel.pdf?attredirects=0 (downloaded on 28.01.2015).

Women.org, USAID, and Australian Aid. March 30, 2012. "Striving and Surviving: Exploring the Lives of Women at the Base of the Pyramid." Available online at http://www.mwomen.org/Research/striving-surviving-exploring-the-lives-of-women-at-the-base-of-the-pyramid (downloaded on 30.12.2014).

Women with Disabilities Australia. 2002. "Bridging the Digital Divide—A Resource Manual of Initiatives Enabling People in Disadvantaged Groups to Gain Access to the Internet." Available online at http://www.wwda.org.au/digital.htm (downloaded on 27.12.2014).

UNCRC. September 2, 1990. G.A. Res. 44/25, U.N. Doc.A/RES/44/25. Available online at http://www.un.org/documents/ga/res/44/a44r025.htmss (downloaded on 28.01.2015).

———. July 1, 2003. "Adolescent Health and Development in the Context of the Convention on the Rights of the Child," 33rd Session, General Comment No. 4 (CRC/GC/203/4).

———. April 18, 2011. "The Right of the Child to Freedom from All Forms of Violence," General Comment No. 13 (CRC/C/GC/13).

———. 2011. "UN Convention on the Rights of the Child," General Recommendation 13.

UNCRPD. "Convention on the Rights of Persons with Disabilities." Available online at http://www.un.org/disabilities/convention/facts.shtml (downloaded on 30.12.2014).

———. December 6, 2006. G.A. Res. 61/611, U.N. Doc.A/RES/61/611. Available online at http://www.un.org/disabilities/convention/conventionfull.shtml (downloaded on 29.12.2014).

———. December 13, 2006. G.A. Res. 61/106, U.N. Doc. A/RES/61/106, art.1. Available online at http://www.unhcr.org/refworld/docid/45f973632.html (downloaded on 29.12.2014).

UN General Assembly. 1996. Resolution 2200 (XXI) Art. 14, 15,16. UN Doc. A/Res/21/2200.

———. 2006. *"Report of the Independent Expert for the United Nations Study on Violence Against Children,"* 61st session, August 29, A/61/299.

———. 2010a. "Keeping the Promises: Realizing the MDGs for Persons with Disabilities Towards 2015 and Beyond," A/65/173, Report of the Secretary-General, 65th Session, July 26, 2010.

———. 2010b. "Realizing the MDGs for Persons with Disabilities Towards 2015 and Beyond," A/65/448 Draft Resolution v., 65th session, November 9, 2010.

UNHRC. March 29, 2000. "Equality of Rights Between Men and Women," Para 19, General Comment No. 28. Art.3, UN Doc. CCPR/C/21/Rev.1/ADD.10

———. 2005. "Legal Capacity," para. 14, unpublished background conference document (on file with author). Available online at http://www2.ohchr.org/SPdocs/CRPD/DGD21102009/OHCHR_BP_Legal_Capacity.Doc (downloaded on 29.12.2014).

———. 2009. Annual Report of the UN High Commissioner for Human Rights and Secretary General: Thematic Study by the Office of the UN High Commissioner for Human Rights on Enhancing Awareness and Understanding of the Convention on the Rights of Persons with Disability, UN Doc. A/HRC/10/48, January 26.

UN Secretary-General. 2012. "Progress in Mainstreaming a Gender Perspective in the Development, Implementation and Evaluation of National Policies and Programmes, with a Particular Focus on Access and Participation of Women and Girls to Education, Training, Science and Technology, Including for the Promotion of Women's Equal Access to Full Employment and Decent Work," Report of the Secretary-General, 62, U.N. Doc. E/CN.6/2011/5.

UN Women. 2014. Commission on Status of Women "Review Theme," 58th Session. Available online at http://www.unwomen.org/en/csw/csw58-2014 (downloaded on 28.01.2015).

———. 2011a. "Priority Theme," 55th Session. Available online at http://www.un.org/womenwatch/daw/csw/55sess.htm#priority (downloaded on 22.02.2013).

———. 2011b. "Preparation," 55th Session. Available online at http://www.un.org/womenwatch/daw/csw/55sess.htm#prep (downloaded on 22.02.2013).

———. 2011c. "Agreed Conclusions," CSW 55th session. Available online at http://www.un.org/womenwatch/daw/csw/csw55/agreed_conclusions/AC_CSW55_E.pdf (downloaded on 22.02.2013).

UNESCO. 2010. "Adult and Youth Literacy: Global Trends in Gender Parity," UNESCO Institute for Statistics. Available online at http://www.uis.unesco.org/FactSheets/Documents/Fact_Sheet_2010_Lit_EN.pdf (downloaded on 22.12.2014).

UNICEF. 2007. "Promoting the Rights of Children with Disabilities," Innocenti Digest No. 13.

World Bank (WB). 2009. *Women with Disability*. Washington D.C.: The World Bank. Available online at http://web.worldbank.org/WBSITE/EXTER-NAL/TOPICS/EXTSOCIALPROTECTION/EXTDISABILITY/0,,cont entMDK:20193528~menuPK:418895~pagePK:148956~piPK:216618~theSit ePK:282699,00.html (downloaded on 23.12.2014).

———. 2011. "Main Report, vol. 1," in *World Report on Disability*. Washington D.C.: The World Bank.

World Health Organization (WHO). 2009. "Promoting Sexual and Reproductive Health for Persons with Disabilities," WHO/UNFPA Guidance Note. Available online at http://whqlibdoc.who.int/publications/2009/9789241598682_eng.pdf (downloaded on 21.12.2014).

UN. "Special Rapporteur on Disability of the Commission on Social Development." Available online at http://www.un.org/disabilities/default.asp?id=183 (downloaded on 21.12.2014).

UN. "Special Rapporteur on Disability." Available online at http://www.srdisability.org/ (downloaded on 21.12.2014).

UN. "Special Rapporteur on Right to Education." Available online at http://www2.ohchr.org/english/issues/education/rapporteur/index.htm (downloaded on).

UN. "Special Rapporteur on the Right of Everyone to the Enjoyment of the Highest Attainable Standard of Physical and Mental Health. Available online at http://www2.ohchr.org/english/issues/health/right/ (downloaded on 28.01.2015).

UN. "Special Rapporteur on Violence Against Women: Its Causes and Consequences." Available online at http://www2.ohchr.org/english/issues/women/rapporteur/ (downloaded on 23.12.2014).

Yale Center for Interdisciplinary Research on AIDS. 2004. "HIV/AIDS and Disability Global Survey." Available online at http://cira.med.yale.edu/global-survey/about_us.html (downloaded on 22.12.2014).

Young, Jonathan, Ari Neeman, and Sarah Glaser. 2011. "Bullying and Students with Disabilities," in *National Disability Policy: A Progress Report*. Washington, D.C.: National Council on Disability.

Web Sources

http://ehrweb.aaas.org/entrypoint/ (downloaded on 20.12.2014).
http://techgirlz.org/ (downloaded on 21.12.2014).
http://www.mcdeanfoundation.org/docs/GIFT_Info.pdf (downloaded on 21.12.2014).
http://www.ndfpakistan.org/ (downloaded on 21.12.2014).
http://www.nsf.gov/funding/pgm_summ.jsp?pims_id=5383 (downloaded on 21.12.2014).
http://www.nsf.gov/funding/pgm_summ.jsp?pims_id=5475 (downloaded on 21.12.2014).

http://www.nsf.gov/funding/pgm_summ.jsp?pims_id=5482 (downloaded on 21.12.2014).

http://www.orcnetworks.com/networks/breakthrough-diversity-network/ news/whats-your-qq-quota-quotient-managing-disability-employ (downloaded on 22.12.2014).

http://www.pacer.org/stc/exite/ (downloaded on 22.12.2014).

http://www.pacer.org/stc/kite/ (downloaded on 23.12.2014).

http://www.piwh.org/pdfs/wc2002.pdf (downloaded on 28.01.2015).

http://www.smrcorissa.org/content.php?id=64 (downloaded on 28.01.2015).

http://www.tsbvi.edu/space/ (downloaded on 28.01.2015).

http://www.undp.org/ (downloaded on 22.12.2014).

http://www.unesco.org/new/en/unesco/ (downloaded on 22.12.2014).

http://www.washington.edu/doit/Stem/about.html (downloaded on 28.01.2015).

http://www.WomenEnabled.org (downloaded on 28.01.2015).

http://www.wwda.org.au/digital.htm (downloaded on 28.01.2015).

10

Gendered Constructions of Work and Disability in
Contemporary India: Discursive and Empirical Perspectives*

Renu Addlakha

This chapter examines the intersections between work, disability,
and gender with specific reference to contemporary India. This
work is the outcome of several years of ongoing research in the areas of
health, gender, and disability from a largely social–anthropological perspective (Addlakha, 2008; Addlakha et al., 2009; and Addlakha, 2011).
It is interesting to note that the impressive volume of research in labor
history and labor economics in India, notwithstanding the issue of disability is more or less invisible in these disciplinary discourses. Indeed,
while subalternity has influenced academic work therein through the
categories of caste and gender, disability continues to be discursively
absent. One of the important questions that this chapter asks is how
one can capture, historically, and cross-culturally, an evolving category
that is itself the product of the interplay of multiple discourses emanat-
ing from diverse arenas, such as biomedicine, identity politics, human
rights, and international law.

There is a general consensus that a core defining parameter of disability
(either as cause or consequence) is functional limitation, be it a product of
physical/mental impairment or social, economic, cultural, and attitudinal
barriers or both. The productive capacities of disabled persons have been
suspect. Historically, in India, as elsewhere in the world, they have been

* The research for this chapter was conducted during October and December
2010 at the International Research Centre for Work and Human Life Cycle in
Global History, Institute of Asian and African Studies, Humboldt University, Berlin
(Germany). I acknowledge with gratitude the support offered by the institute.

portrayed as medical anomalies, helpless victims, and a lifelong burden for family and society. Disability is configured to involve considerable social investment in care work to enable the survival of persons regarded as biologically unfit and economically unproductive. Disabled persons carry the taint of partial personhood, casting them with a die of weakness, incapacity, incompetence, passivity, dependence, and socioeconomic futility. When a gender lens is brought to bear on this configuration, then the situation of disabled women becomes starker, since a disabled woman is also considered incapable of fulfilling the normative feminine roles of homemaker, wife, and mother. Reproductive and care work are critical components of social constructions of femininity, which means that disabled women are not only considered incapable of productive work like their male counterparts, but they are also normatively excluded from the domain of domestic work and child care.

One of the major factors contributing to the segregation of disabled persons in medical institutions, special schools, and sheltered employment is the almost universal and transhistorical association between disability and functional incapacity. That is why the first step toward ensuring equality of opportunity to disabled persons necessarily involves enhancing educational and employment opportunities in order to promote economic self-reliance. Many disability advocates and scholars bemoan the seeming *overemphasis* on issues of education and employment, resulting in the neglect of other critical life issues, such as sexuality, parenthood, leisure, and recreation. But to my reading, beyond facile generalizations, the intersection between work and disability remains largely under-explored. Consequently, the first section of this chapter delineates the multiple intersections between work and disability, with particular reference to the contemporary Indian context.

How does one explore disability and work in a life cycle perspective? Drawing upon my training in anthropology, the author has examined in great detail the work and career aspirations of young disabled persons in Delhi at school and university levels. These include students in special schools, general schools, and school dropouts. Following up the thread of career in the life course, the author has also interviewed a large number of employed and self-employed disabled persons. The resulting data set comprises over 240 in-depth, multiple, qualitative interviews with 80 informants (using the life history method) comprising an equal number of men and women, covering the major categories of disabilities. An attempt has been made to incorporate different age and occupational categories (ranging from college teachers to roadside vendors, housewives, and students, among others), and caste groups. Comparing the aspirations of young people of both genders for career advancement and social mobility with the actual experiences of seeking market integration and surviving in nondisabled-friendly work environments make for a thought-provoking commentary on the contemporary Indian neoliberal economic system and sociocultural realities. Of course, it will not be possible to do a detailed analysis of the data for this chapter, but some broad trends can be observed, which are highlighted in the concluding section of this chapter.

Unpacking Disability

A number of social and historical factors after the Second World War led to disability, being recognized as a valid category of oppression: countries in Western Europe, Japan, and the United States were faced with the challenging task of rehabilitating a huge number of disabled soldiers. The United Nations (UN) Declaration of Human Rights (1948) and the social welfare paradigm dominating the policies of the postwar period, all contributed to the need for social interventions to mitigate the plight of marginalized groups. The Black Civil Rights Movement and the Women's Movement that gained momentum during the 1960s also influenced the emergence of disability activism. The most significant outcome of this process was the organization of disabled persons themselves into a vibrant social movement along the same lines as these movements. Through self-advocacy by disabled persons, the concept of disability was redefined not as personal tragedy necessitating therapy, but as collective oppression necessitating political action (Oliver, 1996). In this perspective, the focus shifts from the inability of persons with disabilities to adapt to the so-called *normal* environment to the failure of the social and structural environment to adapt to the needs and aspirations of the disabled. As advocates for equal rights for disabled persons, these disability organizations lobbied with national governments for a barrier-free environment, inclusive education, and affirmative action in employment, in addition to the whole range of civil, political, social, and economic rights to which all citizens are entitled.

Instead of giving rights to disabled citizens and empowering them, a culture of charity and welfare has been systematically promoted in India since the colonial period. Medical rehabilitation, including distribution of assistive aids and appliances, special schools, vocational training in low-end occupations, and sheltered employment, has been the pillars of State policy for the disabled. Furthermore, electoral politics of caste and gender have pushed them to the margins of the political landscape, making them a weak political constituency. They have, in fact, been systematically disenfranchised by the political system. Things began to change marginally after 1981 (UN International Year of Disabled Persons) when the issue of disability was opened up at the national level. The changing international climate focusing on human rights and empowerment of marginalized groups impelled the government to make some policy changes, such as enhancing token reservations in educational institutions and employment. But real progress in the form of concrete legislation to deliver the promise of equality of opportunity and social justice only came in 1995 with the passage of the Persons with Disabilities (Equal Opportunities, Protection of Rights, and Full Participation) Act. One of the positive outcomes of economic liberalization and globalization has been the introduction of a view of disability as a human right and development issue, rather than simply a matter of charity and welfare. This perspective is slowly entering deliberations primarily due to the efforts of voluntary groups, such as the Disability Rights Group in Delhi that lobbied with the government both for passage of the disability legislation and incorporation of disability in the 2001 Census. In 2007, India signed the United Nations Convention on the Rights of Disabled Persons (UNCRPD) that has the potential of making disability a critical public policy issue.

One of the intractable challenges in scholarship and activism on disability is the problem of definition. Disability is a complex sociomedical reality. In its widest sense, it mirrors the complex interplay between society, culture, and the individual at any given time and place. More narrowly, it refers to a complex set of bodily expressions, social categories, and individual experiences involving multiple criteria of classification. For instance, disabilities may be congenital or acquired: most intellectual disabilities are congenital. Malnutrition, micronutrient deficiencies, and infections may result in childhood disabilities, polio being the most obvious example. When disabilities are acquired later in life due to accidents, injuries, or advancing age, they may be characterized by episodic upsurge of symptoms and/or progressive degeneration. Many mental and psychoneurotic illnesses, such as schizophrenia, multiple sclerosis, and Alzheimer's disease, fall in this category. A disability may be static, such as the loss of a limb due to an amputation. Then, there are hidden and visible disabilities. Diabetes and epilepsy are hidden, while leprosy and blindness are visible conditions. Disabilities may be temporary or permanent. For instance, a mild fracture may result in temporary disablement, while spinal cord injury, sustained in an automobile accident, might result in permanent disability. In addition, there are many gradations of disability ranging from mild to severe.

Keeping in view the sheer diversity of this overarching category, the UNCPRD includes within its ambit those who have long-term physical, mental, intellectual, or sensory impairments which, in interaction with physical, social, and attitudinal barriers, may hinder their full and effective participation in society on an equal basis with others. On the basis of this broad definition, conditions such as cancer, cardiovascular disease, tuberculosis, and HIV/AIDS may also be (and are in parts of the world) seen as disabilities. This underscores the evolving nature of the category of disability itself, making its historical and cross-cultural elaboration extremely challenging. However, broadly speaking, a disability generally has two interconnected components, that is, medical limitation(s) and social prejudice(s), which often get translated into discriminatory behavior toward the affected person.

For purposes of this chapter, the discussion will be limited to disabilities that have legal sanction in the Indian context, namely, blindness and low vision, hearing and speech impairments, locomotor or orthopedic impairment, and mental retardation and mental illness. According to the Persons with Disabilities Act, 1995,[1] a person must be medically certified to have a disability of at least 40 percent to be eligible for State-supported disability benefits.

Work and Disability: Conceptual Issues

Prevailing perceptions and empirical realities appear to confirm the impression that disabled persons are incapable of engaging in productive work. The assumption that disability equals non-employability is reflected in uniformly higher unemployment and underemployment rates. Disabled people are more likely to be looking for work; if working, are more likely to work part time, and be in lower-end occupations, under-paid, and self-employed. Indeed, due to special education and low social expectations, they are not likely to be working at all, highlighting the adverse role of social prejudice and discrimination. Their status in the labor market is iniquitous; they have less bargaining power and are often unable to engage in intense competition because the terrain of exchange is unequal,[2] an intrinsic characteristic of capitalist economies. Most disability scholars are in agreement that industrialization generated the category of disability. Industrial work systematically excluded the disabled because it was not designed for those whose bodies and intellects were not suitable for the average work. Given this legacy, it is not surprising that increasing educational and employment options has been the centerpiece of disability legislation, be it the Americans with Disabilities Act (1990) or the Indian Persons with Disabilities Act (1995). Indeed, it is worth noting that that first disability legislation, namely, the Disabled People's Employment Act (1944) in the United Kingdom aimed to cope with the workforce shortages induced by the Second World War. For the first time, it gave official recognition to the employment potential of disabled persons, opening up public consciousness to accepting that they are employable given suitable rehabilitation and workplace accommodations. This Act is also seminal because it embodies all those elements that continue to be relied upon to enhance the economic status of disabled persons, such as quota schemes, disabled persons' register, designated jobs, special aids, grants for upgrading premises, fares to work, personal assistance, reader services, etc.

While medicine and law are the sources of official definitions of disabilities, empirical surveys and ethnographic studies are better sources for understanding the actual interface between disability and work because a core defining parameter of popular understandings of disability is the diminishment or loss of capacity to engage in productive work. For instance, old age is considered the most common type of disability in rural Tamil Nadu (Harris-White and Erb, 2002). Geriatric conditions and complications were cited by informants as leading to loss of visual, orthopedic, and aural capacities. Other studies have also shown that self-identified disability is largely assessed by adults in terms of their reduced capacity or loss of capacity to work (Klasing, 2007). Disability definitions in many rural areas are not congruent with medical conditions, but directly related to work capacity. For instance, conditions such as pain, alcoholism, and *swelling* are not considered to be disabilities in a Western setting, but are experienced as disabling in an agricultural and rural industrial economy dependent on sustained physical labor (Harris-White and Erb, 2002).

Furthermore, the workplace is a veritable site for causing disabilities, particularly machine entanglements in factories and agriculture. Even though thousands of workers acquire permanent injuries leading to disabilities due to industrial accidents, injury control is not a major focus of disability prevention (Bacquer and Sharma, 1997). Then, there are also numerous occupational environments exposing workers to contracting chronic illnesses and disabilities, for example, silicosis among construction workers.

Expectations of work from disabled persons are markedly reduced, especially if the disability is congenital or since childhood. Against this backdrop, gender impacts the disability–work interface in interesting ways. For instance, Mehrotra (2006) points out that men with intellectual disability in rural areas, such as Haryana, are usually assigned women's work, such as fetching water, weeding, or grazing cattle. Acquiring a masculine identity and proving their manhood (which are both intrinsically linked to one's status in the labor market) are considered beyond the competence of disabled men, who are notionally clubbed in the community of women and children. They are often ridiculed and assigned household chores. On the other hand, women with disabilities perform the usual household chores and child care. They must demonstrate a higher level of impairment to be excluded from domestic work.

Looking at disability from a political economy perspective through work highlights its direct, indirect, and opportunity costs on the household. In addition to the loss of productivity and social status affecting the disabled person directly, other household members also have to contribute to treatment and care. The burden of such ongoing care work is largely borne by the female members, which in turn affects their participation in the labor market.[3] The loss of productive work due strain on household income and care work may lead to downward mobility. This highlights how disability is both a cause and consequence of poverty.

Historicizing Disability and Work in India

> ... disability is everywhere in history once you begin looking for it, but conspicuously absent in the histories we write.
>
> (Baynton, 2001: 52)

Some recognizable social placements of disabled persons are as court fool and jester, objects of amusement for profit in freak shows and carnivals, scientific specimens in museums and medical schools, for example, the Elephant Man, the Hottentot Woman. Apart from accounts of disability in medicine and literature, exploring disability as a historical subject and viewing disabled persons not only as victims but also as agents comes from disability studies, an interdisciplinary field developing since the 1980s that regards disability not as an isolated individual pathology, but as a key sociopolitical category on the lines of race, class, and gender. Disability has had manifold meanings in all world religions through interlinking notions of sin, evil, suffering, healing, faith, and grace. But as rightly pointed out by the pioneers of disability studies, it is the Industrial Revolution and accompanying capitalism that really crystallized the category as we understand it today. Capitalism is embedded in able-bodied ideals of strength, control, mastery, independence, and struggle, which slide into positivist notions of survival of the fittest and progress. During the 18th and 19th centuries, the imperatives of a system of commodity production and exchange demanded non-owners of the means of production to sell their labor power to participate in the industrial process. Those who could not sell their labor power on normal and average terms faced the loss of subsistence and consequent independence, merit, self-identity, and social status. A rapidly developing profession of medicine provided the ideological basis for identifying and classifying devalued differences (cripples, imbeciles, insane, etc.), giving rise to institutional structures, such as workhouses, special schools, sheltered workshops, community care, and rehabilitation. This is the conventional historiography of the disability concept dominating disability studies and forming the ideological basis of the social model that conceptualizes disability not as an individual medical problem requiring treatment and rehabilitation, but as a form of social oppression requiring social structural change, particularly the removal of material, social, and attitudinal barriers that are the real source of the inequities and inequalities between disabled and nondisabled persons (Campbell and Oliver, 1996; Gleeson, 1998; Oliver, 1990, 1996).

The universals of disability history are the documented movement from charity and moral models (largely embedded in religion) to medical and contemporary social models. Another historical continuity is chartered by identifying specific historical events, such as the institutional confinement of madness, industrialization, the Holocaust, and deinstitutionalization to show how contemporary responses to disability, for example, exclusion from formal employment, incarceration in mental hospitals, and disability-selective abortions, are encoded in these events. While using main concepts of disability studies, such as discrimination, exclusion, oppression, and charity, scholarship on the history of disability, in India draws upon major texts of Hinduism, such as the Ramayana, the Mahabharata, and Manu's laws, to depict conceptions of disability and the plight of disabled persons in pre colonial India (Bhatt, 1963; Dalal, 2002; Miles, 1995, 2001; Narasimhan and Mukherjee, 1986). These scholars try to search for comparative moments in Indian history with events in Western history and draw analogous inferences, for example, linking religious interest in disability with the charity approach and institutional care. Such inferences are suspect because the themes under discussion may not carry the same meanings in the different spatiotemporal and cultural contexts, and the sources of data are not exact equivalents. For instance, the above Hindu epics are not equivalent to the Bible which carries greater doctrinal authority. If in its widest ramifications it moves beyond physical mental deficit to map the interface between the individual society and culture at any given time and place, then how are we to capture histories of disablement in other places that have not had the same experiences as the West? Conventional disability studies scholarship assumes both the pan-human existence of disability and a universal template of its historical development (Anand, 2013).

It is noteworthy that while social historians and subaltern scholars have contested Eurocentric narratives by privileging the voices of subjugated groups, disabled persons have been marked by their absence in these discourses. Even gender historians have not incorporated disabled women as a subject of analysis and understanding. On the other hand, Indian disability studies scholars cited above using the Western scholarship as their template have produced works which read more like the histories of disability of Europe and America. Since disability is largely configured in social welfare terms, making its study more the domain of religion and medicine, a political economy perspective that recognizes the contribution of disabled persons as workers can open a window on a historiography of work and disability along the lines of class, caste, and gender. This is only possible when the equation between disability and non-productivity is explicitly contested.

A central issue in such an enterprise is identifying and accessing data sources that could provide insights into the everyday experiences and lives of disabled persons. The challenge is to look for disability in the historical record, and subsequently, look for linkages with work taken in its widest connotations as human activity undertaken for the fulfillment of needs and ultimately survival. Being largely framed as a welfare issue, disability is more likely to be captured through institutional histories of hospitals (mental hospitals, leprosaria), special schools (for the blind and deaf),[4] and missionary and other religious institutions engaged in treatment, training, and rehabilitation of disabled persons. Considering the overlaps between disease and disability, particularly chronic diseases, the history of medicine literature is another important research site.

Given the deep-seated connections between caste and work in the Indian context (that is, hierarchy of tasks coded in terms of a doctrine of purity and pollution), histories of caste groups might contain references to the work expected of and actually done by disabled persons. In addition to institutional and community records, a more fruitful pathway into labor history and disability might be exploring claims and judgments under various Acts (such as the Workmen's Compensation Act, 1923 and the Factories Act, 1948) relating to working conditions, industrial accidents, and injuries. For pre colonial notions of disability, examining state edicts and ordinances of the princely states and the Mughal court could yield insights.

It is unlikely that disabled workers constituted a large segment of the labor force in factories, but Buchanan's (2002) study of deaf factory workers in Ohio during the first half of the 20th century is worth emulating. A neglected, but potentially fertile, source of examining the relationship between work and disability is through the occupation of soldiering. It is impossible to conceive of war without its direct consequences in the form of disability.

While institutional and legal histories are a particularly fertile terrain for exploring disability and work, two other historical contexts would be the history of prosthetics (falling within the histories of science and technology), such as the development of artificial limbs, and visual and hearing aids. A good example of such recent disability history is Raman Srinivasan's (2002) account of the development of the Jaipur foot, a low cost, locally produced prosthetic tailored for use in Indian conditions developed during the 1960s.

Doing a historiography of disability in India necessarily implicates a global history perspective. Its emergence on the global stage in the 1970s is the outcome of a number intersecting currents, such as the human rights mandate of the UN, the community-based rehabilitation discourses of biomedicine, identity politics paradigms of civil society groups, and self-advocacy by disabled persons themselves. These currents translate into global networks of circulation pushed by the Global North into enclaves of the Global South. Notions of spatiotemporal interconnections, entanglements, and fluidity configure the global transactions around disability in which the macro-level actors are bilateral and multilateral institutions such as the World Bank (WB), the UN, and its specialized agencies (especially the World Health Organization), individual nation states, and local-level disability organizations. There are interesting (but unexplored) ways in which disability intertwines with work in a global context characterized by flexibility overcoming some of the accessibility barriers imposed by a rigid factory or conventional office regime. With information technology inputs, such as screen reading software, many physical barriers can also be overcome. On the other hand, as shown by the WB (2007) study, expansion in the private sector and greater informalization and casualization of the Indian economy have adversely impacted disabled people's employment. Exploring disability and work from a global history perspective has the potential to produce inclusive scholarship on both contemporary disability and labor histories.

Disability, Work, and Gender in India: Empirical Situation

While the Indian census provides a macro view of disability and work, a more nuanced understanding of the situation, particularly with reference to gender, is provided by small, area-specific, cross-sectional comparative studies, such as the National Sample Survey Organization (NSSO) 58th round (2002), Harris-White and Erb (2002), Klasing (2007), and WB (2007). The following documentation is based on a comparative analysis of all these data sources.

According to the Census (Registrar General of India, 2001),[5] around 65 percent of the disabled population is classified as nonworking, which means not engaged in remunerative work. Over 50 percent of them are reported to be dependent on their families, followed by another 25 percent falling in the category of students (who are also dependent). This means that a lot of domestic labor, which disabled persons may engage in, especially women, is simply not counted as work. Contrary to the popular view that beggary is the main occupation of disabled persons, only one percent reported it as their occupation, most of who were persons suffering from mental illness.

Of the 35 percent disabled persons reported to be engaged in the labor market,[6] work participation rates are higher in rural areas than in cities. This could be due to higher relative population and greater flexibility of the agricultural economy to absorb a larger number of disabled persons in gainful work. Overall, the highest work participation is among the visually challenged, followed by those with hearing disability, while the lowest work participation is among those with mental disability (mental illness and mental retardation in urban areas)[7] and multiple disabilities.

Seasonal self-employment seems to be the norm among working disabled adults in rural areas. They may only be employed during peak periods when other workers are not available or have migrated.[8] In a survey in the state of Andhra Pradesh, wage labor averaged only 7–10 days per month and never exceeded seven months in a year, resulting in uncertain incomes and seasonal shortfalls (Klasing, 2007). While agricultural wage labor is the dominant occupation, other occupations performed by disabled persons are petty business, selling vegetables, milk, and cloth, carpentry, and mechanics. Agrarian poverty may even drive disabled people into physically strenuous activities, such as bullock-carting and construction work to reduce dependence (Harris-White and Erb, 2002).

Agricultural work puts immense physical strain on the bodies of disabled persons and adversely affects their incomes. Most have to work for longer hours than their nondisabled counterparts, either because they will only be hired if they make up for their disability or simply because it just takes them longer to complete the allocated tasks. Furthermore, there are the physical hardships of going to distant fields on uneven terrain. Hilly areas and flooded fields pose critical accessibility issues in rural areas.

The job profiles change in the urban areas with greater access to special educational institutions and job reservation possibilities. Government employment as orderlies, office clerks, and teachers predominate, with a higher employment rate for disabled women. However, the likelihood of disabled persons being employed is over 20 percent higher in rural than urban areas, and highly significant statistically.[9]

The employment rate of disabled women relative to nondisabled women is significantly higher than for disabled men relative to nondisabled men. A possible explanation is that the gender factor has an important additional effect on employment rates, which dilutes the independent effect of disability among women on their employment rates.[10] According to the WB (2007), having a disability reduces the probability of being employed by 31 percent for males in rural Uttar Pradesh, and 32 percent for males in rural Tamil Nadu. In contrast, it reduces the probability of being employed only by 0.5 percent for rural females in Uttar Pradesh and by 11 percent for females in rural Tamil Nadu. However, there is a considerable gender gap between employment of disabled men and women, ranging from 37 percent to 11 percent in rural areas (NSSO, 2002).

According to Harris-White and Erb (2002), disability pauperizes, and it does so in a gendered way. Around 80 percent of total disabled men in their field site in Tamil Nadu were economically and domestically inactive. Although work-wise unproductive, all these men engaged in community life, were self sufficient in terms of self-care, and were not socially dependent. However, performance of gendered female occupations such as cooking, cleaning, fetching water, and child care would result in their social humiliation. Caring for such men was part of the normal caring role of a female member of the household. Full-time female caregivers cannot take up wage employment, whose loss is an opportunity cost of disability to the individual and the household. Around 45 percent of households with a disabled member reported an adult missing work mainly due to care-related work (WB, 2007).

On the other hand, disabled women could not forfeit their domestic duties, and most of them engaged in some kind of household work. Indeed, they have to show a considerably high level of incapacity to justify their nonparticipation in domestic work and child care. In the aforementioned empirical studies, severity of disability was very high in inactive disabled women with most of them requiring assistance in feeding, dressing, and personal hygiene. Additionally, gender bias in favor of men results in disability being identified earlier in males, and the gender gap in treatment against women is also empirically highlighted. If household expectations regarding female productivity mean that they have to experience and display a greater level of incapacity to be entitled to care and economic dependence, then it also implies that disability is somewhat less impairing for them than for their male counterparts.

Another interesting gender facet of work and disability is the fact that disabled men, such as those with intellectual disabilities in rural Haryana, may engage in domestic labor (Mehrotra, 2006), reversing the sexual division of labor with the husband taking on household responsibilities and the wife taking on more outside wage work.

In addition to residential location, type of disability, and gender, another hierarchy of disadvantage occurs due to caste, which has the same impact on disability as class, with those at the lower end having less financial security and, hence, finding it more difficult as a household to weather the shock of disability. Caste-disaggregated disability data from a range of sources show the concentration of *dalits* (Schedule Castes) and tribals, among the group of disabled beggars, and other employment arenas, such as government and business having an overwhelming representation of disabled persons from higher castes (Pal, 2010). Indeed, self-identified disability prevalence is lower in low-caste areas, due as much to the high incidence of malnutrition and disability-related mortality as to lack of access to health care and dire economic necessity which requires work participation by everyone without exception. But where it does occur in such a context, it is very severe in degree. The impact of lower caste and class on disability can be inferred from another perspective. In his qualitative study of barriers to employment among a subset of locomotor-disabled persons in Bangalore, Upadhyay (2013) found that socioeconomic status and family income were stronger determinants of employment success and quality of work experience than the disability per se. It appears that neither observable characteristics of disabled people nor their productivity account for most of their employment deficit; other factors, such as deep-seated prejudices translated into discriminatory behavior and location within other grids of inequality, such as caste, class, and gender, are more determinative of their poor employment outcomes.

Initiatives for Inclusion

In addition to traditional systems of promoting economic self-reliance among disabled persons through philanthropy and charity, more structured measures in the form of disability pensions, low-credit loans for self-employment, reservations in education, quotas in employment, and the so-called corporate social responsibility (CSR) in the private sector are being implemented in India in an ad hoc way to bring disabled persons into the labor market. Such measures are a combination of low-end occupations in open segregated and self-employment contexts. Often, the initiatives are not accompanied by appropriate environmental modifications, for example, reserving jobs for locomotor-disabled persons in a location that does not allow wheelchair access is both illogical and self-defeating.

In a country in which the culture of public employment reservations is unusually strong, reservation has been a central plank of disability policy since it was first introduced in low-end jobs in the government in 1977. The Persons with Disabilities Act, 1995, mandates 3 percent reservation in public employment (1 percent for persons with visual, speech and hearing, and orthopedic disabilities, respectively). However, linking this provision to identification of specific jobs in government departments considered suitable for disabled persons has contributed to enhancing the perception of such persons as incompetent. The list of identified jobs is based on the assumption that features of an impairment are the exclusive determinants of an individual's ability to hold a position at a particular skill level, ignoring the potential influence of other factors, such as motivation, age of disability onset, access to employment services, and the nature of the workplace and labor market. The arbitrariness of the whole identification process is revealed by such absurdities as, for instance, an agricultural scientist specialized in econometric analysis being suitable for an individual who is blind or has an orthopaedic disability, but not for someone with a hearing disability. Equally baffling is the exclusion of persons with loss of functioning in both lower limbs from positions of accountant, auditor, and postmaster. At the core of the whole job identification exercise is the presumed loss of productivity when the worker is disabled, and providing reservation in those job categories whose suboptimal performance is acceptable.

Apart from reservation, there are other schemes executed by the Ministry of Labor, such as establishment of special employment exchanges, vocational rehabilitation centers (VRCs), and apprenticeship programs incorporating skill development and job placement of disabled persons. In 1997, the Government of India constituted the National Handicapped Finance and Development Corporation (NHFDC) for promoting self-employment through loans at low interest rates to disabled entrepreneurs. This scheme suffers from both disability and gender biases with over 80 percent of beneficiaries being men and nearly 90 percent having orthopedic disabilities. Then, under the vocational rehabilitation program, only about 10,500 persons a year are rehabilitated. In 2001, only 559 persons with disabilities underwent training under the apprenticeship scheme, and that too largely in traditional crafts, such as recaning of chairs, candle making, chalk making, book binding, etc.[11] Furthermore, persons with mental illness are excluded from this program. Each of these approaches suffers from inherent disadvantages resulting in benefiting only a very small number of the target population. Indeed, the facilities offered are largely urban based, excluding the bulk of the disabled population living in rural areas.

An incentive approach for employment of disabled persons in the private sector has not been very successful. Apart from some bulk employment in public sector companies like National Thermal Power Corporation and Titan Watches, employment rates of disabled persons in the private sector is less than 0.5 percent (Abidi, 1999). However, an emerging area of economic opportunity in the private sector, particularly for those with sensory disabilities, is the business process outsourcing (BPO) segment, offering them a new pathway into labor market integration (Friedner, 2009).

The job-market bias against disabled persons is not unique to the government and the private sectors. While the nongovernment organization (NGO) sector is perceived to be an important arm of the State in service delivery through the model of public–private partnership, the situation with respect to hiring of disabled persons also faces challenges. A survey of both mainstream and disability NGOs commissioned by the National

Center for Promotion of Employment of Disabled Persons in 2005 found that more than half had disabled employees constituting only 4 percent of the total workforce. The new strategy in the NGO sector is disabled persons' organizations to enable the critical stakeholders themselves to assume leadership roles and work toward self-empowerment.

Disability, Work, and the Life Cycle: An Ethnographic Perspective from Delhi

Both large-scale surveys and small-scale qualitative studies exploring the experiences of disabled persons in the community have contested stereotypes of total dependence, non-productivity, and general incapacity. In interviews with adolescents preparing to enter the job market and adults engaged in work (including housework), work was found to be a central component of their construction of their identities. While it is true that disability was perceived by most of the interviewees to be a barrier to labor participation, an intense desire and unremitting effort to engage in gainful work was universal and no different from nondisabled persons.

To the query about what they wanted to become, most disabled school students, like their nondisabled counterparts, did not give specific responses, but only said that they wanted to do some *job*. During the last few years of schooling, most were more preoccupied with the specialized courses they would pursue after completing school rather than with specific professions that they would take up. College students, on the other hand, were more specific, opting for a handful of professions, such as teaching (school and college-level), bank probationary officer, call center work, running a business, journalism, etc. Some of these careers choices, such as music or Hindi teaching, are jobs in which there is a history of reservation.

Interestingly, female adolescents (even those coming from rural areas and studying in special schools) put marriage and rearing a family as secondary to the more important goal of acquiring the necessary qualifications to earn a livelihood. Most said that marriage was not a certainty and, hence, it was imperative for them to be economically self-reliant. At the college level, professional aspirations became particularly sharp as the thought of not being able to marry became a distinct possibility.

In the case of disabled adolescents from lower socioeconomic strata going to regular government schools, where the possibility of dropping out was high both due to accessibility issues and their family's precarious economic status, the gender difference was more marked with young men exploring vocational options, such as motor mechanics, tailoring, electricals, carpentry, etc., and girls focusing on fine tuning their housework skills. Marriage was perceived to be more viable by young girls in this cohort than among their middle- and upper-class counterparts.

None of the interviewees voluntarily said they wanted to take up jobs, such as that of clerk, assistant, telephone operator, peon, and orderly, which were the lower-rung jobs initially opened up for reservation in the government sector to persons with physical and sensory disabilities. This could be due to lack of awareness about reservation beyond an idea of its mere existence. Secondly, jobs such as that of a telephone operator are becoming obsolete; and lastly, curtailment of jobs in the public sector due to structural adjustment policies has been highest at the lower rungs of the bureaucracy, adversely affecting disabled persons in the process.

When we look at actual workplace experiences of disabled persons, we find, as Upadhyay (2013) has pointed out, seeking and keeping employment is a corporeal experience, referring to the whole range of accessibility issues ranging from mobility and transportation to staircases and accessible toilets. Then, there is the issue of fatigue management which gets overlooked in debates on accessibility. The fact of the matter is that the bodies of disabled persons do have to exert more than those of their nondisabled counterparts. That is why simple reservation often leads to more frustration when it is not accompanied by reasonable workplace accommodation. While affluent respondents can offset many of the transport-related barriers by having their own vehicles and drivers, negotiating the workplace space itself poses problems which are more intractable. For instance, blind teachers in schools and colleges often sought assistance from students to not only function as escorts but also to read assignments and help them in their routine administrative work.

But perhaps the most subtle and intractable barriers are the attitudes and behaviors of coworkers. While overt discriminatory behavior was not often reported by disabled persons employed in the formal sector, a number of interviewees working in different organizational contexts in which they were often the sole disabled employee reported feeling isolated. They felt they were marginalized because they were disabled which created an unbridgeable gap between them and their nondisabled colleagues. Emotional responses of coworkers ranged from sympathy and pity, on the one hand, to animosity and competitiveness on the other.

Since equal opportunity policies are not yet part of company policies and government departments are not obliged to fill vacancies with disabled candidates, as there is no penalty for non-implementation, disabled persons are loathe to raise issues of access and accommodation for fear of being further marginalized, if not dismissed. For instance, some of the college and school teachers told me that though they were entitled to transport and other allowances due to being disabled, they often did not claim them not only because of the complicated administrative process, but because they felt they would be further humiliated for claiming such entitlements. They got the message that they should be grateful that they had a job in the first place.

The overweening importance of work in the life of a disabled person cannot be underestimated. The following case vignettes are some examples of this overarching reality.

B is a 40-year-old unmarried woman diagnosed with cerebral palsy. After completing her schooling in a special school and the National Open School, she has been trying to engage herself in some kind of (not necessarily gainful) *work*. Being from an upper socioeconomic class, her narrative did not echo dire economic need, but throughout our interview, she kept referring to her *business* of selling cosmetics on commission. She said that she was a salesperson for Amway and Oriflame products, and even encouraged me to buy something from her. Looking at her situation, it was quite clear that there would be very little *work* she could/would be doing, but her mental preoccupation with herself as a working person was remarkable.

S is a 52-year-old unmarried woman suffering from muscular dystrophy that constricts her free mobility outside the home. She has never attended school but managed to acquire some basic education through home tuition, and subsequently went on to study French for a couple of years at the French Cultural Center in Delhi. For the past 10 years, she has been giving home tuitions in French to school children. Her younger sister who also has the same disability, but is able to function with a wheelchair, has gone through normal schooling and even completed a postgraduate degree in psychology from Delhi University. She has not been able to find suitable employment commensurate with her interest and qualifications. She has been working at the Spastic Society as a counselor for the past 15 years, a job for which she is both overqualified and underpaid.

R is a 30-year-old housewife with two children living in a slum in West Delhi. She was identified as a potential candidate for self-employment by a prominent Delhi disability NGO working for economic empowerment of disabled persons in her area. Being mobility impaired and having a household to manage, she had been promised a sewing machine for working from home. I was introduced to her by an employee of this NGO and throughout our interview, she told me all the plans she had made to start earning some money, including liaising with tailors in the nearby market and telling her neighbors to give her tailoring work.

***

Disability cuts across class, gender, nationality, and generation because it can potentially happen to anyone at any time. In the macro-level social welfare domains in India, poverty, caste, and gender outrun disability. Furthermore, the neoliberal vision of suitably crafted and pliant workers does not seem to include disabled persons. But the costs of disability on the Gross Domestic Product are similar to those of under-nutrition.

Work is not only necessary for physical survival, but also vital for self-esteem and psychological well-being. Disability is a crosscutting category that may be explored from many perspectives. This project makes a beginning in looking at their multiple intersections largely with reference to contemporary India.

Notes

1. Presently, there is a revision of disability legislation in India in order to make the legal regime compliant with the UNCRPD that India has signed.
2. It is not as if poverty, unemployment, more part-time employment, and underemployment are only characteristics of disabled persons in developing countries like India. For instance, in the United States, 82 percent nondisabled persons of working age have a job as against 29 percent disabled persons and only 11 percent severely disabled persons. Disabled persons are three times more likely to be poor and suffer discrimination and attrition at the workplace (Russell, 2001).
3. Chakravarti (2008) highlights the opportunity costs of mothers with children with cerebral palsy, who had to forego their careers and incomes in order to provide care to their dependent children.
4. The first school for the blind in India was established in Amritsar in 1887 and the first deaf school in Bombay in 1884.
5. The figures are outdated, but the results of the latest Indian Census conducted in February 2011 are not yet available in the public domain.
6. The gap between disabled persons and general population employment rates has widened for all education levels since the 1990s, coinciding with economic liberalization, with the poorest and illiterate sections being even more

adversely affected (WB, 2007). Shrinking public employment and agrarian crises are cited as contributing factors.

7. Several studies have pointed to higher levels of exclusion and stigmatization on grounds of mental disability in cities contesting the commonsense perception that education and awareness would moderate the effects of disability.

8. Parallels between this situation and employment of disabled persons during wartime may be drawn, highlighting their reserve workforce status in times of crises.

9. Interestingly, disabled people have a 10 percent higher rate of self-employment than the general population (WB, 2007).

10. Addlakha (2013) and Ghosh (2013) have both highlighted the importance to employment accorded by disabled women and their families, perhaps to compensate for their diminished chances in the marriage market on account of the disability. This qualitative finding is corroborated by quantitative data: being married has a relatively strong, positive effect on the probability of being employed for males, but a negative effect for women. Having a postgraduate education has a stronger correlation with employment for women than vocational training.

11. Education for disabled persons has been historically valued not so much for fostering their social development, but to prevent them from becoming social and economic liabilities. Consequently, the emphasis on vocational training has been a strategic approach to enable them to become productive persons at minimum cost to the State and society.

Bibliography

Abidi, J. 1999. "Current Status of Employment of Disabled People in Indian Industries," *Asia and Pacific Journal of Disability Rehabilitation*, 10 (2). Available online at http://www.dinf.ne.jp/doc/english/asia/resource/apdrj/z13jo0400/z13jo0410.html (downloaded on 03.12.2013).

Addlakha, R. 2008. *Deconstructing Mental Illness: An Ethnography of Psychiatry, Women, and the Family*. New Delhi: Zubaan Books.

———. 2011. *Contemporary Perspectives on Disability in India: Exploring the Linkages Between Law, Gender and Experience*. Saarbrucken: LAP Lambert Academic Publishers.

———. 2013. "Body Politics and Disabled Femininity. Perspectives of Adolescent Girls from Delhi," in Renu Addlakha (ed.), *Disability Studies in India: Global Discourses, Local Realities*, pp. 220–240. London, New York: Routledge.

——— (ed.). 2013. "Body Politics and Disabled Femininity: Perspectives of Adolescent Girls from Delhi (India)," in *Disability Studies in India: Global Discourses, Local Realities*, pp. 220–240.

Addlakha, R., Stuart Blume, Patrick Devlieger, Osamu Nagase, and Myriam Winance (eds). 2009. *Disability and Society: A Reader.* New Delhi: Orient BlackSwan.

Anand, S. 2013. "Historicising Disability: Questions of Subject and Method," in R. Addlakha (ed.), *Disability Studies in India: Global Discourses, Local Realities,* pp. 35–60.

Bacquer, A. and A. Sharma. 1997. *Disability: Challenges vs Responses.* New Delhi: Concerned Action Now.

Baynton, D. C. 2001. "Disability and the Justification of Inequality in American History," in P. K. Longmore and L. Umansky (eds), *The New Disability History: American Perspectives,* pp. 33–57. New York: New York University Press.

Bhatt, U. 1963. *The Physically Handicapped in India.* Mumbai: Popular Book Depot.

Buchanan, R. M. 2002. *Illusions of Equality: Deaf Americans in School and Factory.* Washington, D.C.: Gallaudet University Press.

Campbell, J. and M. Oliver. 1996. *Disability Politics: Understanding Our Past, Changing Our Future.* London: Routledge.

Chakravarti, U. 2008. "Burden of Caring: Families of the Disabled in Urban India," in R. Addlakha (ed.), *Indian Journal of Gender Studies Special Issue: Gender Disability and Society,* 15 (2): 341–363.

Dalal, A. K. 2002. "Disability Rehabilitation in a Traditional Indian Society," in M. Thomas and M. J. Thomas (eds), *Disability and Rehabilitation in South Asia,* pp. 17–24. Bangalore: National Printing Press.

Friedner, M. 2009. "Computers and Magical Thinking: Work and Belonging in Bangalore," *Economic and Political Weekly, XLIV* (26 & 27): 37–40.

Ghosh, Nandini. 2013. "Bhalo Meye: Cultural Construction of Gender and Disability in Bengal," in R. Addlakha (ed.), *Emerging Paradigm of Disability Studies: Perspectives and Challenges from India,* pp. 201–219. New Delhi: Routledge.

Gleeson, B. 1998. *Geographies of Disability.* London: Routledge.

Government of India. 2002. *Disabled persons in India.* Report no. 485. New Delhi: National Sample Survey Organisation.

Harris-White, B. and S. Erb. 2002. *Outcast from Social Welfare: Disability in Rural India.* Bangalore: Books for Change.

Klasing, I. 2007. *Disability and Social Exclusion in Rural India.* New Delhi: Rawat Publications.

Mehrotra, M. 2006. "Negotiating Gender and Disability in Rural Haryana," *Sociological Bulletin,* 55 (3): 406–426.

Miles, M. 1995. "Disability in an Eastern Religious Context: Historical Perspectives," *Disability and Society,* 10 (1): 49–70.

———. 2001. "Studying Responses to Disability in South Asian Histories: Approaches Personal, Prakrital and Pragmatical," *Disability and Society,* 16 (1): 143–160.

Narasimhan, M. C., and A. K. Mukherjee. 1986. *Disability: A Continuing Challenge.* New Delhi: Wiley Eastern Ltd.

National Sample Survey Organization (NSSO). 2002. "Disabled Persons in India," Report No. 485.

Oliver, M. 1990. *The Politics of Disablement*. London: Macmillan.

———. 1996. *Understanding Disability: From Theory to Practice*. London: Macmillan.

Pal, G. C. 2010. "Dalits with Disabilities: The Neglected Dimension of Social Exclusion," Indian Institute of Dalit Studies Working Paper, vol. IV, no. 3.

Registrar General of India. 2001. *Census of India*. Available online at http://www.censusindia.net (downloaded on 03.12.2013).

Russell, M. 2001. "Disability, Oppression and Political Economy," *Journal of Disability Policy Studies*, 12 (2): 87–95.

Srinivasan, R. 2002. "Technology Sits Cross-Legged: Developing the Jaipur Foot Prosthesis," in K. Ott, D. Serlin, and S. Mihm (eds), *Artificial Parts, Practical Lives: Modern Histories of Prosthetics*, pp. 327–347. New York: New York University Press.

Upadhyay, A. 2013. "Corporeality, Mobility and Class: An Ethnography of Work-Related Experiences in Urban India," in R. Addlakha (ed.), *Disability Studies in India: Global Discourses, Local Realities*, pp. 169–200. New York: Routledge.

WB. 2007. "People with Disabilities in India: From Commitments to Outcomes," Human Development Unit, South Asia Region. Available online at http://siteresources.worldbank.org/INDIAEXTN/Resources/295583-1171456325808/DISABILITYREPORTFINALNOV2007.pdf (downloaded on 03.12.2013).

11

Legal Capacity and Civil Political Rights for People with Psychosocial Disabilities*

Bhargavi V. Davar

This chapter is drawn from our active participation in the Indian legal reform processes of all disability laws in compliance with the United Nations Convention on the Rights of Persons with Disabilities (UNCRPD).[1] We have been active in these processes as women survivors of psychiatry and studious users of various *alternative* techniques (Davar, 2008), including lifestyles, diet, and spiritual practices, for mental health and overall well-being. During this time, we have encountered several questions, concerns, and dilemmas relating to the basic experience of psychosocial disability, development of identity as women with disabilities, the intersection of rights granted by UNCRPD with CEDAW (Convention on the Elimination of All Forms of Discrimination Against Women), and gender rights. The chapter is concerned with some pivotal rights, which our constituency of persons with psychosocial disabilities has always held dear, particularly in the making of the UNCRPD: legal capacity and civil political rights. The chapter is set within the context of the trials and tribulations of struggles for full legal capacity, both within normative structures (the *harmonization* process led by the government) as well as within civil society, the women's movement, and the disabled peoples' movement (in India and worldwide). However, a broader view of the notion of legal capacity, its scope, and its operationalization leads to complex questions of regionality, history, gender, and context, while not diluting its importance in the lives of women with disabilities.

* Through financial support by the IDA, we have travelled regionally, trying to study institutional relationships that impact lives and rights of people living with psychosocial disabilities.

UNCRPD, Article 12: Right to Equal Recognition before the Law

India was among the first countries to sign and ratify the UNCRPD. In doing so, the Indian government made a commitment to its people and to the international community on its obligation to *respect, protect,* and *fulfill* the equal enjoyment of all human rights and freedoms of all people with disabilities, on equal basis with others. While the UNCRPD has been considered as not providing for any new rights, it melds together socioeconomic and civil political rights in ways that make human rights truly indivisible, inalienable, and universal for all people with disabilities. While some countries have placed reservations on Article 12 in ratifying the UNCRPD, the Government of India did not place any reservations.

Article 14 of the Indian Constitution provides that "The state shall not deny to any person equality before the law or the equal protection of the laws within the territory of India." As *parens patriae* (a doctrine that grants the inherent power and authority of the state to protect persons), the State is obligated to respect, protect, and fulfill Article 14 for all people on equal basis. Article 14 is also related closely to Article 21, which covers constitutional protections on Right to Life and Liberty. Article 21 of the Indian Constitution provides, "No person shall be deprived of his life or personal liberty except according to procedure established by law." Article 22 of the Indian Constitution provides protection against arbitrary and unlawful arrest and detention. It provides for the right to information on the reasons for arrest, for being brought before a judge promptly, the right to have a proceeding before a court, etc. There are no identity or status groups who face restriction or deprivation of legal capacity and liberty in India, *excepting* persons with psychosocial disabilities.

Women were not considered as legally capable until recently, and the feminist movement has played a big role in legal reform on this aspect. Legal capacity was fully denied, for example, in family laws, inheritance, and in laws for political participation, among other areas of life, which continue to challenge feminist legal reformers (Parashar and Dhanda, 2008). A legal interpretation of equal recognition before the law and full legal capacity has been covered in various Conventions, also ratified by India. For example, the International Convention of Civil Political Rights (ICCPR) grants that, "All peoples have the right of self-determination. By virtue of that right they freely determine their political status...." Further, "All persons shall be equal before the courts and tribunals" (Article 14), and that "Everyone shall have the right to recognition everywhere as a person before the law" (Article 16). ICCPR also provides that "All persons are equal before the law, and are entitled without any discrimination to the equal protection of the law" (Article 26). The ICCPR has covered a range of human rights applicable in country situations of emergency, war, or conflict, dealing particularly with access to justice issues in the context of deprivation of liberty.

CEDAW Article 15 provides that, "States Parties shall accord to women equality with men before the law." Further,

> States Parties shall accord to women, in civil matters, a legal capacity identical to that of men and the same opportunities to exercise that capacity. In particular, they shall give women equal rights to conclude contracts and to administer property and shall treat them equally in all stages of procedure in courts and tribunals.

States parties are also obligated under CEDAW to deem *null and void* any existing contracts and private instruments having an effect of restricting the legal capacity of women. Particularly on suffrage and inheritance issues, recognition of equality before law proved to be liberating for millions of women, where the extant social and legal practice of *husband* or *father* as proxy decision maker was seriously challenged.

While CEDAW provides for equal recognition before law, the CEDAW monitoring committee, even in their most recent Concluding Observations at their 54th session,[2] did not comment on the implementation of legal capacity for women in general, or the violations to right to legal capacity found in law in most countries of the world through special legislations, such as the mental health legislations, family laws, and other common laws. The Concluding Observations largely cover women with disabilities under the broader rubric of *underprivileged women*. These cover social, economic, and cultural rights, such as education, employment, social security, etc. Civil political rights including legal capacity have not come up in the Concluding Observations in the context of women with disabilities. The committee has duly noted the multiple discrimination and harmful stereotyping of vulnerable women, including women with disabilities. Legal capacity issues can be obliquely read into the Concluding Observations on domestic violence, referring to the *voluntary consent of rape victims*. Women forced to live within institutions have elicited no comments in these Concluding Observations. Ms Rashida Manjoo, the UN's Special Rapporteur, on her recent visit to India in 2013, has, however, commented extensively on the rights to violations of bodily integrity of multitudes of women in different vulnerable contexts, and also rights violations of women in custodial settings. In the context of women with disabilities, she has mentioned *forced medication* as a rights violation issue.

The international debate on legal capacity, in the context of treatment choices and free and informed consent to medical treatments, can be traced back to the Nuremberg Code of 1947, in the postwar period. The first principle of this code is that

> The voluntary consent of the human subject is absolutely essential. This means that the person involved should have legal capacity to give consent; should be so situated as to be able to exercise free power of choice, without the intervention of any element of force, fraud, deceit, duress, overreaching, or other alternative form of constraint or coercion; and should have sufficient knowledge and comprehension of the elements of the subject matter involved as to enable him to make an understanding and enlightened decision.

The mental health legislation of India (Mental Health Act [MHA] of 1987), a special law which is believed to cover all the human rights of mental health *patients*, does not cover the freedom to choose or refuse treatments, nor any provision on free and informed consent. Contrary to the Nuremberg Code, which largely forms the basis of medical ethics, the MHA of 1987 provides liberally for the forced commitment of persons with disabilities and consent for treatment. Mental health *patients* are the only kind of patients who have been completely denied any coverage under the biomedical ethics frameworks, and they are subject to *special* status as patients.

While these codes and conventions gave a more specific legal framework for concepts, such as *legal capacity* and *discrimination*, it did not specifically address issues of people with disabilities, but as in the case of CEDAW, recent committees have started to mention people/women with disabilities among broader categories of vulnerable groups. Nondiscrimination clauses in these Conventions typically specified "race, color, sex, language, religion, political or other opinion, national or social origin, property, birth or other." Specific incapacity issues of people with disabilities, especially those with mental and psychosocial disabilities, were not addressed. Further, disability itself was considered to be a medical issue, and not a social status, personhood, or identity issue, such as gender or race. The intersection between gender, disability, and civil political rights was also not very much in discussion. Being an invisible constituency, we even had little knowledge about our legal status as women with psychosocial disabilities in India, until the arrival of the UNCRPD.

What Is Legal Capacity?

The International Disability Caucus, a global cross-disability coalition which was instrumental in negotiating Article 12 during drafting of the UNCRPD, said that

> Legal capacity is fundamental to a person's self-determination. We all make choices in our everyday life: what we eat, what we wear, which radio station we listen to and we choose our friends and relationships. If a person does not have legal capacity—including the right to exercise this legal capacity—then a *presumption of incapacity* flows all over an individual's life; not just on issues of medical treatment and contract or financial decisions but all choices of a person are determined by *someone else*.

Legal capacity includes two fundamental components, of holding the right of being recognized as a legal personality, as well as the capacity to act. The International Disability Alliance, an umbrella organization of global disabled persons' organizations (DPOs) declares that *legal capacity* is best translated as the "capacity for rights and capacity to act" (International Disability Alliance, 2008).[3]

> Legal capacity can be described as a person's power or possibility to act within the framework of the legal system. In other words, it makes a human being a subject of law. It is a legal concept, a construct, assigned to most people of majority age enabling them to have rights and obligations, to make binding decisions and have them respected. As such, it facilitates personal freedom. (Nilsson, 2012)

Mental Disability Advocacy Center, Budapest, defines the right to legal capacity as recognition of the

> [C]apacity to be the bearers of rights, and their capacity to act. Capacity to bear rights means the capacity to be a potential holder of rights and obligations, while capacity to act means the capacity to exercise these rights and to enter into legal relationships. (MDAC, 2011: 5)

Legal capacity is in extant legal pedagogy and practice, in India and worldwide, linked to the cognitive dimensions of human consciousness. India has inherited laws from its colonial rulers, and *unsoundness of mind* is a determination of a rational, logically thinking, linguistically and mathematically competent mind that can process cause and effect. Being of *sound mind* has mainly included rational aspects, such as understanding a transaction, understanding the consequences, not coming under undue influence, being able to decide, etc. This may be considered as the masculinization of human faculties by some feminist psychologists (Lloyd, 1984). In the transition to modernity, emotion became associated with the feminine and reason with the masculine, with the latter being legitimized as the sum and substance of the human mind. Jaggar (1989) writes:

> Not only has reason become contrasted with emotion, but it has also been associated with the mental, the cultural, the universal, the public and the male, whereas emotion has been associated with the irrational, the physical, the natural, the particular, the private and, of course, the female. (p. 151)

Another fallacy of modernity is the individualism associated with rationality, actions, and decision making.

While drafting the UNCRPD, advocates for full legal capacity placed legal capacity at the core of personhood, challenging the idea perpetrated through modernity that human capacity should be measured only in terms of rationality. A set of arguments presented and reiterated through the Ad Hoc Committee meeting proceedings, on which further literature has been built, were: Human beings in general do not make decisions based on reason alone (Quinn, 2010). Quinn has questioned the *atomic* view that modernity presents about human beings, emphasizing that decision making is rarely so. We do take support from people who care for us, and who we care about, in the decision-making process. This is more relevant in the context of south countries, where rarely do individuals make decisions by themselves. Furthermore, legal capacity is not about making bad decisions or about taking risky decisions. The range of risk around decision making is made by individuals in association with their social units, such as peer groups, families, etc. Michael Bach (2006), in his presentation at an Ad Hoc Committee meeting, extended the notion of capacity to include not just cognitive capacity, but also reflective capacity, and personal identity (having a narrative about a continuing sense of self).

Legal Capacity Debate Is Contextual

The notion of legal capacity is, as may be evident from the above, a matter about law, justice systems, and courts. It is not about how we perceive or treat each other in family, neighborhood, or society at large, but how we are perceived within the scope and function of law. This is called *legal personality*, *legal status*, etc. in various country contexts. A disqualification before law, however, can have untold consequences in the conduct of everyday life and having personal freedoms, particularly for women. A disqualification before law may build stereotypes and set up discriminatory barriers on enjoying equal opportunities in all walks of life. So having full recognition before law is a fundamental right that must be respected, protected, and fulfilled by law for all people with disabilities, in the post-UNCRPD era.

Different countries have the legality of a person enshrined in their constitution, the civil code, and/or they may have special laws for recognition of or the deprivation of capacity. For example, in the Philippines Civil Code, every person has full legal capacity, but some groups, namely, *mentally ill* and *deaf mute*, are denied the capacity to act. In the making of the UNCRPD, DPOs struggled for both the right of and the right to act for *all* people with disabilities. In India, while the Constitution does not universally deprive capacity, the right to vote is not available for people *of unsound mind*. This is further reflected as provisions of the Representation of People Act, 1951. Various specific Acts may also deprive people of legal capacity (as discussed below). Women with psychosocial disabilities may face double or multiple discrimination through the existence of these special provisions of exclusion.

Who a *legal personality* is may also be determined by the received legal legacy through colonization and reformative changes made, if any, following independence. For example, Nepal was not colonized by any country, so they do not have universally applicable incapacity laws, as we have in India and parts of Africa, that were colonized by the British. Commonwealth nations in general have a legal legacy of incapacity provisions. Indian legal drafters post Independence did not examine the incapacity concepts or legal provisions, and those provisions were literally copied almost verbatim from the past in over 150 laws, leading to some improbable neocolonial (Davar, 2012), or what Bruno Latour (1993) calls, *hybrid* legal text. The *insolvent*, the *criminal*, on the one hand and the *defected*, *infirm*, or *insane* on the other were all equally considered as legal nonpersons, excluded from various rights to civil and political life in post-Independence India, and found clustered together as a disqualified group within various laws as incapacity provisions. Bangladesh is a country where Muslim personal law is more dominant than the received legal traditions (Indian or British). Bangladesh also does not have an overarching legal incapacity regime, even though those laws may be discriminatory for women (Kamal, 2010), while, in free India, whole constituencies of people with physical and mental disabilities may be considered to have died a *civil death* through such normative exclusion. Philippines has a different legal structure because the country was colonized by the Spanish. Nepal and

Philippines, unlike India, do not have a MHA, do not have mental asy-lums,[4] and do not have legal clauses over patient consent or treatment choice, as we have in India (Davar, 2012). Thus, inherited legal systems and efforts made by ruling government or nation-builders post indepen-dence may determine the legal capacity status of women with psychosocial and other disabilities in a country.

Further, even in India, legal capacity may be an urban–middle-class issue, in families which deal with property, banking, contracting, marriage, divorce, custody, maintenance, business law, taxation, and other civil, eco-nomic, and family matters more rigorously within the scope of law, than, say, communities living within a large city slum, in rural, pastoral, hilly, nomadic, mountainous, forest, or tribal families, or in culturally diverse and complex inner city slums of a metropolis. It is the urban (lower and upper) middle class which has a higher stake in this area of law in present times, and it is debatable whether women of all classes of society are equally affected by the incapacity laws. However, these laws may come into play in order to manage civil matters, for example, their inheritance rights or family rights often through guardianship arrangements. Jurisprudence on *insanity* may render people deserted, dispossessed, or homeless and poor.

Illustratively, Hon. Justices Dinakaran and Regupathi noted in a pre-amble to their Judicial Order of 2007 concerning the illegal detention of Mr Deenadayalan thus: "This petition has an unpleasant history. We are grieved at the turn of events in this case, viz., making a normal man, a mentally ill person, in order to grab his property fraudulently, by per-verting or subverting the provisions of the MHA, 1987."[5] Several such examples may be found in Indian case law, of deprivation of liberty and capacity in the context of various civil matters. In another illustrative case, Jaydeep Ladkat[6] of Wanawadi, Maharashtra, filed for guardianship of person and property of his father, Vitthal Ladkat, on grounds of *mental illness*. Within six months of this order, Jaydeep Ladkat also got the court to notice the *mental illness* of his mother, after institutionalizing her in the same year for four months. The mother was diagnosed consecutively with *occasional depression, major depression, schizophrenia,* and *paranoid schizophre-nia,* the same diagnoses applied on the father. Huge properties involving hectares of prime land and several city properties, under litigation already, were involved in this matter before the court. Even so, the court did not make further inquiries upon receipt of doctor certificates, did not have independent examination of the senior Ladkats, and pronounced guard-ianship. In both these cases, a private mental asylum owner from Pune city has been involved in the certification process and institutionalization. The court, in fact, went so far as to declare the senior Ladkats not even capable of going before any court of law. In this way, *incapacity* provisions have served third-party interests.

Finally, *legal capacity* is a social and cultural construct, encoded in law through modernity, and determined by the social perceptions and attitudes of peoples, as they are reflected in popular, scientific, and social determinations of capability. Considering these variations in local histories, ways of understanding, perceptions, social organization, and cultures, a contextual perspective on the legal capacity debate is needed, and we must be wary of *master narratives*. We need to better understand the role of *legal incapacity* in determining the right to a range of family rights, where contests for power and control may run high. In much of the emerging international literature, cited in this chapter, this contextualization is unfortunately not found, leading to a North–South debate on legal capacity, and bringing up the sensitive topic of colonialism and its aftermath.

The World Network of Users and Survivors of Psychiatry (WNUSP) have brought the spotlight on Article 12, strategizing advocacy around two related issues: achieving full recognition before the law and fighting the regime of force and coercion found within the mental institutions of the West (the United States and Europe). In contrast, the non-Western world is quite bereft of any kind of mental health systems, including mental institutions, and the issue of force and denial of capacity is not felt so sharply at the ground level. In the West, the postwar period saw the emergence of masses of victims of mental institutions, resulting in the *Ex-Patients' Liberation Movement, Mad Pride Movement*, and national users and survivors' networks. However, in the non-Western world, since mental institutions did not exist to such a major extent, being survivors of the institution system also did not emerge as a victimization or trauma experience. Therefore, the debate in this part of the world is whether to focus on the issue of force and legal capacity, or to focus more on building inclusive and community-based mental health care (Article 19 of the UNCRPD) for people with psychosocial disabilities.

India, like China, is more complex in the Asian region, however, with institutions and involuntary treatment being considered as *modern* mental health care and favored by families and the government. India is a hybrid culture of the modern and the traditional, where, in the last 10 years, private business of running colonial-type asylums has been encouraged by liberalizing licensing norms under the MHA. Otherwise, until 2000, there were only 6,000 or so institution-based beds within mental asylums, which were largely public institutions. Today, as described in Davar (2012), there are over 600 private institutions in the country, mostly in urban or semi-urban areas, and slowly spreading even to district level.

Legal Capacity in India: A Double Bind for Women with Psychosocial Disabilities

As *medical patients*, persons with psychosocial disabilities should be fully protected by medical ethics of patient consent and choice, which is also provided for by UNCRPD Article 25,[7,8] on equal basis with others. However, traditionally for 200 years, some persons seen as being *unsound* have been subjects of public works, prisons, and then finally the health department, through the Indian Lunatic Asylums Act of 1858 and the Indian Lunacy Act of 1912. *Unsound* mind, found both in mental health law as well as incapacity laws, was a legal category which allowed the colonial courts to determine the level of safeguards and protections the State needed to provide for society and for imperialist power (Ernst, 1991; Mills, 2004), and included a broad social category of people. As Mills (2004) writes, various incapacity laws, for example, marriage and divorce laws, allowed for filtering out some people as *unsound* and incarcerating them through the lunacy legislation. This notion became strongly medicalized when the Indian Lunacy Act of 1912 was changed to the MHA in 1987, following strong advocacy by the Indian Psychiatric Society post Independence. The courts saw the emergence of *medical evidence* and the role of psychiatrists to provide medical opinion on capacity following this legislation. By the late 1980s, the parents' groups of children with mental disabilities, such as Parivaar, organized to have their own separate legislation, within the disability department, viz. the National Trust Act of 1999. The category of *idiots* was dropped from the subsequent version of the MHA, which contained its focus only to *mental illness*.

In India, variants of *idiocy*, *insanity*, and *unsound mind* leading to determination of *incapacity* and denial of human rights are found not only in mental health law but in all classes of laws (civil, criminal, and civil commitment laws); when so found *incapable*, decision making is largely left to guardians and custodians (families, private institutional authorities, state authorities, and other proxy individuals as appointed by the State). Other laws such as the Bombay Prevention of Beggary Act, Criminal Procedure Code, Police Act, and the MHA support these procedures of involuntary commitment into custodial facilities. While not every incapacity judgment or guardianship arrangement may result in institutionalization, involuntary institutionalization is often a precondition for substituted decision making or disqualification as a person before law. If nothing, such incarceration provides the necessary evidence before the courts and strengthens the case for such disqualification and/

or guardianship. Within custodial institutions, therefore, we can expect to find people not only in a regime of care and treatment, but also with concomitant legal problems relating to bank accounts, property matters, divorce, custody of children, etc.

The incapacity provisions, the guardianship provisions, and the involuntary commitment provisions may act together or separately as the biggest legal barriers to the full and effective participation of women with psychosocial disabilities in society. Abled women, dalits, and others have, over the last 50 years, slowly gained release from a regime of total legal erasure as persons; the legal barrier for people with disabilities is the last frontier to cross. The violence and atrocities perpetrated against people with psychosocial disabilities, taking advantage of their legal status in India as *incapacitated* people, is more fully described in Davar (2012). Analogous to the situation of the deaf, the mentally disabled, and the multiply disabled, people with psychosocial disabilities have been subject to beatings, custodial rapes, sexual assault, murder, neglect, chaining, fraud, and deceit, especially in marriage and property matters, and being passive subjects of nonconsensual clinical trials and treatments. We continue to endure inhuman, degrading, and torturous treatments, such as forced electroconvulsive therapies, direct electroconvulsive therapies, solitary confinement, and forced medication, in the name of medical cure. Our access to justice is severely curtailed because we are seen as incapable.

While one set of laws and grassroots practices recognize the disability in a negative manner, as above, through denial of full legal capacity, on the other hand, questions have been asked whether mental illness is at all a disability in the first place. The Parivaar group is advocating that "mental illness is a disease, and it is not a disability," much to the chagrin and ire of people with psychosocial disabilities.[9] In this, Parivaar is allying with the mental health professionals who for long have not perceived the relevance of the UNCRPD for mental health sector and see only the *disease* point of view. It is granted more easily that intellectual, cognitive, and developmental disabilities are disabilities, while there is skepticism regarding mental illness. So within medicolegal and policy environments, we run the risk of *not* being recognized as a legitimate disability constituency, *or* being viewed from a forensic medical perspective of having a violent and dangerous mental condition that can only be contained by forced treatments and crime-handling methods, and not methods more suitable for managing a health crisis. Either perception undermines our dignity as human beings and as persons with disabilities. In the first instance, our periods of vulnerability are not recognized, and in the second instance, such vulnerability is overly medicalized using inhuman, degrading, and torturous treatments (Davar, 2008). Such a situation prevails because of the complex intersectionality between custodial laws, incapacity laws, and guardianship laws.

Case Law Illustrations

What is the impact of the incapacity laws on women? How does it affect their lives? To answer this, we provide some recent case law examples, referring only to case law in the post-UNCRPD period. Within the family court system, a sample reading of judgments shows that *unsound mind* continues to be used to invoke nullity of marriage or divorce matters. These lower courts typically do not follow judicial safeguards, and unless the case reaches the High Court, access to justice for women so rendered *incapable* is a concern. The lower courts rarely challenge the doctors' evidence, taking it as necessary and sufficient condition to grant divorce or nullify a marriage. The High Court of Chennai has noted that for the purpose of grant of a decree of divorce, the petitioner charging insanity must establish that,

> [U]nsoundness of mind of the respondent is incurable or his/her mental disorder is of such a kind and to such an extent that the petitioner cannot reasonably be expected to live with his/her spouse. Medical testimony for arriving at such a finding although may not be imperative, but undoubtedly would be of considerable assistance to the Court. However, such medical testimony being the evidence of experts would not leave the court from the obligation of satisfying itself on the point in issue beyond reasonable doubt.[10]

Case outcomes on incapacity/*insanity* petitions are usually poorer for women in the lower courts. At the High Court level, women are subjected to periods of observation, repeated court public hearings on her *insanity* and psychiatric evaluation, and the bodily and mental integrity and privacy of the woman is violated through this process. In the Chennai case above, the court, which redressed the harm done to the woman by psychiatric labeling for purpose of nullifying the marriage, however, noted discriminatorily: "Both the petitioner husband and the respondent wife stick at their respective stands and hence, the activities of the wife have to be looked into to draw inference as to her mental illness." Considering that the woman has already gone through a battery of examinations at the lower court level, the courts have not shown any sensitivity to the question of needless medical inquiries. As there are no valid pathological tests or somatic diagnostics for mental illness, psychiatric opinions given by two or more doctors before a court leads to situations of legal debate and uncertainty, the negative outcomes of which are borne by the woman. In one particular case in Rajasthan,[11] the husband had filed for nullity of marriage based on *abnormal behavior of wife*, which included kissing him in an auto-rickshaw, using a loud tone of voice, and other such matters. The husband claimed that his wife was suffering from *paranoid schizophrenia and Gilbert's syndrome*. The marriage was annulled at the family court level. The sitting Justice in the High Court, when the case reopened there, confronted by the contesting psychiatric reports, prepared his own treatise on *the mental diseases*, and based on his own research, revoked the judgment of the lower court. While *unsound mind* in earlier times involved the strictest of court vigilance, recent case law on such petitions is derived from anything ranging from *sleep* problems, *stress* to *paranoid schizophrenia*, tying legal capacity with diagnosis more tightly.[12] It may also be the case, from the few cases reviewed here, that petitions for rendering the marriage null and void are presented by the husband, adding charges of *adultery, fraud, nondisclosure of mental illness* or *deceit* to the petition (see note 15), sometimes added to evade the fact of a second marriage, obligations for maintenance, custody of children, or confiscation of articles such as gold and money received at the time of marriage.[13]

One marriage in Pune was annulled by a lower court on the basis of a finding of *moderate depressive episode with somatic syndrome*.[14] The history of this case shows that the husband filed a nullity of marriage petition on grounds of insanity and fraud due to nondisclosure, in the Pune family court. He alleged that his wife has had "as many as six previous sexual relationships" and had kept him in the dark about it. Not revealing these past relationships was construed by the lower court as *deception*, the ground of *insanity* admitted, and the marriage was rendered null and void. The judgment was squashed by the High Court, which, however, engaged in serious violation of the right to bodily and mental integrity and the right to privacy. The woman was repeatedly sent for different gynecological and psychiatric tests. The husband had alleged the woman's *abnormal* behavior (promiscuity) and some other events (crying spells, poor sleep). He alleged that her "vaginal opening was enlarged and vaginal muscles laxed." After two independent gynecologists found that the vaginal muscles were indeed *laxed*, the gynecologists directed that *both* of them should see a psychiatrist. The woman in question had reported child sexual abuse by a male cousin who had raped her in childhood, which the court noted in its judgment. Other than this, the woman also was evidently distressed, and had herself mentioned sleep disturbance, crying spells, etc. before the court. The words "petitioner was shocked" have been used in the final judgment several times by the sitting judge in the Mumbai High Court, in the context of the woman's past sexual/ intimate relationships. Not empathetic at all to the history of childhood sexual abuse nor to its mental health consequences in the woman's adult life,[15] the court ordered several medical tests. After several subsequent referrals, she was diagnosed with *severe subjective distress* and *moderate depression with somatic complaints*. Tussle between two courts and between two psychiatrists or more resulted in serious violations of right to bodily and mental integrity, consent to medical interventions, and right to privacy.

Similar legal situations of medical disempowerments prevail on the guardianship jurisprudence when *insanity* is brought in. A sample reading of judgments in 2011 on *guardianship* done for the purpose of this chapter suggests that district courts are regularly giving guardianship over people mainly in the context of property matters, pensions, etc.[16] Guardianship granted is not for a specific cause (e.g., management of property), but of a *person* found to be *mentally ill*. In a judgment of November 18, 2011, the District Court noted in their judgment that, "Certainly there needs to be someone to take care of this fellow," handing over the person of Bhimaji Kulkarni to his brother.[17] In the sample of 10 cases reviewed, in two cases, a person of *mild mental retardation* was found to be *mentally ill* by the court and granted guardianship under the MHA. Even though the MHA specifically excludes mental retardation, section 52 of the MHA on guardianship was applied.[18,19]

Harmonization Efforts on Legal Capacity

In each country case which has come up before the UNCRPD monitoring committee, the Concluding Observations have been very forthright on directing States Parties toward ensuring both the right to legal capacity as well as the right to exercise such capacity. The UN Monitoring Guidance report gives monitoring guidelines for

> [E]liminating disability as a ground for depriving someone of his or her legal capacity—for example, by eliminating the practice of appointing guardians who make decisions on behalf of persons with disabilities and, instead, providing support to persons with disabilities so that they can make their own decisions. (UN, 2010)

The Concluding Observations have also considered the relationships between Articles 12, 14, and 19, and have directed the abolition of institutions especially for persons with psychosocial disabilities and coercive mental health legislations, particularly in the context of China.

Following the ratification of the UNCRPD, the Indian government is obligated "to adopt all appropriate legislative, administrative and other measures for the implementation of the rights recognized in the present Convention," and, "to take all appropriate measures, including legislation, to modify or abolish existing laws, regulations, customs and practices that constitute discrimination against persons with disabilities." Harmonization efforts are underway with respect to the MHA, 1987, to address the issue of incapacity found with respect to medicolegal matters, especially consent to treatment, though these efforts have come under much criticism from self-advocates and human rights groups (Davar, 2012): the National Trust Act, with respect to the full legal capacity of people with autism, cerebral palsy, mental retardation, and multiple disabilities, and a new law is pending before the government, titled Rights of Persons with Disabilities Bill, 2012.

On the one hand, people in governance, the caregivers' organizations, the legal drafters of these legislations, and various other actors within civil society more easily assume that full legal capacity is a special feature of people with psychosocial, intellectual, and mental disabilities (see, for example, Narayan et al., 2011). For people with mental disabilities also, parents' groups, such as Parivaar, have found it difficult to give up the familiar paradigm of guardianship despite efforts to move toward the new paradigm.[20] However, world experience on guardianship is available, showing how guardianship results in the nullification of all rights of persons with disabilities (MDAC, 2007).[21] A recent Czech court decision is also noteworthy.[22] The court has ruled that every person has a right to a *legal personality*, and that just a finding of intellectual disability/mental health problem cannot be the justification of denying legal personality. The court has declared plenary guardianship as *obsolete*. In the context of Czechoslovakia, the MDAC, Hungary, notes that parents have had a choice of choosing plenary *or* partial guardianship arrangements. Even though both options have equal probability, plenary guardianship has been the more frequently exercised option by communities. The reasons for this are that within the court system no reasonable accommodation is provided to hear and understand the wishes of a disabled person, and support mechanisms to exercise legal capacity have not been made available.

In India, as presented above, we have growing evidence of the abuse of incapacity provisions, guardianship, and substantial procedural limitations or lapses within the legal system. The Persons with Disabilities Act, 1995, did not cover a single one of the civil political rights, including legal capacity. The National Trust Act (also presently being *harmonized*) also restricted recognition before the law on equal basis with others, by providing guardianship arrangements, where needed, for people with mental disabilities: autism, mental retardation, cerebral palsy, and multiple disabilities. The National Trust Act did not include other disabilities. While the UNCRPD mandates inclusive laws and policies, the parents' organizations have mobilized strongly against inclusion of people with other disabilities. On the basis of the UNCRPD, the Supreme Court[23] has recently upheld the personal autonomy of a woman with intellectual impairment and ordered the continuation of her pregnancy, as per her wish and choice, clearly stating that, "Consent of the pregnant woman is indeed an essential condition for proceeding with the termination of a pregnancy as per Medical Termination of Pregnancy Act 1971." However, the apex court has made a distinction between a *mentally ill* person and a *mental retarded* person in this instance, noting that full legal capacity may be reinstated in the case of the latter only; and not the former. This amounts to discrimination against a certain group of people with disabilities.

Recently, the National Legal Services Authority of India Scheme 2010 for *mentally ill persons and persons with mental disabilities*[24] provides thus:

> It is obligatory for our legal system to ensure the human rights and fundamental freedoms of persons with disability (including mentally ill persons and persons with mental disabilities) are enjoyed on equal basis with others and to ensure that they get equal recognition before the law and equal protection of the law.

To our knowledge, this is the only salutary recognition of equal recognition before the law for persons with psychosocial disabilities, other than the general constitutional guarantees, in the post–UNCRPD period. However, these guidelines do not provide for voluntary treatment for persons *not capable* of giving consent to treatment. Further, among the services offered, *support for exercising legal capacity* in all legal domains is not found. There is a clause on rescue of people who are being treated by force within institutions. We are not aware how many women have been helped by this scheme or have been rescued from *forced treatment* by this agency.

The topics of legal capacity, *high support need*, and *guardianship* elicited heated debate and polemics in the high-level committee appointed by the Ministry of Social Justice and Empowerment to write the new Disability Rights legislation. In the various deliberations on legal capacity, there was unanimous agreement that people who get marginalized and excluded are those who may have a *high support need* and that their needs must be protected. The parents and caregivers' group held that people may not be able to take decisions, however much we may provide support. Some people may be able to make small decisions, but may not be able to make big or better decisions, according to them. Families are extremely anxious about removing guardianship. This group felt that guardianship plus minimum provision for substituted decision making should be there in the new disability Act.

Representatives of DPOs in the subcommittee argued that *high support need* is contextual and time-bound. We must work with an evolving concept of disability and provide equality of opportunity. When someone is seen as *high need*, their abilities are not recognized and they get deskilled further. We should look at protections through the concept of *indivisibility of rights*, but not overprotection, by legally taking over decision making. A person on the *high support* side needs all kinds of support, to make decisions relevant for his or her life. We must be skilled in receiving different kinds of communication on the person's expressed needs. In the end, the quality of life of all persons with disabilities should be ensured.

Eventually, the group recommended that plenary guardianship should be abolished, and supported decision making should be put in place. To ensure that this process is seamless, the law must carefully lay out the transition process. We should have some intervening steps (timeline for nullifying existing guardianship arrangements, providing enough public information, counseling families, creating alternative mechanisms, etc.). The group also placed expectations on capacity-building of organizations and families on the new paradigm, along with experiments, piloting, and model-building. Further, funds should be allocated to promote self-advocacy and assertion of persons with disabilities through community-building programs. While a ring of support from others is needed, this cannot substitute for the assertion of persons with disabilities. The subgroup strongly proposed that the new Act must fully and unequivocally recognize legal capacity, that all people are equal before the law and have the capacity to act.

The last but one draft of the "Rights of Persons with Disabilities Bill," presently being dressed up for the Parliament, carried these recommendations in full, in all three core aspects: abolition of plenary guardianship, transition pathway, and creating legal alternatives. However, to the great disappointment of the disability movement, particularly people with psychosocial disabilities, when the final draft was released, lo and behold, there was a provision for *limited guardianship*, without any kind of further legal articulation or safeguards, and contradictory to the rest of the provisions on legal capacity. The Mental Health Care Bill, also adopted by the Cabinet at the point of writing this chapter, is incapacity legislation, having forced treatment at its core. Other incapacity provisions found in all classes of law have not been noticed as requiring legal reform by the Government of India.

In this chapter, we have tried to capture the knowledge around Article 12, and to show up the big gaps between the inspirational mandate of the UNCRPD and ground-level realities of women with psychosocial disabilities. We have also tried to describe the implementation aspects of Article 12, particularly relating to the Rights of Persons with Disabilities Bill, 2012. The struggles of the disability movement go on, on this key Article, without which no other human right can be realized.

Notes

1. India signed the UNCRPD on March 30, 2007. On October 1, 2007, the government ratified the UNCRPD, and in doing so, made a commitment to the people of India and to the international community on its obligation to *respect, protect,* and *fulfill* the equal enjoyment of all human rights and freedoms of all people with disabilities, on equal basis with others.
2. The CEDAW Committee COs, 54th session. See http://www2.ohchr.org/english/bodies/cedaw/cedaws54.htm (downloaded on 11.07.2013).
3. Also refer to http://www.disabilityrightsfund.org/resource/legal-capacity.html-0 (downloaded on 26.12.2014).
4. In our recent *missions* to the Philippines and Nepal, which have also ratified the UNCRPD, we found that they were starting to promote a MHA, and were in the process of building more institutions, as a way of *modernizing* the nations.
5. Habeas Corpus Petition No.1334 of 2007, dated September 14, 2007, *Uma Manickam vs The Inspector of Police and Ors* on 14 September, 2007, Madras High Court. Petition filed under Article 226 of the Constitution of India praying for issue of writ of habeas corpus directing the respondents to produce Deenadayalan, Son of Balu Reddiar, aged about 54 years, now under illegal custody of the respondents before this Court and set him at liberty.

6. District Court of Pune, in Civil Suit No. 1640 of 2009; M. A. No.: 681/2009, under MHA 1987; Judgment Date: January 31, 2011; Civil Suit No.: 680/2009; Order Date: June 18, 2011.

7. Article 25 (d) requires health professionals to provide care of the same quality to persons with disabilities as to others, including on the basis of free and informed consent by, inter alia, raising awareness of the human rights, dignity, autonomy, and needs of persons with disabilities through training and the promulgation of ethical standards for public and private health care.

8. When the Erwadi tragedy happened in Tamil Nadu in 2001, people in the neighborhood did not rush to help the dying inmates, because they thought that the cries of the inmates were the ravings of mad people.

9. The chief of Parivaar, a parents' organization, on mental illness as disability; see http://www.dnis.org/print_interview.php?interview_id=125 (downloaded on 28.08.2012).

10. L. Hemalatha vs N. P. Jayakumar, judgment delivered January 24, 2007; appeal against the order passed on January 3, 2002 in FCOP No. 40 of 1999, in the court of P. D. Dinakaran, Chennai High Court.

11. Prakash Kumar Bachlaus vs Smt. Chanchal alias Jaya on January 23, 2007, RLW 2007 (3) Raj 2306; Bench: G. S. Misra, V. Kothari; Judgment by V. Kothari.

12. Kerala High Court, in Rajesh vs Shiji, Mat. Appeal No. 211 of 2010, OP.406/2006 of Family Court, Malappuram, Kerala; Justice Baboo Mathew Joseph had an array of psychiatrists testify to the fact that Shiji, as alleged by Rajesh, her husband, did not suffer from any mental illness.

13. John vs Mercy Kuriakose on May 26, 2009, in the High Court of Kerala at Ernakulam, A. S. No. 61 of 1997, John vs Mercy Kuriakose, in the court of Justice SurendraMohan.

14. Mr Vinand Vilas Arabale versus Ms Shilpa Vinand Arabale, Petition A. No. 487/2011, for annulment of marriage under section 12(1)(c) in the court of Principal Judge, Family Court of Pune. Judgment delivered on July 29, 2012.

15. The Child Welfare Information Gateway in Washington, D.C. has useful resources on the subject of childhood sexual abuse. See https://www.childwelfare.gov/pubs/issue_briefs/cm_prevention.pdf (downloaded on 26.12.2014).

16. On May 2, 2011, petition M. A. 578/2010, Pune district court, guardianship over person and property of *mentally ill person*, Sriram, given to Mrs Meena Dubey, under MHA, 1987.

17. Civil Application No. 618/2011, by applicant Vijay Pandurang Kulkarni, in Pune District Court.

18. Misc. Application No. 387/2009, Sandesh Gajanan Bhave, receiving pension and managing property of brother Prashant Bhave, found to have *mild mental retardation*; decided on June 18, 2011.

19. Civil Application No. 109/2010, by Deepak Shridhar Bhalerao; order on July 13, 2011.

20. See http://www.inclusion-international.org/wp-content/uploads/JPG-PRESENTATION.ppt.f (downloaded on 01.09.2012).
21. See http://www.mdac.info/en/Hungary (downloaded on 07.09.2012).
22. See http://www.mdac.info/en/czech-republic-constitutional-court-finds-deprivat (downloaded on 08.09.2012).
23. Supreme Court of India, Record of Proceedings C. A. No. 5845 of 2009, *Suchita Srivastava & Anr vs Chandigarh Administration*, August 28, 2009.
24. A national legal authority which enables cadres of legal aid services in all states of India adopted the "Legal Services to the Mentally Ill Persons and Persons with Mental Disabilities Scheme of 2010," in the Meeting of the Central Authority of NALSA held on December 8, 2010 in the Supreme Court of India.

Bibliography

Andrews, Jonathan and Anne Digby (eds). 2004. *Sex and Seclusion, Class and Custody. Perspectives on Gender and Class in the History of British and Irish Psychiatry.* Amsterdam: Editions Rodopi B. V.

Bach, Michael. Jnauary 2006. "Legal Capacity, Personhood, and Supported Decision Making," presentation at the Ad Hoc Committee Meeting, Canadian Association for Community Living. Available online at http://www.un.org/esa/socdev/enable/rights/ahc7docs/ahc7ii3.ppt and http://www.lco-cdo.org/disabilities/bach-kerzner.pdf (downloaded on 07.09.2012).

Braslow, Joel. 1997. *Mental Ills and Bodily Cures: Psychiatric Treatment in the First Half of the Twentieth Century (Medicine and Society).* California: University of California Press.

Cremin, Kevin M. 2007. *General Hospital Psychiatric Units and Rehabilitation Centers in India: Do Law and Public Policy Present Barriers to Community Based Mental Health Services.* Pune: Bapu Trust for Research on Mind & Discourse.

Davar, Bhargavi V. 2008. "From Mental Illness to Psychosocial Disability: Choices of Identity for Women Users and Survivors of Psychiatry," *Indian Journal of Women's Studies*, in R. Addlakha (ed.), Sp. Vol. on *Disability, Gender and Society*, 15 (2): 261–290.

———. 2012. "Legal Frameworks for and Against People with Psychosocial Disabilities," *Economic and Political Weekly*, XLVI (52): 123–131.

Dhanda, Amita. 2000. *Legal Order/Mental Disorder.* New Delhi: SAGE Publications.

Ernst, Waltraud. 1991. *Mad Tales from the Raj: The European Insane in British India 1800–1858.* London: Routledge.

Foucault, Michele. 1965. *Madness and Civilization: A History of Insanity in the Age of Reason.* New York: Pantheon.

Goffman, Erving. 1961. *Asylums: Essays on the Social Situation of Mental Patients and Other Inmates.* New York: Anchor Books, Doubleday and Co.

International Disability Alliance. 2008. "Article 12, Principles of Implementation," a position paper prepared by International Disability Alliance. Available online at http://www.internationaldisabilityalliance.org/en/ida-position-papers-and-statements (downloaded on 01.09.2012).

Jaggar, A. M. 1989. "Love and Knowledge: Emotions in Feminist Epistemology," *Inquiry*, 32 (2): 151–176.

Kamal, Sultana. December 2010. "Law for Muslim Women in Bangladesh," UN Statistics Division. Available online at http://unstats.un.org/unsd/vitalstatkb/Attachment390.aspx (downloaded on 07.09.2012).

Latour, Bruno. 1993. *We Have Never Been Modern*. Harvard University Press.

Lloyd, Genevieve. 1984. *The Man of Reason*. Minneapolis: University of Minnesota Press.

Mental Disability Advocacy Center (MDAC). 2007. *Guardianship and Human Rights in Russia: Analysis of Law, Policy and Practice*. Budapest: MDAC.

———. 2011. "Supported Decision Making as an Alternative to Guardianship," Policy Paper 4, MDAC with Civil Rights Defenders, Budapest. Available online at http://www.mdac.info/sites/mdac.info/files/English_Supported_Decision-making_An_Alternative_to_Guardianship.pdf (downloaded on 16.08.2012).

Mills, James. 2004. "Body as Target, Violence as Treatment: Psychiatric Regimes in Colonial and Post Colonial India," in James Mills and Satadru Sen (eds), *Confronting the Body: The Politics of Physicality in Colonial and Post-Colonial India*, pp. 80–101. London: Anthem South Asian Studies.

Mills, James H. 2004. *Madness, Cannabis, Colonialism*. New York: Macmillan St. Martin's Press.

Minkowitz, Tina. 2011. "Why Mental Health Laws Contravene the CRPD—An Application of Article 14 with Implications for the Obligations of States Parties," *Journal of Critical Psychology, Counseling and Psychotherapy*, 11 (3): 165–172.

Minkowitz, Tina and Amita Dhanda (eds). 2006. *First Person Stories on Forced Interventions and Being Deprived of Legal Capacity*. Odense: WNUSP/Pune: Bapu Trust.

Narayan, C. Laxmi, M. Narayan, and Deep Shikha. 2011. "Ongoing Process of Amendments in MHA-87 and PWD Act-95 and Their Implications on Mental Health Care," *Indian Journal of Psychiatry*, 53: 343–350.

National Human Rights Commission. 1999. *Quality Assurance in Mental Health*. New Delhi: National Human Rights Commission.

Nilsson, Anna. 2012. "WHO GETS TO DECIDE? Right to Legal Capacity for Persons with Intellectual and Psychosocial Disabilities," CommDH/IssuePaper(2012)2, for the Commission for Human Rights, Council of Europe, Strasbourg. Available online at https://wcd.coe.int/ViewDoc.jsp?id=1908555#P222_13324 (downloaded on 16.08.2012).

Parashar, Archana and Amita Dhanda. 2008. *Redefining Family Laws*. New Delhi: Routledge India.

Quinn, Gerard. 2010. "Personhood and Legal Capacity: Perspectives on the Paradigm Shift of Article 12 CRPD," concept paper, presented at the HPOD Conference, Harvard Law School, February 20, 2010.

Scull, Andrew. 1989. *Social Order/Mental Disorder: Anglo-American Psychiatry in Historical Perspective.* London: Routledge.

Szasz, Thomas. 2001. *Pharmacracy: Medicine and Politics in America.* Connecticut: Praeger.

UN. 2010. *Monitoring the Convention on the Rights of Persons with Disabilities: Guidance for Human Rights Monitors,* Professional Training Series No. 17. New York: UN. Available online at http://www.ohchr.org/Documents/Publications/Disabilities_training_17EN.pdf (downloaded on 01.09.2012).

WNUSP. June 17, 2011. "Legal Capacity as Right, Principle and Paradigm," submission to the Committee on the Rights of Persons with Disabilities in response to its call for papers on theoretical and practical implementation of Article 12.

Epilogue: Transforming Invisibilities and Obscure Directions

W omen with disabilities like all other women are of many colors, ethnicities, classes, sexual orientation and are usually sited in a world that privileges men. The hegemonic realities, which disadvantage women, also subject them to develop agency which is a crystallization of women's subjectivities in juxtaposition with the prospect to act. The subjectivities have been developed through historical attribution and masculinist circumscription. Different historical constructions have contributed to women with disabilities' personhood, which despite the peripheralization of their issues augmented the development of a rich feminist culture and identity.

Private and Public Spaces

The entrenchment of discrimination toward women largely lies in the patriarchal system present in countries across the globe. Patriarchy is a major factor that is responsible for discriminatory practices against women in general, and women with disabilities in particular. It unfortunately is excluded from discourses in most countries, and even in the United Nations (UN), which plays an important role in setting the standards for gender equality. The resultant gendered problématique, referred to are a range of issues that derive from the patriarchal core of hierarchal social organization. It places the highest social value on those who control the order and manage it to their advantage, at a higher cost to those at the lower levels of the hierarchy. Patriarchy is a germinal ideology, and the global gender order is its organizational form (Reardon, 2008). It is the sociopolitical order in which public policy is made, and established on an unequal order. Among the most important research carried out on the interpretation of gender and patriarchy are the studies of R. W. Connell and Betty A. Reardon (Connel, 2000; Reardon, 2008). Catherine A. MacKinnon's *Toward a Feminist Theory of the State* remains an important reading on the arguments on the public and private space for women. Though not specifically linked to disability, the arguments remain valid (MacKinnon, 1989).

Patriarchy remains the underlying ideology paradigm for most human organizations where the small elite groups of power holders are the greatest users of power and, therefore, make most decisions for women. They may be men or women without disabilities or men with disabilities. In this order, groups of powerful males (in some cases, even women) dominate their interests, perceptions, and values over humans at a lower position in the power-based hierarchy. Patriarchy is a system based on hierarchy, oppression, and inequality. Inequality in societal hierarchical arrangements, such as gender, race, class, and caste, are strengthened through the persistence of patriarchal thinking. Patriarchy fears the sharing of power, and this nature of the system requires the beginning of a discourse even within the field of disability. We must critically understand within the disability conceptual framework the bases of the strength of patriarchal norms and its inconsistencies to create change toward gender equality.

We need to change the concept of power from a misogynistic way of domination to a community of equals where power benefits all and does not produce a hierarchy. To move women with disabilities outside the patriarchal paradigm, we must, therefore, gain a critical understanding of it so that it can be replaced by a democratic system of human rights and structure of equality. The discourse should not only challenge the markers of patriarchy, but also (through creative and imaginative critical analyses) negotiate toward full equality using numeric markers to designate the new frontiers. We might be able to draw strength by linking with the antislavery movement, as women were enslaved earlier than men. The antislavery movement has also supported feminist workers in their search for political rights, as these rights are related to the essential attributes of freedom and democracy.

Patriarchy must be considered as a major barrier generally and specifically in the ability of women with disabilities to access their rights. Its linkage with disability will lend strength to women's search for autonomy and leadership roles. As patriarchy is not yet identified as a major barrier in the life of women with disabilities, and research has rarely examined its complexities, this is one analytical trajectory that needs our endorsement. The patriarchal-power syndrome exists everywhere, including in the disability movement where women's leadership is put down so that they cannot exercise the authority which is theirs by right. If we bow down to misogynist hate speeches by disability power holders and not complain about it because we will be derided/frightened, then we only deserve the leadership we deserve and the lower hierarchy we are placed in.

The Gender Essentials in a World of Diversity and Marginalization

The volume speaks of a correction of inequities through an enabling environment and enhanced leadership. This is possible through the positive impact of women's agency and removal of entrenched social practices, which create discrimination. The provision of security in the public space, for instance, will provide the basis of the establishment of a new gender-equal world order.

In this gendered world of disability, the heterogeneity of disability issues is linked to the diversity of disability groups and situations. In the persisting hierarchy, some groups find themselves at the bottom. Among these near-excluded groups, as we have observed in this book, are women with multiple disabilities and those with psychosocial disabilities. Besides, disability as observed gender also cuts across ethnicity, such as in the case of women from indigenous populations who find little space in our writings. Indigenous identity is culturally construed and must be understood from that standpoint. The disability and women's movement has been ineffective and inconsistent when faced with the issue of indigenism due to a lack of understanding of the culture. Though both men and women from indigenous communities face problems, women face many layers of discrimination imposed upon them (United Nations, 2013: para 40). With globalization and the expansion of capital into indigenous areas for the exploitation of minerals, petroleum, gas, water, and other resources, many groups face displacement, forced migration, severe poverty, and the end of their cultural lifestyles. Women with disabilities in many indigenous areas are mostly illiterate, have little or no access to health care and work, and suffer the most in crisis situations. Globalization has resulted in displacement from their homes and migration to insecure places in search of livelihood. The increased militarization of these areas has also left women open to extreme violence. It is imperative to the feminist study of disability that inclusion remains an important marker of equality.

Disability identity can be situational, and research needs to cover this unspecified aspect. One important situation, for instance, is related to disaster and conflict situations. The United Nations Convention on the Rights of Persons with Disabilities (UNCRPD) gave due emphasis to disability issues under Article 11, which covers armed conflict, humanitarian emergencies, and the occurrence of natural disasters (United Nations Enable). Countries are affected by both conflicts and disasters in which rights are not allowed to be accessed, especially if they are gendered.

The vulnerability of women and girls who are already disabled increases in conflict situations. The long years of conflict in various parts of the globe have left several communities bereft of the peace and development that they rightfully deserve. Today's wars are fought differently as State forces target insurgents and civilians equally. Landmines have a gendered impact as men have better access to health and rehabilitation services, leaving women disabled and excluded from society. Evidence-based research is required, for instance, on the impact of landmines on persons with disabilities and the creation of disability among women, which may have specific gendered consequences.

Peace and conflict include and exclude women differently. While women face specific types of violence in conflict situations, not much work has been done in relation to this aspect in the context of disability. In peace negotiations, the right of women was recognized in 2000 by the UN Security Council Resolution (UNSCR) 1325, "Women, Peace and Security."[1] This was followed by a series of other articles that addressed extended issues, such as protection from sexual abuse. Security Council Resolution (SCR) Resolutions 1894, 1960, and 2016, which are related to protection, include all women, though they do not mention disability. None of the six resolutions mentioned women with disabilities as peace builders or peacemakers. In fact, UNSCR 1325, which is the most important and especially relates to participation, does not pay any heed to women with disabilities. Disability feminists and disability organizations also have not paid attention to UNSCR 1325. The disability leaders have to wake up to this call and make sure that women with disability are part of the peace processes in their countries. There is also a need for women with disabilities to strengthen their alliances with women around the world who are working toward achieving the goals of UNSCR 1325.[2]

There are several issues in conflict situations that require further attention. For instance, both men and women with disabilities are more dependent on health care than others. In conflict situations, health services break down and many persons acquire a disability, which largely affects the quality of life of the persons affected. Women who require reproductive health services and those with disabilities face neglect. Field visits to conflict areas by the editor of this volume to collect data for the CEDAW (Convention on the Elimination of All Forms of Discrimination Against Women) India Alternate Report, especially in Manipur and on the border of Jammu and Kashmir, highlighted the plight of innumerable women with Post-Traumatic Stress Disorder and injuries due to war.[3]

During any movement (whether displacement due to conflict, disasters, or forced migration), women with disabilities may lose wheelchairs, hearing aids, and prosthetics, reducing their mobility. However, specific problems such as inaccessible toilets become not only a physical barrier, but also contribute to increased sexual violence against them. UN High Commissioner for Refugees (UNHCR) recognized the requirements of persons with disabilities in refugee situations after the UNCRPD was opened for signature. After the adoption of the UNCRPD, UNHCR commissioned a study on the issue, which concluded that women with disabilities "are more likely to be exposed to sexual exploitation and physical abuse" (Women's Refugee Commission, 2008: 7). The limited research on the issue has proved enough evidence for us to take it further. The wars in Afghanistan, Syria, and Ukraine are testimony to our need for more knowledge and action.

Gendered research of disasters has been quite limited globally. These issues must be understood as part of the inherent inequalities in society that exist even during disasters. It has been observed that during humanitarian emergencies, women have less access to resources that are essential in disaster preparedness, mitigation, and rehabilitation, including social networks and influence, transportation, information, skills (including literacy), control over land and other economic resources, personal mobility, secure housing and employment, freedom from violence, and control over decision making (Anderson, 1994; Krishnaraj, 1997; Myers, 1994). This situation is exacerbated when linked to women with disabilities. We must ask certain questions in carrying out research linked to contributions that women with disabilities make to hazard mitigation, emergency preparedness, response, and long-term recovery. Studying issues related to women with disabilities as a homogeneous group is not adequate methodologically because they might represent different disabilities, races, classes, or religious groups.

Women Matter: Response and Change

An uncaring society, social indifference, and noninclusion, as we have seen in all the chapters, create gender asymmetry and require a reexamination of policies and their implementation. The feminist disability movement and research needs to respond to the issues discussed above. The present chapter is built on the different contributions of the volume and the gaps in research, policy, and action. An inclusive movement and extended legislation built on women's voices, we all as writers believe, would provide the foundation to transform women's lives.

Change will come with adoption of not only new and existing laws on disability but also inclusion in alterative laws. Along with the UNCRPD, we must also mainstream disability into other UN conventions. One of the important conventions that monitors the implementation of women's rights is CEDAW. Reporting to CEDAW in the context of disability must include data on women with disabilities and the various fields, especially health (Article 12), employment (Article 11), education (Article 10), equality before law (Article 15), marriage and family life (Article 16), and economic and social benefit (Article 13). The CEDAW Committee should consider the equality and autonomy interests of women with disabilities as equal to those of other women when applying its analysis to the abovementioned articles. In the 60 reports to CEDAW, there was very little reporting on women with disabilities. The CEDAW Committee, however, as per its General Recommendations (GRs), stated that states should report temporary special measures that address issues related to women with disabilities (GR 25). For example, as per Article 15 of CEDAW, legal capacity laws should be developed—a matter of particular concern to women with intellectual or psychosocial disabilities. The CEDAW General Comment 24 on health is also not inclusive of all disabilities, mentioning physical and mental disabilities only. Although the GRs by CEDAW specifically requested information on different types of violence, states have reported little or no information on forced hysterectomy on women with disabilities.

Social change within a patriarchal system is difficult when combined with a feudalistic trend in governance. The system provides not only symbolic representation to women but also keeps out those men with disabilities who protest against this top-heavy feudalistic system—an order in which (so-called) urban, *elite* men dominate at the cost of many men and all women with disabilities. The marginalization of women with disability in the feminist movement is again visible. In 2004, the author attempted to create space for disability issues in the Indian Association of Women's Studies (IAWS) Conference, the largest women's academic–activist forum in India. However, two rather different results emerged. One of the women who attended the conference as part of the disability group was elected as the IAWS President; however, IAWS could not draw other women with disabilities into its main forum, thus, negating the 2004 exercise of inclusion.[4] In the 2014 IAWS meeting, women with disabilities were invited, but only to a special pre-conference meeting, resulting in limited interaction with other women.

We need to ask the following questions: Why are women with disabilities marginalized in both the women's and disability movements? Why is it that when women raise their issues, the movement sees it as a threat and a dividing force? Strategies for inclusion must be designed and adopted by the women, who must challenge the movements' stand that "Now is not the right time" or "You will break up the movement." Rather, the slogan should be, "By inclusion, we gain strength" and "Nothing about women without women."[5]

***

The existing asymmetrical environment where women with disabilities find themselves extends beyond social inequities. An uncaring society based on social indifference and a nonfunctional judicial system create gender unfairness. If there has to be correction of inequities, it will require a reexamination of gender policies and their implementation. Bringing in a new equal order can only work if there is reexamination of values and entrenched practices. What should be clear from any analysis of the situation is that any theory of identity, thus, provides women with disabilities with a nonessentialist view. Some of the queries always are, Why women with disabilities? Is this an essentialism of sorts in which women with direct experience of disability are believed to have that experience and the knowledge even different from those of men and women without disabilities? Is felt experience the last word in privilege? The crucial question is, Do women as a category, which faces elevated and different discriminations and oppressions and experiences of these, have the right to define their oppressions? Agnihotri's subtitle in his article "Where does the shoe pinch?" is significant.

The first question defines the right and knowledge of women with disabilities to define their own experiences and decide on the trajectories of their choice. The second question is whether their work, strategies, and tactics are appropriate in the proper context when there exist global and national disability networks.

The answer to this query may also lie in reply to another question. What have women with disabilities as a group achieved? It is obvious from the chapters that they have achieved a great deal both in the past and in the immediate present, and are laying the trajectories for the future. If the ultimate aim is democratic transformation of social relations of gender, then women with disabilities have to decide on the method to achieve their rights.

Notes

1. There are six UN resolutions on women, peace, and security, the most important being UNSCR 1325 (2000) which called for the participation of women in peace processes and the improved protection of women in conflict zones. 1820 (2008) reaffirmed commitment to 1325 and linked the prevention of sexual violence with the maintenance of peace and security; 1888 (2009) mandated peacekeeping missions to protect women and girls from sexual violence in armed conflict; 1960 (2010) reaffirms the commitment to fulfill UNSCR 1325 and is the second UNSCR to mention persons with disabilities. 2016 (2103), the latest, also mentions disability. Besides, UNSCR 1894 (2009) called for the protection of civilians in armed conflict and for assistance with the social reintegration of victims of armed conflict, including persons with disabilities, and is the first resolution in this series to mention persons with disabilities.
2. On July 19, 2013, Shanta Memorial Rehabilitation Center where I work organized a meeting on SCR 1325 where women with disabilities had participated from Northeast India. At the UN level, Stephanie Ortoleva has been working on the issue.
3. Visit to Manipur (December 18, 2012) and Jammu and Kashmir's Anantnag District on May 2013.
4. At the IAWS meeting, the women with disabilities' subtheme group resolved, among other things, the following:

   - We appreciate the contribution made by IAWS in creating a historic event by including its disabled members.
   - Disability should be a part of the general theme of women's studies and movements in India in the future IAWS conferences.

   Shanta Memorial Rehabilitation Center, Bhubaneswar has been making a continuous effort to create various platforms for women with disabilities to participate. This was one such common intersecting meet. In 1991, it had invited leaders of·the disability movement to Bhubaneswar at a meeting on women with disabilities and media to discuss their concerns and promote their common ideology. For the last four years (2010–2014), it has been attempting to get women to come together on common issues at the national level through the formation of the Women with Disabilities India Network. Among the work it has done is preparing (a) a chapter on disability as part of the India Alternate Report for CEDAW (2014), (b) report for the Special Rapporteur on Violence Against Women 2013, and (c) input into the Verma Commission constituted to recommend amendments to the India Criminal Law to provide for quicker trial and enhanced punishment for criminals accused of committing sexual assault against women.

5. By women with disabilities at a consultancy organized on the intersection of CEDAW and UNCRPD in Bangalore on February 4, 2013, by Shanta Memorial Rehabilitation Center.

References

Anderson, Mary B. 1994. "Understanding the Disaster–Development Continuum: Gender Analysis Is the Essential Tool," *Focus on Gender*, 2 (1): 7–10.

Connell, R. W. 2000. "Masculinities and Globalization," in I. Breines, R. W. Connell, and I. Eide (eds), *Male Roles, Masculinities and Violence: A Cultural of Peace Perspective*. Paris: UNESCO.

Krishnaraj, M. 1997. "Gender Issues in Disaster Management: The Latur Earthquake, Gender, Technology and Development," *Gender Technology and Development*, 1 (3): 395–411.

MacKinnon, Catherine A. 1989. *Toward a Feminist Theory of the State*. Cambridge, MA: Harvard University Press.

Myers, M. 1994. "Women and Children First: Introducing a Gender Strategy into Disaster Preparedness," *Focus on Gender*, 2 (1): 14–16.

Reardon, Betty A. 2010. "Toward a Gender Theory of Systemic Global Violence: Exposing the Patriarchal Paradigm," in Ma Elena Diez Jorge y Margarita Sanchez Romero (eds), GENERO Y PAZ, pp. 219–259. Icaria, Barcelona: .

United Nations (UN). 2013. "Study on the Situation of Indigenous Persons with Disabilities, with a Particular Focus on Challenges Faced with Regard to the Full Enjoyment of Human Rights and Inclusion in Development," Permanent Forum on Indigenous Issues, Twelfth session, February 2013, document no. E/C.19/2013/6, para 40.

United Nations Enable. http://www.un.org/disabilities/default.asp?id=150 (accessed on June 18, 2012).

Women's Refugee Commission. 2008/2010. *Disabilities Among Refugees and Conflict Affected Populations*. Geneva: Women's Refugee Commission. Available online at http://womensrefugeecommission.org/resources/document/609-disabilities-among-refugees-and-conflict-affected-populations (downloaded on 28.01.2015).

About the Editor and Contributors

Editor

Asha Hans is the former Director, School of Women's Studies, and Professor of Political Science, Utkal University, India. She is the author and editor of many publications related to women's rights, the latest being *The Gender Imperative*, coedited with Prof. Betty Reardon (2010). Her book *Gender, Disability and Identity* (2003) is a globally recognized seminal work coedited with Annie Patri. An advocate of women's rights, she has participated in the formulation of many conventions in the United Nations. A leading campaigner of women's rights in India, she has initiated many campaigns on the inclusion of women with disabilities in the mainstream women's movement. She is also the founder of Women with Disabilities India Network.

Contributors

Renu Addlakha is currently Professor and Deputy Director at the Centre for Women's Development Studies. She is presently engaged in research on health, disability, gender, and development. Renu did her Master's in Social Work and MPhil in Sociology from Delhi University, and her PhD from Delhi School of Economics. She has trained in medical anthropology, and her areas of specialization include mental illness and the psychiatric profession, public health systems, bioethics, gender, and family. Her latest, most important publications are *Deconstructing Mental Illness: An Ethnography of Psychiatry, Women and the Family* (2008), *Disability and Society: A Reader* (coedited with Stuart Blume, Patrick J. Devlieger, Osamu Nagase, and Myriam Winance, 2009), *Contemporary Perspectives on*

Disability in India: Exploring the Linkages Between Law, Gender and Experience (2011), and *Disability Studies in India: Global Discourse, Local Realities* (2013).

S. B. Agnihotri is an officer of the Indian Administrative Service and a distinguished alumnus of IIT, Bombay. He has a Master's degree in Physics, in Environmental Science and Engineering, and in Rural Development, followed by a PhD from the University of East Anglia, Norwich, UK, on "Sex Ratio Patterns in the Indian Population." His work has been approvingly cited by scholars, such as Amartya Sen, Ashish Bose, Barbara Miller, Veena Mazumdar, and others. His PhD thesis has been published by SAGE as a book. He has a number of publications to his credit in *Economic and Political Weekly* and other reputed journals.

Upali Chakravarti is Assistant Professor, Department of Elementary Education, Miranda House, New Delhi. She is a member of the Course Development and Review Committee of Action for Ability Development and Inclusion (AADI), Post Graduate Diploma in Special Education (PGSE) recognized by Rehabilitation Council of India (RCI) and affiliated to Faculty of Education, University of Delhi (November 2011), Delhi. Her areas of specialization include Psychology, Developmental Psychology, Disability, Special, and Inclusive Education. Her recent publication of 2013 is "Burden of Caring: Families of the Disabled in Urban India" in Disability Studies in India: Global Discourses, Local Realities.

Malini Chib is a freelance writer, activist, and advocate of equal opportunities and full participation for the disabled. She is the Chairperson of the ADAPT Group, formerly The Spastics Society of India. Malini has travelled extensively globally and has many publications to her credit. She has presented papers in international and national conferences, and conducted Training and Empowerment Courses on Disability Issues and helped create awareness on disability. A graduate in History Honors from Bombay University, Malini has an Advanced Diploma in Publishing from Brookes University, Oxford. She has done her first Master's in Women's Studies at the Institute of Education, University of London, and her Second Master's in Management Technology from London Metropolitan University. Malini is a recipient of a National Award by the President of India for her book *One Little Finger*.

Bhargavi V. Davar, PhD (1993), is a social science researcher in mental health. She has authored *Beyond Foundationalism: Psychoanalysis as a Human Science* (with P. R. Bhat, by SAGE, 1995), which was on the epistemological foundations of mental and behavioral sciences. Her other books include a monograph on *Mental Health of Indian Women* (SAGE, 1999), *Mental Health from a Gender Perspective* (SAGE, 2001), and she coedited *Gendering Mental Health: Knowledges, Institutions and Identitites* (2014). Bhargavi Davar is a survivor of psychiatry and is a trained Arts-Based Therapist. She established the Bapu Trust for Research on Mind and Discourse in 1999.

Santoshi Halder is an Assistant Professor in the Department of Education, University of Calcutta. She has a Master's degree in Education and a PhD in Applied Psychology. She has more than 12 years of research experience on disability. In her work, Halder has explored and represented various aspects, interventions, and challenges faced by various persons with disabilities in India and abroad. She is also a project consultant to various international projects with leading researchers worldwide. She has received the Governor's Medal from the Governor of West Bengal, India, for her contribution toward community and its people.

Sandhya Limaye has experience of working with the disabled population for the past 29 years. She is a qualified social worker in the field of disability, and has an MPhil and a PhD in the field of disability social work. Currently, she is working as Associate Professor and Chairperson at the Center for Disability Studies and Action, School of Social Work, Tata Institute of Social Sciences, Mumbai. She has been awarded many fellowships, such as the Erasmus Mundas Fellowship in 2009 in Germany, the Fulbright-Nehru Fellowship in 2012–2013 at the University of Buffalo, New York, USA, and the Rockefeller Foundation's Bellagio Residency Program in Italy in 2014.

Nilika Mehrotra teaches Social Anthropology at Jawaharlal Nehru University, New Delhi. She has been engaged in disability research for over a decade. She is the author of *Disability, Gender and State Policy* (2013). She has completed a study of Disability Studies Programs in the United States and India as a Fulbright Senior Research Fellow at UC Berkeley, USA (2013-2014).

Tina Minkowitz was one of the drafters of the Convention on the Rights of Persons with Disabilities, and has contributed extensively to the development of norms related to legal capacity, the freedom from disability-based detention, and the freedom from forced psychiatric interventions as a form of torture and ill-treatment. She is the international representative of the World Network of Users and Survivors of Psychiatry, and the founder and president of the Center for the Human Rights of Users and Survivors of Psychiatry.

Mahima Nayar has been working in the areas of gender, violence, and disability for the past 10 years. After being trained as a psychiatric social worker, she completed her doctoral work in the area of women and psychosocial disabilities in an urban, low-income neighborhood. Her areas of interest include urban health issues and medical anthropology. She is currently teaching in the School of Social Work at Tata Institute of Social Sciences, Mumbai.

Stephanie Ortoleva, a highly recognized international human rights lawyer, consultant, author, and researcher on women's rights and disability rights, is the founder/president of Women Enabled, Inc., an international NGO which educates and advocates for the rights of all women and girls, focusing on and collaborating with women and girls with disabilities worldwide. Her work focuses on human rights programming and training in developing, transition, and post-conflict countries, and consulting for governments, nongovernmental organizations, and international organizations. As a woman with a disability herself, she brings the development, academic, and legal perspectives to her work and her personal experience. She has a JD from Hofstra University School of Law with outstanding honors.

Amrita Patel is a researcher, teacher, and trainer of Women's Studies and Gender. She has conducted research on issues related to gender, specifically gender budgeting, gender development index/gender indicators, women and media, gender and disaster, women self-help groups, land rights for women and gender, and governance, displacement, and migration issues affecting women. Amrita is the Honorary Secretary of Sansristi, a gender research and advocacy organization based at Bhubaneswar. Earlier, she had taught at the School of Women's Studies, Utkal University. Presently, she is the Project Advisor, State Resource Center for Women, Government of Odisha.

Shubhangi Vaidya teaches at the School of Interdisciplinary and Trans-Disciplinary Studies at the Indira Gandhi National Open University (IGNOU), New Delhi. She has been educated as a sociologist at the Center for the Study of Social Systems, Jawaharlal Nehru University, New Delhi. She has published extensively on the issues of disability, care, and gender. She has also written teaching materials for IGNOU's Master's degree programs. Shubhangi is the parent of a teenager with autism, and is actively involved in lobbying for the rights of persons with developmental disabilities and their families. Her current research interests include disability studies from a cross-cultural perspective.

Index